Disaster Psychiatry

Disaster Psychiatry
Intervening When Nightmares Come True

Edited By
Anand A. Pandya and Craig L. Katz

In Conjunction With The
Disaster Psychiatry Outreach
Book Committee

Carol Bernstein
Christine Lehmann
David Rimmer
Marianne Szegedy-Maszak

 THE ANALYTIC PRESS
2004   Hillsdale, NJ   London

Published by
The Analytic Press, Inc., Publishers
    Editorial Offices:
    101 West Street
    Hillsdale, NJ 07642

    www.analyticpress.com

    Designed and typeset by
    Christopher Jaworski, Bloomfield, NJ
    qualitext@verizon.net

    Typefaces:
    Goudy Old Style & Zapf Humanist

Library of Congress Cataloging-in-Publication Data

Disaster psychiatry : intervening when nightmares come true / edited by
    Anand A. Pandya and Craig L. Katz ; in conjunction with the Disaster
    Psychiatry Outreach Book Committee
p.cm.

Hardcover   ISBN 0–88163–389–5   Paperback   ISBN 0–88163–418–2
    1. Psychic trauma—Treatment. 2. Grief therapy. 3. Disasters—
    Psychological aspects. 4. Crisis intervention (Mental health services).
    I. Pandya, Anand A. II. Katz, Craig L. III. Disaster Psychiatry Outreach
    Book Committee.

RC552.P67D528 2004
616.85'210651—dc22

      2003062894

Printed in the United States of America

10 9 8 7 6 5 4 3 2 1

*To our families, Howard, Linda, and Maya,
who have enabled us to engage in this
taxing but rewarding work*

*Especially to the many disaster survivors
who have taught us so much
about dignity and courage*

Contents

(Continued)

Anand A. Pandya, M.D. graduated from Harvard College with Honors in Mathematics and Philosophy and received his medical degree from New York University School of Medicine. Dr. Pandya received his general psychiatric training from Columbia University and forensic psychiatric training at New York University. Cofounder of Disaster Psychiatry Outreach, Dr. Pandya runs the ADEPT Program at Bellevue Hospital and is a member of the Department of Psychiatry of New York University School of Medicine. He is active in the American Psychiatric Association and serves on the board of directors of the National Alliance for the Mentally Ill.

Craig L. Katz, M.D. graduated from Harvard College and received his medical degree from Columbia University. He completed a psychiatry residency at Columbia University and a fellowship in forensic psychiatry at New York University. Dr. Katz is Director of Acute Care Psychiatry Services and Clinical Assistant Professor of Psychiatry at Mount Sinai School of Medicine in New York City. Cofounder and President of Disaster Psychiatry Outreach, he has most recently directed the World Trade Center Mental Health Screening and Intervention Programs that address the mental health needs of Ground Zero workers and volunteers. Dr. Katz serves as cochair of the American Psychiatric Association's New York County District Branch Committee on Disaster, is a member of the advisory panel of the Aircraft Casualty and Emotional Support Services, and is a contributor to the Committee on Terrorism of the Group for the Advancement of Psychiatry.

About Disaster Psychiatry Outreach
Disaster Psychiatry Outreach, Inc. was founded in 1998 by Craig L. Katz, M.D., Anand A. Pandya, M.D., and two colleagues. The only organization in the world exclusively devoted to disaster mental health services, DPO has responded to the Swissair Flight 111 crash; the Egypt Air Flight 990 crash; the 2001 earthquakes in El Salvador; the American Airlines Flight 587 crash; the 9/11 terrorist attacks in New York City; and the anthrax scare (at Rockefeller Center and ABC studios in New York) that followed 9/11. DPO received the Tom Levin Award for Community Activism for its response to the September 11 terrorist attacks. The award was jointly presented by the World Association and the American Association of Psychosocial Rehabilitation at a special ceremony at the United Nations on March 13, 2002.

Foreword

Robert Coles

What follows are the words of psychiatrists who have witnessed the human consequences of disasters, whether of a natural cause or, alas, wrought by in-dividuals intent on hurting people and destroying the places where those people live and work. As I read through these accounts of suffering wit-nessed and of healing attempted, I kept remembering the words of two psy-choanalysts who had come to terms with an enormous disaster, one that would ultimately lead to the death of millions of men, women, and children caught up in the murderous workings of a hate-ridden ideology become a nation's war machine put relentlessly to use. Here, in that regard, is Anna Freud, who gave us child psychoanalysis, going back in her mind to the 1930s, when the Nazis seized power in Germany (1933) and, soon enough, invaded Austria (1938):

> I recall that time only too well—nightmares stay with us, and this one (military and political, both) was a disease spreading across all Europe, person by person, nation by nation. I especially recall my father's deter-mined effort to keep doing his work—see his patients, write about psy-choanalysis for his own satisfactions as a doctor, a writer. He knew the growing danger we faced, but he did not want to admit defeat, surren-der, flee, as some were beginning to do, well before Hitler's troops marched into Vienna, greeted (appallingly) by crowds of cheering people. Once, more hopeful than the facts justified, he told us—and his colleagues—"that this will pass." I remember him adding: "All

disasters do"—though he quickly said that "the cost will be high" [personal communication].

Anna Freud was moving back and forth from the German she had heard spoken at the time to her own direct, forceful English (which had an elegant simplicity we all had come to appreciate). In sum, she was taking us back in time to an awful moment in the world's 20th-century life—and then, after a pause, a deeper than usual intake of air, a sigh, a shaking of her head, a shudder, really, she resumed with a small lecture, and we began to recognize a shift in her tone from the foregoing personal remarks to those of a veteran teacher, a vigorous and knowing psychological theorist:

My father was no stranger to the darker side of life—where there was Eros, there was Thanatos around some corner, he knew. We seek love (each of us in a way that has to do with our particular life), but we can be all too out for ourselves, all too indifferent to glance at the newspapers, and look outside, where swastikas were already being carried by people who could hardly wait for the annexation Der Fuhrer was screaming to the world as absolutely necessary and soon to come. I noticed my father looking not outside and not toward us, but at the floor, then he muttered to himself: "terrible—a disaster that historians will try to understand. For us, a disaster that will challenge us." We stood there silent—aware of what might soon be happening, but as it is put (in English so often by the parents of the children I see) "hoping against hope." In a few words, in second's time, he had let us know that he saw clearly what lay in store for us—even though he intended to carry on with dignity, meet each day's responsibilities ("stoicism," as some say) [personal communication].

A break for her talking self, a cup of coffee slowly sipped, then a look toward Albert Solnit, the head of the Yale Child Study Center, and a trusted friend of hers, whose pioneering work in child psychoanalysis she much admired—even as we knew that she would soon want to be listening rather than speaking, and, maybe, leaving for the spell of quiet rest she much wanted. Then, all of a sudden, these few words (one sentence), and she would be up on her feet: "A terrible disaster visited us in Vienna—and shortly thereafter I was talking with children in London who had also experienced disaster, seen it happen again and again. (The Blitz, we then called it, the daily bombing by Hitler's Luftwaffe.)"

One disaster led to another—and out of all that jeopardy, vulnerability, came Anna Freud's brilliantly accomplished, instructive work and writing (*War and Children*)—hence, another aspect of social, political, and psychological crisis: duress prompts the reflective inwardness of those affected or those who are near enough at hand to try to be of help, yet also be able to stand back a bit with written thoughts and ideas that let others come to understand what happened here or there, back then in time and place. Indeed, Erik H. Erikson, Anna Freud's one-time analysand and colleague, recalled the following in 1980, as he let himself go back to a disaster that also came to bear on his life as well as that of his fellow lay child psychoanalyst:

We were witnessing such growing horror there in Germany, in Austria—the rise of unparalleled evil—that we were "knocked off course," as some of my students now put it. What to do—now, when, where? In a few years of time a whole world was assaulted, destroyed, banished into cemeteries, concentration camps or (for the lucky) exile—"a continent's nightmare" some of us said and said. When I arrived in America, I tried to tell people about this nightmare; but it was hard, at first, for them to appreciate how much tragedy would be coming, even to England and France and America and Russia, which in the middle 1930s seemed relatively safe, at a distance from the disaster Miss Freud and I had observed, and then (yes!) fled [personal communication].

Both Anna Freud and Erik H. Erikson knew to tell others in person or on paper what had transpired—a disaster became a subject of description, of consideration: the tragic summoned from past experience, turned into an instrument of communication and education. So, now, with those whose words await today's readers of this book: ahead are personal tales, lyrical reports, statements both objective and subjective, in the tradition of Anna Freud and Erik H. Erikson remembering the past. Ahead, too, are moments of perplexity, alarm, and very important, a kind of autobiographical candor worthy of St. Augustine's *Confessions*. "I immediately got lost and disconnected," a doctor doing work on the Gaza Strip recounts—and then this: "It seemed that every stare, even from a child, came from a terrorist who was about to kill me. I was sweating and began trembling."

If danger threatened these doctors attending the tragedies that disasters bring, there were other times of gritty, inventive, and imaginative response—clinicians determined to make do, to fulfill the possibilities and the responsibilities that accompany their work. These are stories of disasters that evolve into times of healing, caring—stories of the redemptive side of medical work. In a sense, the trials and traumas told in this book become sources of sober, deeply felt reflection—men and women putting their knowledge and skills to work but in doing so being given much to ponder (about their own purposes as well as the perils they encountered, that they tried hard and long to take on). Put philosophically, here are contemporary existential dramas, accidents, and incidents that come crushing down on lives, but also decided moments that mark a medical presence aimed toward the survival and endurance of others. Across this planet, disasters have struck, often to people's surprise and dismay; yet all over some doctors have rallied to offer help to fellow human beings (a term that is perhaps more appropriate in this context than "patients"). They have rallied secure with stethoscopes and ears open, minds and hearts responsively attentive.

No wonder Anna Freud once told us that she owed so much of her life to the disasters that struck her and others she knew so well, and no wonder the psychiatrists who grace us with these psychological narratives are telling us, in their own way, the same story: that a whole new life started in their thinking, feeling lives as a consequence of what happened to them as they contended with what had been visited on others by fate, chance, or circumstance. No wonder Dr. William Carlos Williams gave us such affecting, stirring "Doctor Stories," and no wonder Dr. Anton Chekhov's medical stories are so vividly compelling. They both knew (and had experienced) whereof they wrote. For the psychiatrists who have gathered their stories for this book, the same holds true: what once occurred now goes on the record for others to realize, to take to heart.

Robert Coles is a child psychiatrist who teaches at Harvard University. He has worked with children who have had to endure various social and political struggles in the United States and abroad.

Introduction

What do psychiatrists bring to the human response to disaster? This book addresses this simple question through the voices of psychiatrists who have provided services during, and in the aftermath of, a variety of disasters, both natural and man-made.

Surely disaster psychiatry needs to be informed by the rich literature of grief and trauma. But most of this literature ignores the systems issues and outreach that are integral to disaster response. The literature of military psychiatry acknowledges the role of psychiatrists within a specific type of community at risk for trauma and grief. This literature is highly relevant to disaster psychiatry, a fact to which Mark Dembert's contribution to this volume ably attests. Yet, there is no parallel in civilian society to the structure of military organization and the degree of control implemented through a military hierarchy. Thus, disaster psychiatry necessarily differs from military psychiatry in crucial ways.

So how are these diverse literatures integrated into clinical practice? And how do transcultural psychiatry, child and adolescent psychiatry, occupational psychiatry, and other subspecialties interface with disaster psychiatry? A traditional approach to such questions would include a systematic review of the literature (Katz, Pellegrino, Pandya, et al., 2001) or the preparation of a textbook. However, since so much clinical wisdom falls outside the peer-reviewed literature, we deem it valuable to consider what psychiatrists actually do in responding to disasters and, equally important, to consider how they think about their interventions, both during and after the events in question.

If we define disaster broadly as traumatic events that overwhelm the resources of a community, we may profitably draw on a wide range of tragic events in order to develop a clinical and public health model for future events. Disasters have continued to occur for millennia. We may hope and strive for an end to such tragedies, but it is reasonable simultaneously to prepare for them.

Every disaster is unique. Traumatic events encompass natural disasters, industrial accidents, and disasters of human contrivance, such as wars and criminal activity. And the fine details of a particular disaster can shape its impact in dramatic ways. For example, the World Trade Center attacks have had a tremendous impact on the way certain survivors experience going to work, since the attacks occurred at a work site at the beginning of a work day. How would the meaning of this event be altered if it had occurred an hour earlier? And how would the meaning be different if the site had been a residential building or a recreational center?

Equally, every community is unique and hence uniquely affected by disaster. It is a matter of a community's previous experiences with similar and different disasters, with its rates of baseline medical and psychiatric morbidity, with its cultural beliefs about the event in question and about death, and also with the socioeconomic demographics that determine the resources available to cope with disaster. Owing to this great variability among disasters and the communities that must cope with them, it is no easier to reduce disaster psychiatry to a treatment algorithm than it is to arrive at algorithms for psychotherapy in general. Perhaps the best we can do at present is to learn from psychiatrists who have responded to disasters past and present, near and far.

Reference

Katz, C. I., Pellegrino, L., Pandya, A., Ng, A., DeLisi, L. E. (2001), Research on psychiatric outcomes and interventions subsequent to disasters: A review of the literature. *Psych. Res.*, 110(3):201–217.

I

September 11, 2001

Given the time and place of this book's publication, it is inevitable that the response to the events of September 11, 2001 have a privileged place in it. Our organization, Disaster Psychiatry Outreach (DPO), coordinated the volunteer psychiatric response to the attacks in New York City. Some 700 volunteer psychiatrists, assisted by 350 nonpsychiatrist volunteers, provided over 7,500 hours of service, logging over 7,000 separate contacts with individuals affected by the disaster. These figures do not include DPO's simultaneous responses to other disasters, such as the crash of American Airlines Flight 587 in the Rockaways and the anthrax-contaminated letters discovered at both the NBC and ABC studies in New York City. In sheer magnitude, DPO's response to the events of 9/11 dwarfs the civilian psychiatric response to any other known disaster.

The unique scale of 9/11 makes it difficult to generalize from this event to other disasters. Some of the more elaborate psychiatric services that arose in the aftermath of 9/11, such as the Kids' Corner described by Desmond Health in Section IV of this volume, would not be appropriate to smaller disasters. Nonetheless, psychiatric observations arising from 9/11 and its aftermath illuminate aspects of disaster psychiatry that are relevant to disasters of more conventional scale.

The essays in this section introduce the diverse levels at which disaster psychiatry operates. Interventions may assist large populations, as described by Joseph Merlino and Joseph Napoli, or they may take the form of a series of individual encounters, as described by Kristina Jones and Claudia Sickinger. Both types of work may be limited to a single day or extended over several months. Inevitably, the locus and duration of intervention will shape the depth of therapeutic engagement and, by implication, the psychiatrist's conception of his or her role.

1

A Woman Named Katherine

Claudia T. Sickinger

The 9/11 experience touched us all in the most extraordinary of ways. Like many, I wanted to do something. In the midst of the chaotic circumstances, I sought to find a useful place for myself among different roles as physician, human being, and New Yorker. As a community-oriented, public-sector psychiatrist with outreach training, I hoped I would be somewhat prepared. Yet disaster psychiatry in general, and this disaster in particular, had me questioning this, and, although I felt I should do more as a trained mental health professional, I wondered whether I actually could. The stories told by survivors, witnesses, families of fallen victims, and rescuers were, at times, horrifying and often humbling. I was keenly aware of the line between professional participant and voyeur. It is a line we often walk when dealing with the out of the ordinary. Fortunately, early in my volunteer experience, I realized the link between what I ought to do as a disaster psychiatrist and what I do in my everyday practice. A remarkable woman named Katherine helped me with this.

On the day I met Katherine, I was already "experienced," meaning I had actually been a volunteer at the Pier 94 Family Center once, with some idea of what was going on. Disaster Psychiatry Outreach (DPO) was at the center to provide on-site voluntary psychiatric services, consistent with their mission to mobilize the unique skills of psychiatrists in disaster situations. In such circumstances, we may perform various psychiatric assessments, certain nonpsychiatric medical interventions, liaison with

3

other agencies and professionals who may confront such concerns, provide information to those who might need it, and, most of all, see that those who need such assistance receive it on site, as well as from follow-up with their local resources. On arrival for my shift that day, I learned I would be among those volunteers escorting families by boat to Ground Zero. In a corner curtained off for privacy, we received a brief orientation from the Port Authority officer in charge of the transport. We were advised to be proactive in terms of approaching those who might appear to need some support, which is typical of working in an outreach capacity. As I emerged from behind the curtain and entered the area where the family members waited, I searched faces looking for a group I might join. A Red Cross volunteer, who discreetly gestured toward a woman with a tear-stained face, soon approached me. "She's alone," the volunteer said in a loud whisper. "She lost her brother, and she's in pretty bad shape. I think she may be dissociating[1] or something. She told me she doesn't feel like she's really here."

Katherine was an attractive woman, who looked to be somewhere in her late 40s. She was dressed casually, but nicely. Her appearance suggested privilege without pretension. Although she was clearly upset, she managed to offer a warm smile as the Red Cross volunteer brought me over. During the Port Authority orientation, the officer had suggested that we not necessarily introduce ourselves as psychiatrists. Perhaps this was to avoid having people feel as if they were being singled out for psychiatric care, which might be perceived as intrusive, as opposed to just needing appropriate emotional support. All the volunteers of varying mental health disciplines wore generic "Mental Health Volunteer" tags. I told Katherine my first name, said I would be riding in the same boat over to Ground Zero, and asked if I might join her. She nodded, seeming glad to be asked, and then apologized for being "such a mess."

"I'm afraid I may have frightened that other volunteer," she said. "I told her I didn't feel like I was actually *here*, meaning this is all still so hard for me

---

[1]*Dissociation* is a defense mechanism exhibited by people under a variety of circumstances and within the context of a variety of psychiatric conditions. It generally refers to an unconscious "disconnect" between certain thoughts or behaviors and the rest of an individual's conscious activities. Usually precipitated by situations of intense physical or psychological stress, dissociative states can range from brief periods when a person may feel unreal or disconnected from his or her own body, to more long-term states of amnesia with confusion about one's own identity (Kaplan and Sadock, 1972; Andreasen and Black, 1995).

to believe, and it has a surreal quality, like a dream that I hope I'll wake up from." She added, glancing at my "Mental Health Volunteer" ID, "I guess it may have sounded a little crazy?" I smiled, shook my head, and reassured her such feelings were what many experience in early stages of grief.

The group was led out to the pier where the boats waited. We were all handed a hard hat and given some brief instructions about what we would see, where we be allowed to go, and how long we would be allowed to stay. We boarded the boat, and from that moment on, I was Katherine's companion. We began with small talk. I learned she was a mother of four children, who were now high school and college aged. She was originally from the New York area but now lived in Dallas. Although she had worked before becoming a mother, she had always been home with her children. Her husband was a businessman. Katherine talked freely and easily. She had excellent social skills and seemed intent on keeping the conversation going. I was grateful for this. After all, something terrible was awaiting us just down the river. Perhaps we both preferred not to think about it quite yet.

She spoke about her children with great enthusiasm. She described their personalities and strengths, as well as problems each had overcome. She appeared to enjoy them as individuals and seemed to take great pride in the young adults they had too quickly become. At some point while chatting about them, she paused and said that she hoped she could do something her kids would be proud of. She wanted to be a role model for them. I asked her if she was sure she wasn't already. She smiled and changed the subject.

She spoke of her own mother, who had criticized her coming to New York to visit Ground Zero. "How could you bear to go there?" was her mother's question. Katherine had two surviving siblings, who had also chosen not to come. Her father had died several years ago. It had been her "baby" brother, a 46-year-old employee of a brokerage firm, who had been on an upper floor of 2 World Trade Center when the second plane hit. As she spoke about him, she pulled a "MISSING" flyer out of a folder she carried, which had his photograph and description on it. It described and pictured a tall, handsome, healthy-looking man in the prime of life.

"I still can't believe he didn't get out," she said. "My brother was a very smart guy, very big and strong. He had experience as a volunteer fireman. He knew everything about fires. A few other people from his firm did make it out. One of his coworkers, this tiny little woman who always wears high heels, was somehow able to get down and get out. How is it possible that he couldn't?" She looked at me as if she hoped I had the answer. I wished I did. My expression most likely betrayed that I had none, that I, too, was at a loss.

She continued, seeming to want to help me, as well as explain it to herself. "Probably, knowing my brother, he was trying to help others get out. It was his fireman mentality. He probably figured he'd be OK, and it was all the others who needed help." I nodded. Like her brother, Katherine also appeared to be someone who wouldn't hesitate to jump in and assist.

"Over the past week and a half," she said, "we tried to remain hopeful that, by some chance, he made it and is injured in a hospital somewhere. By now, we all believe he's gone. It's been hard to accept. For the last few days, since I've been here in New York, I've tried to tie up some loose ends and make sure my brother's affairs are in order. It just helps to feel like I'm doing something. My mother thinks I'm terrible to focus on things like that. She's upset with me because she thinks I'm not spending enough time with her. My other siblings decided to stay with her and not to come here today. She told me that I don't seem to care how much she's suffering." I offered that she was suffering, too. She nodded. "Well, I guess she feels her grief is greater than mine and my siblings' because she lost her son. Do you think it's callous of me to do these things?" My reply was essentially that everyone's grief is very personal. I reassured her that different people respond to loss differently. Maybe she had been trying to maintain some order and normalcy in a very abnormal situation? I told her that there was nothing wrong with this and that it could perhaps be helpful in her healing process.

The downtown area of Manhattan was becoming more visible. We would soon be at Pier 11 and Ground Zero. As we approached, I attempted to orient my view, which was definitely difficult without the towers. The first landmark I recognized was the World Financial Center building. Its magnificent atrium, badly damaged by fallen debris, appeared fractured like carelessly handled crystal. From the river entrance to downtown, it had served as a shimmering gateway to the World Trade Center. Now its shattered glass and twisted metal presented an empty space where the towers had stood. As we docked, we were told we would first go to the site designated as a temporary memorial for families wishing to leave tokens at Ground Zero. As we left the boat, we were warmly greeted by rescue workers from all disciplines, who stood along the walkway for the purpose of offering support to the families. Once we passed this group of well-wishers, we became aware of the relative quiet around us. The streets were empty, the buildings dark. It was as if we had entered a lost city.

At the memorial site, the volunteers stepped back, giving the families some privacy. Katherine was one of the few who had come alone. Most others had someone to lean on or cry with. As she placed flowers at the site, I wished at least one person from her family could have been there with her. As with some of the other areas around the city where families had put up flyers, flowers, and notes, this site resembled a shrine, but because of its unique, protected location and proximity to the place where so many perished, it had an even more sacred quality. All around were physical reminders of those whose lives had been interrupted. By this time, there had been some cleanup, but plenty of scattered office materials still remained and clinging papers peppered tree branches. The walkway had been cleared, although thick, gray dust still blanketed the surrounding area.

After some time at the memorial, we were guided toward the towers. As we drew nearer, we became increasingly acquainted with the powerful and terrible smell. While impossible to accurately describe, it combined the musty, dank scent one gets a blast of when a subway underground pushes air up through a grate in the sidewalk, mixed with a pungent smoldering smell of material that was never meant to be burned. More than anything I experienced that day, it was that smell that I am least likely to forget.

We were led up to a platform above the street level where we could view the collapsed towers. From this vantage point, the extent of the destruction could be appreciated in its fully horrific form. We all stared, transfixed by the devastation. I reminded myself I was there to work. It was all I could do to resist being swept away by the sights. There were the enormous, jagged mountains of debris. Many surrounding buildings were badly damaged, and some were shrouded in a black netting to catch dangerous falling pieces. In the middle of all this chaos, the seemingly fearless workers with their machines tackled the seemingly untacklable mess. Katherine asked me where exactly Tower 2 had stood, of which I wasn't sure. I turned to ask a nearby rescue worker. He was knowledgeable and kind. It was extremely noisy on the platform because of the work going on below. With practically all senses on overload, it was a bit overwhelming. It seemed like we were there for quite some time. Then we were told it was time to go, so that they could make room for the next group.

On the way back to the boat, I felt a heaviness on my heart. No one seemed to be talking very much. We boarded. We sat down. Katherine eventually broke the silence. "My brother was living with a woman," she said. "I really wish he had married her. Actually, I think he was finally considering it. My sister and I married and had children, but neither of my brothers did. It's interesting. Since my brother's death, I've wondered about it. Before this woman, he was involved with someone else for years. She eventually couldn't wait anymore and is now married to someone else. I can't blame her, of course, he could have married her, but didn't for some reason." Katherine then began to share with me a painful tale about her childhood, her relationship with her brother, and their mother.

She had recently realized, from some comments her brother had made when she last saw him, that their mother had abused him. She had been both saddened and somewhat liberated by this realization. She, too, had been abused both emotionally and physically by her. She recalled many instances as a child when her mother berated and beat her for what seemed to be small annoyances or infractions of house rules. She remembered being cornered in front of the refrigerator on one occasion and being hit in the face repeatedly until her nose bled. Her mother had been unhappy and resentful of her husband's work and golf schedule, which often left her home alone with the children. Katherine recalled that these beatings seemed to occur when no one else was around. Because of this, she had always assumed she was the only one who was "bad," the only one with whom her mother had reason to be angry. She had always been too ashamed to tell anyone. She now believed that her mother had likely abused all of them in the same way and had managed to have it be a secret that none of them would share. Of her siblings, she had always felt closest to her little brother who was now gone. They had been great and inseparable playmates as young children. She had taught him things. She had felt like his protector. As they grew older, a distance grew that she didn't understand. They didn't share the way they used to. She sought to explain this: "Maybe, because of Mom, he decided he didn't want any more women to have that kind of control over his life?"

She had tried to rewrite this scenario with her own children. Unlike her mother, she hoped her children felt that she enjoyed being with them. She described the excitement of being their teacher and friend. They had grown into wonderful people. She felt lucky in many ways, but now they were almost grown up. Would she still be useful to them? Perhaps this was the time for her to pursue her own interests? For years, she and her husband had lived their lives in parallel. Now they were suddenly colliding. Had she ever really felt he appreciated and understood her? In some ways, perhaps he reminded her of her mother. He was always irritated with her. Was it a mistake that they had ended up together in the first place? I listened and advised her to take her time with big decisions, offering that at times like this, many feel somewhat estranged from other people and thus may question their relationships.

We arrived back at Pier 94, still talking. As we left the ship, we ran into the Red Cross volunteer who had been initially concerned about Katherine. Katherine reassured her. "I'm OK now, thanks to this lady." Things weren't busy for the moment at the DPO booth. We found an empty table and talked some more. Katherine's grief over the loss of her brother had led to her processing a lifetime of grief. Under these hostile circumstances in the middle of the crowded, bustling warehouselike atmosphere of the pier, she was rapidly piecing together answers to many previously unanswered questions. She was making many new connections. For her, this tragedy appeared to be perhaps as elucidating as it was debilitating. I gave her some information about what the next few weeks and months might be like. I explained that there might be times when things would seem more difficult or not to be moving forward. I urged her to make sure she took proper care of herself and suggested she might find comfort and continued benefit from additional grief counseling or other psychotherapy.

Before she left, Katherine told me the reason she had come to Ground Zero when no one else in her family had. "When my father was dying, it was my little brother who, more than anyone, was by his side. He was there with him when he died. I had only been able to go back and forth between here and home a couple of times. It gave me great comfort to know he was there for Dad. I wanted to do the same for him." I was impressed with Katherine's insightfulness and courage. As we said farewell, I wished all the best for her as she faced this difficult time in her life.

On the occasions that I volunteered, I had varying types of contact with victims, families, and other workers. Not all the people with whom I would come in contact would express the types of insights that Katherine had but, thanks to her, I felt I was more aware of what kind of process they might be going through. In each case, my function was to give whatever support and guidance was appropriate. In some ways, the work was similar to what I usually do as a psychiatrist, but in other ways it was dissimilar. On a typical day, I am sought out specifically as a physician of mental health to assess someone (a patient) who is seeking treatment. In contrast, as a disaster psychiatrist, while keeping a watchful eye for signs of trauma, complicated grief, or other psychiatric symptoms warranting concern, my only actual intervention might be to provide information, offer a chair, or lend a supportive ear. Such interaction doesn't necessarily lead to a diagnosis or treatment recommendation. In fact, my role is generally not to provide treatment in the usual sense but to assess carefully and guide someone toward treatment elsewhere if needed. Because of this, it is equally important to know when and how not to intervene.

As a physician who has taken the Hippocratic oath to "do no harm," I am wary of overzealous interventions that can potentially be more harmful than helpful. It is important to recognize the limitations of a brief disaster-related contact. To attempt to engage someone as a patient in the usual way, potentially opening up psychological wounds and lowering defenses, could leave that person more vulnerable and without the necessary support that is only available in an ongoing treatment relationship. With Katherine, it seemed clear she was at a point in her life on that day with me where she was perhaps more receptive to psychotherapeutic intervention. I tried to listen, support, and gently guide her with the view that, although she might wish for more from me in terms of advice and interpretive feedback (which I might also wish to give), I needed to be mindful of my role, of Katherine's vulnerable state, and her longer term needs with which I would not be able to help.

With this experience, my skills have developed in different ways. The disaster setting can be as seductive as it is chaotic and stressful. As a mental health professional in such a situation, one senses the critical nature of the work. It can bring about feelings of urgency to "make a difference." Under such circumstances, it is important to recognize that, at times, this sense of urgency may be more reflective of the needs and feelings of the person offering assistance than of the needs of those on the receiving end of it. As a result, psychiatrists in the disaster setting must often work harder to remain focused with regard to assessing people's status in terms of what kind of assistance they require or want, while maintaining awareness of their own needs and desires.

This, of course, speaks to many issues, including those of transference and countertransference.[2] The interaction Katherine and I had was certainly affected by her response to me as a person and mental health professional and by the circumstances under which we met. Initially, from the tag I wore, she knew only that I was a "Mental Health Volunteer." Later, after we had returned to the pier from Ground Zero, she asked me exactly what I did, and when I told her I was a psychiatrist, she exclaimed that she had "hit the jackpot." Obviously, a different person might have a different response to this information. For Katherine, it seemed to be a positive one, which likely contributed to her response to me. Likewise, my response to her in terms of my

---

[2]*Transference*, a term used in psychotherapy, generally refers to the expectations, beliefs, and emotional responses that a patient has in relation to a therapist that are based on experiences of significant persons from his or her past. Conversely, *countertransference* is the term used to describe a therapist's reactions to a patient based on relationships with significant persons from his or her past (Kaplan and Sadock, 1972; Gabbard, 1994).

sympathy for her loss, empathy as a person sharing in this national tragedy, and desire to reach out to a woman I admired also affected our interaction. Such powerful circumstances might lead one to stray from standard practice, potentially resulting in care that is not in the recipient's best interest. I felt, however, that my psychiatric training, with all of its dimensions, had prepared me for the task. It supported and steadied me despite my lack of previous disaster experience. It is impossible to say but perhaps even before she knew exactly what my professional background was, Katherine felt supported by it as well.

As the anniversary of 9/11 approached, there was a request that DPO volunteers be present for the memorial service and families' visit to Ground Zero. Apart from the impact that anniversaries of loss typically have on those who are grieving, there was also concern that some visitors might experience delayed grief reactions, which have a tendency to be more severe. I decided to participate. Security was high, and we were required to be there at 5:00 a.m. for clearance. It was still dark as the DPO volunteers gathered on an appointed street corner. The air was summer warm and uncomfortably humid. At the check-in, Federal Emergency Management Agency and City Hall personnel were making sure that we knew where we would be stationed, had proper identification, and had a rough idea of the schedule. As this was going on, the sun was rising. There was suddenly a breeze. It felt wonderful. I looked around, noting the changes that had occurred since my last visit. The area was clear of debris. The smell was gone. Certain buildings, like the World Financial Center, had been restored. Its magnificent atrium was again intact and gleaming in the sun's rays. Where the twisted metal mountains of the fallen towers had been, a cavernous pit several stories deep now existed.

The DPO volunteers were divided into groups, each assigned to different locations where visitors would be gathering. My group's assigned location was the "bottom of the ramp," down inside the pit itself. We had been told that there probably would be no food available, and the DPO medical director was thoughtfully distributing energy bars. The day would be long, and it wasn't clear if there would be any opportunity for breaks beyond necessary visits to the portable restrooms.

From the edge, one could really gain an appreciation for the vastness of the crater. The ramp down was long and pitched at an uncomfortably steep incline. I descended with caution, wondering about the problem this might present to less able visitors. The breeze, initially welcome, had suddenly become a powerful wind. Despite the depth and high walls, there was no shelter from these gusts, which swept down to the pit's floor, whipping the dirt in cyclonelike twists. In a way, these unusually high winds served as a grim reminder of the violence of a year ago. The atmosphere for the ceremony was sparse. A large wooden circular ring to hold visitors' flowers and tokens of remembrance was all that stood on the ground. The circle was located within the footprint of where 1 World Trade Center had stood. Much of the pit, including where Tower 2 had been, was cordoned off. There were certain restricted access areas, where only government, military, and volunteer personnel were allowed to go. Within these, there were several tents and portable restrooms. Bomb-squad teams with their dogs vigilantly canvassed all corners.

As we stood and waited for the ceremony to commence, the sun was high in a clear blue sky, eerily reminiscent of the year before. The bagpipers were the first to descend into the pit, marching and circling as they played their music. The emotion in the air was thick and tangible. Many of us blinked back tears. As the ceremony progressed, the names of those lost were read. I listened for the names of people I knew and thought of their families. At a certain point, the family members began to come down, trickling at first, later by the hundreds. As they came, we looked for any sign that we might be needed. Most came in groups, mourning the same person or people. In many cases, when you saw a group, it was obvious who was missing. A mother stood with her son and daughter, but no husband and father. Two parents arrived with their adult daughter, who was holding a picture of her brother. The members of one large group all arrived wearing T-shirts picturing a young couple and a flight number.

Despite the intensity of the emotion that just being there had for these people most closely affected, the majority seemed remarkably composed. When there were tears, we offered tissues. Some took them and thanked us; others waved us away, wishing to grieve without interference. I wanted to remain accessible, but avoid intruding on those who had come to pay their respects. I later learned from some of my colleagues that there was one person who needed assistance after collapsing in an apparent delayed grief-reaction. Fortunately, this was the only situation of this kind that I heard about.

People were placing flowers, pictures, and tributes on the ground in locations other than the wooden circle. At first, it wasn't clear to me why this was so, but someone mentioned that many were attempting to place memorials in locations, based on the official recovery grid map, which documented where remains had been found. People also gathered at the entrance to the restricted access area, where the footprint of 2 World Trade Center was. Security guards stationed there prevented them from entering and this was causing some distress among these families. They were devastated that they were not being permitted to place their tribute in a location near where they believed their loved one had died. Understanding the importance of this gesture for some, several psychiatrists succeeded in persuading the guards to let us bring the memorials into the off-limits area and place them in a particular location based on each family's instructions.

Sometimes as disaster psychiatrists, we intervene in ways that may seem small. At one point, a distraught woman approached me. Her little boy needed to use the bathroom but portables in the pit were in the restricted area. The security guard had told her she would have to take him to the portables at the top of the ramp, outside the pit. Because of the massive lines of people both coming and going, this would take a long time, plus the family would most likely be unable to return, and thus be forced to leave before they had finished paying their respects. I knew the security guard was just doing his job, but I felt it was also important to help make sure that the families, for whom this event had principally been held, were treated with appropriate sensitivity. Eventually, I was able to persuade the guard to let me take the boy into the restricted area.

Personal feelings aside, I believe professional judgment was what ultimately led to my decision to intervene on behalf of this family. Although I'm not sure it mattered whether I was a psychiatrist in terms of my being able to persuade the guard, I do know that as a rigorously trained professional, I am respectful of rules and the reasons for them. I am keenly aware of risk and danger, and my job involves attempting to keep my patients, many of whom face real risk, safe on a daily basis. As a psychiatrist, however, I couple this responsibility with the task of being attuned to people's emotional needs, which have the potential to have a significant impact on their lives. Guided by these purposes, and also by experience in assessing a situation and potential psychological factors motivating the individuals involved, I am comfortable advocating for such exceptions when appropriate. When I returned with the boy, his mom addressed the guard and me, her face expressing relief and tearful gratitude. "Thank you and God bless you," she said.

After hours of exposure to the windswept dirt, we were all coated with it from head to toe. Looking at my colleagues was reminiscent of how those who had escaped the burning towers one year ago today had looked as they emerged covered in ash. At this time, it was nearing the end of the ceremony. All of the names of those lost had been read aloud and many people were now beginning to leave. The wooden circle had been completely covered with memorials. Everywhere on the ground and against the walls were tributes. I circled the area as I had all day, carrying a supply of tissues and energy bars.

Over the course of the year since I had met her, I had thought of Katherine many times. I wondered if she might be at the anniversary, and if I might see her. Given the thousands who had visited, however, I believed I would likely have missed her. I watched the remaining people around the memorial circle. Many were now helping each other climb over its wall into the center, in an effort to find some additional room for pictures and flowers. Suddenly, I thought I saw Katherine. While I believed it was she, I decided to be certain by loudly calling out her name. As I called out, she immediately looked in my direction. There was a glimmer of uncertain recognition in her eye. As I began to introduce myself, she remembered, and flung her arms around me in a big hug.

She was not alone this time but with someone who appeared to be her sister and several young women, who I imagined might be her daughters and nieces. I asked her how she was. "Oh," she said, " I'm doing so much better now than I was on that day." I told her I was so glad, and remarked on how nice it was that family could also be here with her. She attempted to introduce me to some of her family as "the lady I told you about," but it was so crowded and loud that they didn't seem to hear. "I've been very involved with other victim's families who have been trying to find out what happened and why certain people didn't get out," she said. "Remember I told you I couldn't believe so many smart people didn't make it? Well, it turns out, several of the stairwells were blocked, and many people weren't aware of the alternative exits. Valuable time was lost. Some people were guided to the other side of the building where there was an open stairwell." I nodded.

As we stood there, I wanted to ask her other questions related to how she was doing now. For instance, how her family was, the situation with her husband, her mother, did she ever seek counseling back home? Unfortunately, I knew the circumstances wouldn't allow it. I was happy I got to see her again and know she was well. Katherine's sister was now calling her from across the crowd, telling her they had to go. "We have to go now and pick up my other brother who's waiting for us," she said. "It was so nice to see you. Thank you again for all of your help!" She hugged me again quickly and then was gone.

What I know as a psychiatrist—that who we are is greatly shaped by early experiences—seems to become even more evident when disaster strikes. We all enter the world with certain vulnerabilities, some genetic, others created by early relationships we've had with those closest to us. Because of this, uniquely personal reactions and defenses emerge when each of us is confronted with situations creating stress. Under such circumstances, we are our most vulnerable. As a medical doctor, I seek to treat patients based on my understanding that there are biochemical changes and neuro-endocrine responses, sometimes precipitated by psychological stressors, which can lead to illness. As a psychiatrist, however, I am equally aware of the fact that medicine alone can't always solve the problem. As a disaster psychiatrist I have seen how a catastrophic event can appear to have the effect of compressing a lifetime of psychic distress into one day.

I felt privileged to have met Katherine early in my volunteer experience. She was insightful. She was brave. I am extremely grateful to her. Her ability to articulate feelings about her life and family in the wake of grief exemplified the complex and personal reflection that tragic loss can bring about for each individual touched by it. Being there with her during this process helped further elucidate for me the sort of work disaster psychiatry involves. As a result, I was able to hone my everyday work skills, and develop new ones, to better serve people. I am equally grateful to DPO. The opportunity to serve as a volunteer in my chosen profession has given me great satisfaction. To have been able to participate in the 9/11 relief effort was a great honor and an experience I have grown from both personally and professionally.

References

Andreasen, N. C. & Black, D. W. (1995), Introductory Textbook of Psychiatry, 2nd ed. Washington, DC: American Psychiatric Press, pp. 363–364.

Gabbard, G. O. (1994), Psychodynamic Psychiatry in Clinical Practice: The DSM–IV Edition, 2nd ed. Washington, DC: American Psychiatric Press, pp. 11–13.

Kaplan, H. I. & Sadock, B. J. (1972), Synopsis of Psychiatry, 8th ed. Baltimore, MD: Lippincott Williams & Wilkins, pp. 6–8, 285.

2

Life at the Pile

Joseph C. Napoli

Luckily for me, I was not at the World Trade Center. I was not in the vicinity of the Twin Towers. I was not even in New York City, although I was scheduled to be later in the afternoon on September 11. There are many ironies about that day. Many people who lived through it have said, "But for . . . I would have been in the Trade Center." One of the most public of these "but for's" was the CEO who would have been with the 658 who died in his firm on the 101st and 103rd through 105th floors of Tower 1 but for the fact that he had brought his son to kindergarten. With relief and thankfulness, various individuals have related their stories to me. In providing disaster mental health outreach services to the personnel of the Port Authority of New York and New Jersey in the days and months after that day, I listened to many reasons why, by chance, each person was not at the World Trade Center that fateful day: "I would have been there if I didn't recently transfer . . . if I weren't out sick . . . if my weekly meeting at the Trade Center hadn't been canceled," and so on. Although my irony on 9/11 was a matter of chance, it was not a matter of life and death. Nevertheless, it triggered my thoughts about the relationship between "chance events" and being dead or alive. Ironically, when I was a volunteer firefighter I almost died. On October 15, 1967, by chance, I was at a bowling alley fire that killed five firefighters.

Ironies, "but for's," chance meetings, and matters of chance occur all the time. When they happen in relation to surviving a disaster, they become an indelible part of our memory. Disasters might traumatize us and shatter our beliefs. Nevertheless, how each of us appraises these happenings when they occur in association with a disaster gives meaning to a horrible experience.

What does this have to do with being a disaster psychiatrist? A disaster psychiatrist may also be a victim of disaster, either by direct exposure or by attending to those who were directly traumatized. *Vicarious traumatization*[1] and *compassion fatigue*[2] are terms that refer to the negative impact on professional caregivers as they listen to the trauma of others. This is the risk of being empathic and compassionate. This "secondary traumatization" may be so severe that it destroys meaning and purpose for the disaster psychiatrist, leaving him or her with nothing but doubt. Therefore, why expose oneself to this risk? I believe that psychiatrists should be self-aware so that they may not only better understand and care for those who are traumatized, but also protect their own mental health. Two questions disaster psychiatrists should answer for themselves are: What are the personality traits that are necessary to be a disaster psychiatrist? What are the reasons that I do or would do this work? In addition, novice disaster psychiatrists need to consider what they might experience while doing this work.

This essay has a threefold purpose. First, it shows how disaster psychiatrists should be self-reflective to give attention to meaning, empathy, and self-care and to answer the questions that I have posed. Second, it demonstrates that disasters dramatically confront us with matters of chance and the significance of human connections and attachment in the face of death. Third, it supports my belief that the devastation and death caused by disaster affirms life. I illustrate these three points by describing some of my experiences as a disaster psychiatrist, as well as relating my close encounter with death as a volunteer firefighter. By disclosing my experiences and feelings, I hope that the lay reader will better understand those who do this work and that the professional reader will benefit by my example of self-reflection. In addition, I hope this essay will encourage those psychiatrists who have the potential for this work to join the ranks of disaster psychiatrists.

When I woke on the morning of September 11, I immediately thought about the lecture I would be presenting to the medical students at the College of Physicians and Surgeons in Manhattan. After breakfast I did some preparation for another project that was due the following week. While I gathered up my slides and notes for my lecture, I heard the news blaring from the radio. "An unidentified plane has crashed into the north tower of

---

[1]First discussed by McCann and Pearlman (1990).
[2]Concept introduced by Figley (1994).

the World Trade Center." I wondered, "How could this happen? It's a clear day!" I further thought, "When the military B-25 crashed into the Empire State Building in 1945, there was a very soupy fog. The pilot had lost his bearings and apparently mistook crossing one river for the other—maybe the East River for the Hudson." Being a disaster psychiatrist, I often think in terms of disasters—historical ones and hypothetical ones. Immediately, I called out to my wife and daughter, "A plane crashed into the World Trade Center!" I checked my Breaking News Network (BNN) pager. I needed some confirmation from another source that this had really happened. Usually, this occurs in the reverse order. First my BNN pager buzzes with a report of the latest fire, serious motor vehicle accident, shooting, "jumper up" (the emergency radio lingo for a person about to attempt suicide by jumping), stabbing, and so on—that is, the ordinary "garden variety" violence, mayhem, accidents, and crises. Then, depending on the newsworthiness of the event, it may or may not be broadcast to the public by TV and radio stations and, the next day, described in the newspaper. Even on a slow news day, a BNN-reported event may take time to find its way to the attention of the general public or may never be reported.

A psychiatrist need not be a specialist in disaster psychiatry to provide care for the individuals who experience these "quiet" traumatic events. Psychiatrists treat the survivors of such events in hospital emergency rooms or their offices when these individuals develop mental disorders. Disaster psychiatry adds an outreach dimension consisting of screening for those at risk and providing very early interventions. This may involve rendering care in the midst of chaos at the disaster scene or at a nearby location, for example, an evacuation center. Why do this? Why extend oneself in this way?

Although most trauma and tragedy never come to the public's attention, our protectors—emergency medical technicians, firefighters, paramedics, police—are regularly exposed to the extremes of human suffering. Those who work in disaster mental health and many in emergency services and law enforcement acknowledge that our protectors need to be protected and supported for the sake of their psychological well-being. This was not always the prevailing view. When I was a volunteer firefighter no one paid any attention to the emotions of emergency personnel. If a critical incident such as a line-of-duty death occurred, no one really spoke about it. When our company returned to quarters from any fire, whether it involved a critical incident or not, our members assembled at the bar in the firehouse lounge to smoke, drink, and watch sports on TV. A significant development over the last 20 years has been the recognition that it is essential to care for the emergency responders. More recently, the pendulum has swung to the opposite extreme of individuals rushing in to perform mandatory group psychological debriefings. What had begun as a support for emergency workers has become a method applied indiscriminately to everyone for any kind of traumatic event.

Now we are debating whether to debrief or not. Some research data demonstrates that psychological debriefing may be harmful for those who are highly distressed in the aftermath of a disaster. In May 2001, the New Jersey Psychiatric Association and the Department of Psychiatry of the New Jersey Medical School at the University of Medicine and Dentistry of New Jersey sponsored a full-day symposium on this debate. In the presentations and during the panel discussion, the consensus of the faculty was not to "throw the baby out with the bath water" but to concede that there are problems with and limitations to psychological debriefing. Based on my experience as a volunteer firefighter and work as a disaster psychiatrist, I agree with this conclusion. On one hand, if a crisis counselor conveys the expectation that an emergency responder will likely develop complications after exposure to a critical incident, the responder may more likely develop a debilitating reaction. On the other hand, I would loathe a return to the days of not acknowledging the detrimental impact of traumatic events on emergency workers. To "first do no harm," we need to employ evidence-based interventions. Aggressively jumping in and administrating interventions may interfere with the normal process of coping with a traumatic experience. Nevertheless, it would be inhumane to suspend all interventions while further research is undertaken. Common sense dictates that we should be present, bear witness, and be emotionally supportive. These are basic aspects of the work of disaster psychiatrists.

Although media organizations contract for the BNN service, I sometimes wonder, why do I? I think that it is necessary for the work that I do. The mission of the Fort Lee Office of Emergency Management (OEM) Crisis Response Team, which comprises mental health professionals, clergy, and peer counselors, is to respond and provide mental health services at the time of a crisis or disaster. We voluntarily serve the citizens and support emergency personnel in Fort Lee, New Jersey. In addition, we deploy to other locations when requested to assist other municipalities—that is, to provide mutual aid. Therefore, as chief of this team, I need to be aware of any emergency that happens in my locale. But I know this is an intellectualization. It may be my way of maintaining a sense of control. To know is to control. Therefore, if I know about the disasters and dangers around me, I feel more secure. These events do not "come out of left field" and surprise me. These events are not shocks; they are ordinary.

But it is obviously an illusion to believe that one can control the uncontrollable. In addition, Murphy's law—what can go wrong will go wrong—often prevails, and some say Murphy was an optimist. For example, even with my BNN pager, I almost missed the general alarm blaze in Edgewater, New Jersey, on August 30, 2000. While almost the entire west side of Manhattan was able to see the flames light the sky above the Hudson River, I was home on vacation and I let my BNN pager's battery run down. Fortuitously, I was watching TV when a breaking news caption started to march across the bottom of the screen: "NBC News reports that a fire is burning out of control in the Hudson River community of Edgewater, New Jersey. Stay tuned for the 11 o'clock news for further details." As the Channel 4 News helicopter transmitted live video that showed flames shooting 100 feet into the sky, I was out the door. After passing through the staging area where fire and EMS personnel and equipment from almost every municipality in Bergen County were preparing for action, I arrived at the fire scene. The fire had jumped across a street from its origin in a 400 unit townhouse complex under construction and blew out the windows of a 24-unit garden apartment, demolished nine private homes, destroyed utility lines and poles, and incinerated numerous cars. A fire engine from Edgewater that was among the first to arrive was caught in the heat as the fire leaped over what should have been a natural firebreak. The engine company crew had to pull back quickly as the soaring temperature melted the lenses of the engine's head and emergency lights and cracked its windshield. Although I am the chief of the Fort Lee OEM Crisis Response Team, at this fire I jockeyed ice water along with another OEM volunteer to the exhausted and dehydrated firefighters. Pitching in and performing simple tasks like this is an excellent way for a disaster psychiatrist on the scene to relate to the emergency personnel. While I provided them with water, I chatted and checked how they were doing. Similarly, disaster psychiatrists might hand out food and set up cots in a shelter. While taking care of the basic needs of the survivors, disaster psychiatrists are also attending to their psychological needs and well-being. In addition, when disaster psychiatrists pitch in to do these tasks, they are being team players at a time when teamwork is essential. A disaster psychiatrist needs to have the willingness to pitch in and the capacity for teamwork. Finally, although one does not do these tasks for self-gratification, performing such tasks may be very gratifying for the disaster psychiatrist because this might be the only useful action to take at a particular time.

The day after the fire, as an American Red Cross volunteer at the victim reception center temporarily set up at the Edgewater recreation building, I provided mental health disaster services for some of the 67 people who had lost their homes. Here, too, there were quirks of fate. Unlike the "but for's" of 9/11, these intensified the trauma and loss rather than providing a sense of relief in escaping death. For example, one of the homeowners had just completed an extensive home renovation. Another had just finished restoring a classic car. Like lightning striking a place twice, a woman tearfully described how a short in a power transformer two years before had caused a blowout of all the appliances in her apartment just as this fire had once again damaged all of her appliances by causing an electrical surge in the circuitry of her apartment building. Nevertheless, there was also good fortune. It was life-sparing that this fire broke out in the early evening instead of later when these families would have been asleep.

My use of a BNN pager may merely be a manifestation of my voyeurism. Dr. Gidro-Frank, a psychiatrist distinguished in the annals of the New York State Psychiatric Institute, taught me that there are three traits essential for being a psychiatrist—voyeurism, paranoia, and narcissism. It was his dramatic way of saying that a psychiatrist needs sufficient curiosity to pursue a patient's story despite its being depressing, disturbing, or horrible; sufficient suspicion to doggedly investigate the source or sources of a patient's malady; and sufficient self-esteem to enjoy one's treatment successes and tolerate the failures. Some would also add the trait of masochism to this profile. The psychiatrist has to be a sufficient glutton for pain and suffering to listen repeatedly to horrific tales of human misery. These traits also serve the disaster psychiatrist very well. It is not only altruism that motivates disaster workers, including psychiatrists, to respond to a scene of destruction. We need to see for ourselves and be part of the action. Given the inherent danger, the drive to be there must be strong enough to override our instinct for self-preservation. But here is where paranoia may be life-preserving. By being suspicious and hypervigilant, psychiatrists might be able to sense danger and thus be protective of themselves and provide safety and security for those they are caring for in the aftermath of a disaster.

Voyeurism and paranoia, curiosity and suspicion, drove me on that Tuesday morning of September 11. What happened? Why did it happen? I was not satisfied just hearing about this news; I needed to also see it. Unknown to me then, I also would be driven to smell and feel it. I turned the TV on. Smoke was drifting from Tower 1. The anchorperson calmly and professionally reported what was known, which was not much. No activity was depicted. It reminded me of a "sleeper"—a fire that doesn't show much on the outside but is furiously raging inside. Witnessing a sleeper is like seeing only the tip of the iceberg. Activity outside the fire building is moving gradually and in an orderly manner while beneath the surface, inside the structure, a variety of factors are rapidly brewing to erupt into total chaos and catastrophe. I thought, "The bowling alley fire was a sleeper." I stopped watching the TV, ostensibly to continue getting ready for the day. On reflection later, I realized that I stopped watching because that was not the time for me to be distracted by memories of the tragic fire that occurred in 1967.

My daughter, however, continued to watch the broadcast, saw the second plane fly into Tower 2 and yelled, "A second plane just crashed into the other tower!" Simultaneously, the three of us—my wife, daughter, and I—concluded that it had to be a terrorist attack. Our surprise changed to shock. I exclaimed, "All the bridges and tunnels will be closed. They'll close down the city." I confess that my next thought—"How will I get to Columbia to give my lecture?"—was narrow-minded and selfish. It is natural, however, for one, even a disaster psychiatrist, to have thoughts that are self-centered even as others might be suffering. The irony, which began my thinking on 9/11 about matters of chance, was that my lecture, which would not be presented that day, was titled "Traumatic Stress: Respect, Recognition, and Prevention."

Although I calmly drove to Englewood Hospital and Medical Center and saw my patients on the in-patient unit, I was suddenly caught up in the response to the terrorist attacks. Our hospital command post was already in full operation, thanks to the expertise and dedicated work of Steve Gaunt, director of safety. I was called to the command post and directed to open a crisis counseling center for the staff. I propelled myself into a whirlwind of activity. Crisis counseling was necessary; some of the hospital staff had difficulty functioning because they had friends and relatives at the World Trade Center. We used the PIE method—proximity, immediacy, expectancy—that was first used in World War I for combatants suffering with shell shock. We immediately provided crisis intervention near to where staff members worked with the expectation that they would return to their tasks. This "immediately getting back on the horse" approach was beneficial for our staff. It was also advantageous for our patients because it allowed Englewood Hospital to continue its efficient operation during this state of emergency. We also set up a family assistance center to receive the families and significant others of the hundreds of casualties we were told would be coming, but never did.

Leaving what I had set up in good hands, I rushed to my office to call my patients scheduled for the day to inquire how they were doing and to make alternate appointments. Next, the Fort Lee Office of Emergency Management paged me. I responded to Fort Lee High School and organized the response of 13 crisis counselors. The Fort Lee Emergency Medical Service (EMS) in collaboration with our Fort Lee OEM coordinator and my buddy Joe Licata, and MICCOM (Mobile Intensive Care Communications) for Northern New Jersey, established a huge medical triage and hazardous material decontamination operation on the high school athletic field. Approximately 40 ambulances and crews were standing by, along with four paramedic units. The emergency medical service incident commander of this operation was told to expect nearly a thousand people needing emergency medical care to cross to New Jersey via the George Washington Bridge. After all, many injured evacuees were being transported via a flotilla of ferries to Jersey City, directly across the Hudson River from the World Trade Center.

In Fort Lee, however, no patients arrived. Therefore, like other emergency personnel, disaster psychiatrists need to cope with "hurrying up and waiting" and the frustration of not feeling useful because there is no one that requires their help. Instead, on the evening of 9/11 there was an eerie scene of dazed people, silhouetted by the light from the streetlights and stores, walking in slow motion and milling around on the sidewalks near the George Washington Bridge. Commuters returning from New York City were desperately trying to get home. They did not spend time at the Fort Lee OEM reception center and shelter that had been opened for the public. This would have been only a brief respite after their walk up most of the length of Manhattan and across the bridge. Instead, they wandered aimlessly about, many with cell phones to their ears trying to make contact with their loved ones. Others queued at public telephones and waited their turn to call home. This was an impressive scene of survivors seeking to connect to someone with whom they had an attachment.

The next day, the need for mental health support escalated. I spent the rest of the week directing and providing disaster mental health services, and receiving telephone calls as the chairperson of the New Jersey Psychiatric Association Disaster Preparedness Committee in addition to caring for my patients. The numbness and detachment of the first 24 hours had worn off. People flipped into excitation. I worked with Port Authority police officers assigned to the George Washington Bridge command including those who were at the World Trade Center when the towers collapsed, employees of the Port Authority, and broadcast journalists and other staff at CNBC and MSNBC. Everyone was in a state of hyperarousal. My colleagues and I worked hard to restore calm, order, and a sense of safety.

On Saturday I crashed. I hit the marathoner's wall, only I was not running a marathon—or was I? Surely I was not among the terrified who had run from the collapsing Twin Towers. But I was among the many who were confronted with being vulnerable to another terrorist attack. I dealt with all of this by mobilizing. Now I had nothing to do. By slowing down I was able to feel. I felt sad, irritable, anxious, and angry. I railed at the terrorists.

For no apparent reason, the Port Authority did not accept my offer to have the Fort Lee OEM Crisis Response Team continue to work through the weekend. Maybe it was for the best because I could turn my attention back to everyday concerns. I had to complete my lecture on "Posttraumatic Stress Disorder: The Role of Serotonin—Psychobiology and Treatment" that was scheduled for Thursday, September 20. I tried to work on it, but I could not concentrate. I was experiencing an emotional letdown. I became angry with my wife. It is difficult to return to the ordinary after a disaster. I had worked intensely with dedicated mental health professionals and clergy under very trying conditions. We were a great team, and I missed them. I did not want to let go of being part of the aftermath of 9/11. There is a scheme that describes the sequential psychological and biological reactions of the disaster worker. Its phases are alarm, mobilization, action, and letdown. I was in the midst of the letdown phase—that is, the transition from emergency mode to normal work routine and usual life. I was not satisfied with only hearing about it and seeing it on TV. I needed to go to Ground Zero to experience it firsthand. I had done a lot but I felt I needed to do more. I had to do something, anything. I could not be inactive. I could not tolerate being "on the bench" for the weekend. I yearned to get "back in the game." I called a number of contacts who could possibly get me access to Ground Zero but I had no luck. Then I called Diana Brown, my friend and colleague from the American Red Cross (ARC). We have worked together as ARC Disaster Mental Health volunteers. Seemingly, I called her to get to Ground Zero via the New York Chapter of the ARC. But it soon became apparent that I called her just to make a connection and talk to someone who was a disaster mental health veteran and would understand. I felt much better after I spoke with her, even though it did not get me to Ground Zero. As a disaster psychiatrist I have observed, over and over again, the powerful force of human attachment. While at fire scenes, I have witnessed individuals breaking through police barricades to find their loved ones. Even during the drills of our Fort Lee School System's Community Crisis Response Team, the parents did not require a script for their role play as they ad libbed their urgent desire to be reunited with their children. On 9/11, I took a break from the bustle at Englewood Hospital to return home and hug my wife and daughter. The next day my daughter fielded heart-wrenching telephone calls at Englewood Hospital from individuals frantically seeking their relatives or friends. Facilitating the reunion of disaster survivors with their families and significant others is an essential task for the disaster psychiatrist. The intensity of this attachment extends to one's pets. This was evident at an occupied multiple dwelling house fire at which our Fort Lee OEM Crisis Response Team assisted. This fire occurred on Sunday, September 16 during a community memorial service in Fort Lee for 9/11. So I was back in action. We aided a boy and his family who feared for their two cats that were trapped inside the burning building. Fortunately, one was rescued.

When I finally got to Ground Zero as an observer with the Port Authority, it was not what I expected. I anticipated only death and devastation. Instead, it was like an anthill—a colony of activity. Crews of steel and demolition workers, firefighters, police, and recovery teams swarmed over the area. Four-wheel "Gators"—all-terrain transport units—scurried hither and yon. The movement of cranes, backhoes, and trucks, along with a multitude of human voices, created a cacophony. Trucks pulled in, were loaded with wreckage, and pulled out. Shanties circled the periphery on the southwest side. Ground Zero was an entire village filled with life. I felt safe and protected because I was in the good hands of the Port Authority police officer assigned to me. I did not require a Ground Zero ID badge. Whenever a National Guardsman or police officer approached to check my ID, I just pointed to the officer at my side. Each time we were immediately ushered along until someone yelled at us, "Hey! Hey! This a hard-hat area!" A man dressed in coveralls, heavy boots, and a hard hat who appeared to be a foreman approached us. He signaled for one of the Gators to stop. He took two yellow hard hats from the cardboard box on back of this vehicle and handed one to each of us. As my escort turned to me, he said, "I forgot. Maybe we should've stopped at the Port Authority headquarters on the way in to pick up some gear." My protector had slipped up. It was unfair of me to have placed this responsibility on him. We stood weeping by the wall of remembrance, where there was an abundance of flowers, stuffed animals, and letters, in addition to photographs of the missing members of the New York and Port Authority police departments and the city's fire department. Perhaps because of his loss I should have been protecting him. We then made our way back to the other side of the pile.

"Joe! Joe!" I heard my name being called. It is amazing what flashes through a person's mind in a matter of seconds. There was no apparent source. Being a psychiatrist, I really did not want to admit that I was hallucinating. Because of the weirdness of my surroundings, my mind certainly could have perceived something that did not exist. I was unable to use the excuse that it was an illusion—an actual sensory stimulus that my mind was distorting, like when the wind whistling in the leaves sounds like someone calling your name. There was dead silence at this location. Next, I saw someone running from the top of the pile. In a flash, he was next to me. He was clad in Ground Zero fashion de rigueur—hard hat, khaki clothes, work boots, a necklace of official ID badges, and a particle filter mask dangling by its straps from his neck. With much relief for my sanity I knew who had been calling my name. It was Tony Ng, a psychiatrist and the medical director of Disaster Psychiatry Outreach. He was not only a life, but a life that I knew personally. Therefore, meeting Tony was not only an example of a human connection but represented the ultimate "proof" that there was "life at the pile."

It was life affirming as Tony and I made contact with a firm handshake. Statisticians assure us that meeting someone we know from back home while visiting a distant location is highly probable and not bizarre. Nevertheless, we are amazed when we have one of these "it's a small world" experiences. Certainly, it would be an even greater probability that I would encounter Tony at Ground Zero. We are both dedicated to the same work. Why wouldn't we both be drawn to this place? Yet it was a very odd experience. I did not anticipate that I would see him at Ground Zero. A corollary to this unexpectedly-running-into-someone-you-know phenomenon is meeting-someone-who-you should-already-know-but-don't. Here at the pile, after I introduced my PAPD escort, Tony introduced me to Dr. Carlos Almeida. I should have already known him because he is the director of the Comprehensive Psychiatric Emergency Services at Columbia-Presbyterian Medical Center (CPMC), and I teach emergency psychiatry to the medical students assigned to that service. I suppose not meeting someone in my own backyard could be attributed to the fact that CPMC and the College of Physicians and Surgeons are large organizations but this encounter was an example of how we are connected in many unknown ways. Hence, I contemplated the variations of human connections and the strangeness of chance encounters.

There at Ground Zero Tony and I chatted. He told me about his work as the medical director of DPO in New York City. I filled him in about what I was doing in New Jersey in response to 9/11. Meanwhile, Carlos and my police officer engaged in a conversation. As if prompted by a square-dance caller, we swapped partners and our talking resumed. Finally, we formed a group of four and exchanged comments. Despite being surrounded by death and destruction, we were engaged in lively human interaction.

In addition to coping with witnessing the remains of the dead, disaster psychiatrists need to tolerate chaos and destruction. Veterans need to prepare rookie disaster psychiatrists for what they will face. During our mundane conversation amid the devastation, my mind pictured another pile—the result of the bowling alley fire in 1967. Like this pile, the pile that I remembered consisted of building material detritus. Here and now, the wreckage was large, twisted beams of steel, pulverized concrete, and other destroyed construction materials; there and then, the rubble was broken cinder blocks, splintered wood, and plaster dust. Although not composed of the same inanimate materials, the difference between the two piles was mainly a matter of magnitude. Although the other pile was much smaller, it, too, was a burial mound. Here the count would approach 3,000, including 343 NYFD firefighters, 23 NYPD officers, and 37 PAPD officers. Under the debris of the other pile were the crushed, mangled bodies of five firefighters.

We bade farewell and continued to circle around to the north side. On our way we met a PAPD officer whom my officer knew well. They chatted. We continued on. By now I was beginning to taste Ground Zero. I could feel the dust in my throat. I wondered how the workers who were there day in and day out were able to survive. I began to question. Did I really want to be at Ground Zero? Isn't it too risky? Why do this work?

I also began to think how I happened to be at that fire in 1967. I was not supposed to be there. I should not have been out of my bed. The siren was clear and loud when its sound jolted me out of my slumber. It was a little after four o'clock in the morning. Still half asleep, I quickly got dressed. As I left my house, the cold air hitting my face fully awakened me. I drove to my firehouse. It was dark and the door was locked. Our siren was silent. No one else was responding. Could I have dreamt that I heard the siren? At that moment I heard a siren in the distance. The sound was coming from the neighboring town to the south. I was curious. I thought that since I was up anyway, I would check it out. I drove until I came on the fire scene. It was a sleeper. There was no visible fire. The movement of the firefighters seemed to be in slow motion. They were getting ready to attack the fire through the front door. I went around to the side of the building where an engine company from a neighboring town was working in an alley. I encountered the chief of my department. He was there even though none of our Fort Lee companies had been called out. I was present at a place where I should not have been, at least not yet. My chief and I talked as we stood adjacent to the hose crew who were about to make an entry through the door on the north side of the building. It was a 20-foot-high, 100- by 150-foot structure constructed of cinder-block walls with a bowed roof supported by trusses composed of huge wooden beams and struts. For some inexplicable reason the chief and I turned simultaneously and started to walk away. There was a thunderous boom. We reeled around. Without warning the entire structure collapsed and crashed down on the crew of five. Instantly, the chief radioed the dispatcher to call out my company. I heard my firehouse's siren wail. This would have been the alarm for me to heed. This would have been the time for me to start out.

Joining the flurry of activity by emergency personnel, I went into action and helped fight the fire. When the fire was extinguished, like the disaster survivors that I have since worked with after various disasters, I yearned to be with those I loved after this close call with death.

In conclusion, the serendipity that occurred in relation to the two piles separated by years but linked in meaning affirms the fragility and precious-ness of life and the healing bond of human attachment. My experiences with disasters and the survivors of disaster confirm for me that exposure to trauma may be a positive life-defining experience. Although disasters harshly confront us with death and despair, they paradoxically affirm life and purpose. Nevertheless, because providing outreach for disaster survi-vors might be traumatizing for disaster psychiatrists, they should properly prepare. This preparation includes answering the following questions: What might I experience? Do I have the necessary personality traits to do this work? What are my motives? I have shared some of my experiences as a model for answering these questions. Interwoven in the narrative of my ex-periences I have described some characteristics that I think are necessary for being a disaster psychiatrist. Obviously, each psychiatrist should deter-mine his or her own motives for doing this work and the meaning of being a disaster psychiatrist. When I reflect on the bowling alley fire and remember my grief for my brother firefighters and their families and friends, I know why I am a disaster psychiatrist.

References

Figley, C. R. (1994), Compassion fatigue. Presented at: Premeeting Institute of the annual meeting of the International Society for Traumatic Stress Studies, Chi-cago, IL.

_____, ed. (1995), *Compassion Fatigue: Coping with Secondary Traumatic Stress Disorder in Those Who Treat the Traumatized.* New York: Brunner/Mazel.

McCann, I. L. & Pearlman, L. A. (1990), Vicarious traumatization: A contextual model for understanding the effects of trauma on helpers. *J. Traumatic Stress,* 3:131–149.

3

The Other Ground Zero

Joseph P. Merlino

Ground Zero is where the World Trade Center (WTC) towers once stood; the "other" Ground Zero is where the remains of the towers' occupants and visitors, at least those who were not immediately incinerated in the atrocity of September 11, rest until—and if ever—they are identified. The attacks at the World Trade Center on September 11, 2001 claimed 2,823 lives.

From the early days of this atrocity, we at Bellevue Hospital Center were concerned about our neighbors up the street at the Office of the Chief Medical Examiner (OCME), also known as the city morgue. Clearly, this staff must have been going through hell. Between the never-ending shifts dealing with efforts to identify the remains of the WTC victims, they also had to contend with the air crash of American Airlines Flight 587 in Rockaway, New York, on top of their routinely busy daily responsibilities of processing the homicides, suicides, and accidents that occurred in New York.

Bellevue's efforts working with the OCME took many forms, from joining the New York University staff volunteering in the dining room to offer staff support, to offering support groups on all shifts at the morgue, to providing on-site counselors daily to staff wishing to access help, to roaming the street alongside the morgue, which had been setup specifically for the 9/11 efforts.

Bellevue Hospital, New York University (NYU) School of Medicine, NYU Medical Center, and the OCME are contiguous structures along New York City's First Avenue near the East River. The 30th Street side of the

OCME serves as a short cut for staff coming from Bellevue to enter the NYU School of Medicine. From 9/11 until a year later, that simple street was transformed into an alley of death protected by the New York City police and swarming with cops, firefighters, FBI agents, and others. What had been a quiet thoroughfare was now a high-security, heavily patrolled, war-like restricted zone.

Soon after September 11, I became one of the living who inhabited this surreal space more often than I ever imagined. After receiving my clearance and the necessary photo ID tag identifying me as a member of the OCME, I was allowed to pass the police guards and access 30th Street.

"Death Alley" was now a long narrow block flanked on both sides largely by trailer-home–type structures. These were occupied by the various teams of professionals whose services were required in such numbers that they did not fit in the existing OCME building. These teams had signs on the trailer doors reminiscent of the movie trailers so common in New York with actors' names on dressing-room doors. These names, however, seemed bizarre and macabre. Titles included "medical anthropology" and "postmortem dental identification." These trailers were juxtaposed with equally bizarre areas including "massage" and the Salvation Army canteen truck that served plates of what became known affectionately on the block as "mystery meat." A sign of the "gallows humor" that belied the covert fear and anxiety of these professionals used to dealing with death, but not death of this magnitude and cause, was the rumor claiming that the meat was actually sent up to the DNA lab and came back as "unidentifiable."

Weaving throughout this morbid alley bustling with activity were chaplains, Salvation Army volunteers, and mental health counselors quietly offering any assistance they could provide to the living who were surrounded by hours and hours each day with death that resulted from the unimaginable. Making contact and initiating a dialogue with staff was a delicate proposition. One needed to be always mindful of not being invasive, of not intruding on the private space and time of those tremendously overworked and overwrought. At the same time, we were cognizant that those in need of emotional help were not necessarily active in seeking it. We therefore were left with a mixture of training, experience, intuition, and luck. Innocuous contact was begun with social pleasantries to gauge, as best we could, the emotional status of the individual and his or her openness and accessibility. Such contact would occur while a staffer or volunteer was having a cup of coffee or a smoke or over a meal in the canteen. Sometimes conversation would start during the long walk from First Avenue down 30th Street.

Two recollections come to mind. On a beautiful sunny day, I was standing outside the canteen with a volunteer from the Midwest. We were both remarking on what a glorious day it was when it suddenly dawned on me how I completely forgot where I was and what I thought I was supposed to be doing. On reflection, I was touched by our ability to transcend the moment and still be touched by the beauty that still existed.

On another occasion, I naively went to the morgue on a Sunday afternoon to facilitate a previously scheduled support group. The OCME assigned us to the staff lunchroom in the morgue building. Walking past numerous closed doors, trying to imagine what was behind them, I settled in the empty lunchroom. Soon three or four burly guys came in with their lunch. The Sunday football game was put on the television and the men began to eat with gusto. I looked at my coleader, and he looked at me. Neither of us dared to say a word. We put out a couple of comments to see if they were there for the group; they were not. I sure as hell wasn't going to turn off the football game. After all, this was one of the few breaks these people had in a 12- to 24-hour shift. We decided to use the television commercials to briefly introduce ourselves and distribute information sheets we brought that explained symptoms and reactions to stress and trauma as well as how to deal with this at home with the spouse and kids. I noticed that each of the sheets we handed out were folded and put in each man's pocket. I felt we had a successful, if totally improvised, intervention. I left knowing more than when I entered that lunchroom.

The bustle of Death Alley every now and then would suddenly stop and an eerie silence would blanket 30th Street. Quietly, solemnly, everyone on the street would form two columns, one on either side. They stood at respectful attention as an ambulance-hearse slowly backed down the street. The commanding officer would signal a salute, the ambulance door would open, and a stretcher would be slowly and reverently slid out. The chaplain would offer a blessing, and the black shiny bag would be wheeled into the tent-extension of the morgue to begin the methodical process of cataloging—and hopefully of identification. Once the remains were out of sight, Death Alley returned to its bustle until another ambulance silently approached, and the exact procedure was repeated again, and again. I learned early on that the contents of those bags rarely contained an entire human body.

One of the other things that struck me about this street was the tall stack of red containers, which reminded me of closed milk crates. I found out that these were used by the OCME staff to store the more than 20,000 body parts that were recovered from the WTC site. They were housed in

16 refrigerated tractor-trailer trucks aligned in two rows with their backs opening into a huge, white tent that became Memorial Park. This tented cemetery was located directly opposite the very swank Water Club on the East River, yet another symbol of how death permeated every aspect of New Yorkers' lives post-9/11.

Memorial Park officially became the cemetery for the World Trade Center's Twin Towers after the closing of the Trade Center site and the ending of recovery efforts at the Fresh Kills landfill on Staten Island where more than a million and a half tons of debris from the WTC had been sifted for clues. Families and friends were permitted to visit, very much as they would a funeral home. The sides of each trailer would be wreathed with flowers and candles, like 16 large caskets in a huge funeral home, each containing the countless body parts of those destroyed by the planes of September 11. So successfully did this create a funereal setting for me personally that I found myself reciting a silent prayer each time I entered this sacred space.

Visitations were permitted by reservation during morning and early-afternoon hours. The times were structured and fixed so that the professional activity related to the identification of the remains of this "working cemetery" would stop for specified times, the mausoleum-trailers' doors would be closed, the huge tent entrance opened so that the stench of decaying remains would be diluted, and only then would the families be escorted in. Each small group of family and friends would be greeted at one end of 30th Street and walked to the Memorial Park tent by a member of our mental health team. Emotional support, comfort, counseling referrals, and direction were provided as requested or needed.

Members of the OCME staff were always available to assist in providing technical answers to families' questions about the procedures involved in identifying their loved ones. The family members found great consolation in the caring professionalism of the OCME staff. It must be noted that the staff of the OCME always acted in a dignified and respectful manner in all dealings with the dead and the living. This was never lost on those who volunteered at the OCME and interacted with its staff.

Just as 30th Street had to change and adapt to the needs of September 11, so, too, did my approach to doctoring. As a medical administrator and academic psychiatrist formally trained as a psychoanalyst, it may seem that I should have known just what to do. Well, I didn't. Things were different from anything else I did since graduating from medical school nearly 25 years ago. This was not the setting in which the typical doctor–patient relationship applied. Nor were the groups I facilitated based on the psychotherapy model I've practiced previously. The main difference as I saw it was that the people I was with were *not* my patients. To me they were victims pure and simple. Clearly the dead in Memorial Park were the primary victims, but weren't the loved ones left behind also victims? In fact, weren't those working endless hours for endless days at the OCME also victims? Weren't all New Yorkers, including me, and not just geographic New Yorkers, victims as well?

The working model that I became most comfortable with was akin to that of the physician who has a very close family member or neighbor who is seriously ill; I call this the "physician–neighbor model." The doctor in this scenario is not "the" doctor but an informed and caring participant simultaneously affected by the neighbor's or relative's medical crisis. Adopting this approach enabled me the freedom to have the feelings I had without guilt, to walk away when I needed to, to share my sadness openly and to be as much a neighbor as a doctor. The physician–neighbor model became my way of conceptualizing the role of the early-phase mental health response to 9/11.

In this role I could still draw on my medical and psychiatric skills to identify individuals in need of traditional psychiatric assistance and referral. Utilizing my role as physician and neighbor allowed me to make such a referral while simultaneously advocating for and facilitating this referral. Direct linkages to Bellevue Hospital, NYU Medical Center, Disaster Psychiatry Outreach, and Lifenet proved invaluable.

An important service the mental health team also provided was the sharing of information about recognizing symptoms of *secondary trauma* and reducing the human costs such trauma exacts on the OCME staff's personal relationships, general health, and job performance. Small groups were offered as well as one-to-one contacts with mental health professionals. We also provided grand rounds for the 90 scientists of the DNA division of the OCME on how they could identify signs and symptoms of stress in themselves and in colleagues—and what to do about it. Small discussion groups followed this presentation and continued for some time afterward.

In one of the small groups, an OCME staffer recalled a nightmare she would have in which the various body parts she worked on were made of steel and would slowly come together to form a robotlike monster that moved menacingly toward her until she woke in a panic. Her nightmarish dreams condensed into two major themes for her: the destruction of the Twin Towers and the horrifying realization of her loss of innocence in relation to the meaningfulness of her work and her previously taken-for-granted safety and security.

Other groups demonstrated the importance of identifying anger and directing it constructively. Anger was often identifiable in groups we conducted, and this anger was usually directed against the organization or its leadership. We saw this whether it was at the OCME, in our work at area firehouses, or at various corporations for whom we consulted. Such anger often seemed displaced from the attackers, with the resultant feeling of helplessness. Thus the leadership of the OCME, the fire department, or the corporations became targets of this anger and frustration. This was not helpful because alliances had to be strengthened within each setting for people to move forward out of the 9/11 despair. Identifying these feelings and then working with the group to facilitate constructive dialogue enabled a more optimistic mood in the groups.

One such group featured a number of dentist volunteers and DNA scientists. As the group progressed, we were able to identify the anger the dentists held against the scientists whom they believed looked down on their rudimentary techniques of identifying dental records rather than the cutting-edge science of DNA analysis. The dentists were gratified and relieved to discover that the scientists, on the contrary, valued the dedication, hard work, and scientific contributions they each made toward their common goal of identifying the 9/11 dead. Thus the groups served many functions, from distributing information, dispelling misconceptions, identifying feelings—including anger, and directing the feelings toward a constructive outcome.

My colleagues and I learned a great deal during our time at the OCME. We came to respect and admire the work and dedication of these silent heroes of September 11 and to appreciate, after all, how people can come together in the worst of times to help one another, to be selfless, and to appreciate the simple grandeur of a beautiful day.

I believe the mental health team's work at the OCME will need to continue long after the final 9/11 remains are identified and Death Alley once again reverts to an ordinary street. However, for those of us who were privileged to walk that street, it will never be the same again.

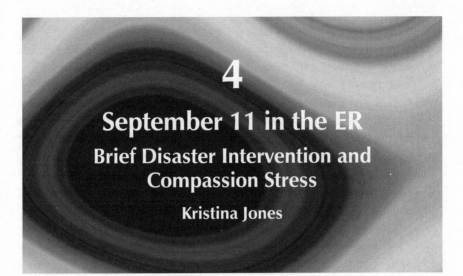

4

September 11 in the ER

Brief Disaster Intervention and Compassion Stress

Kristina Jones

On September 11 I arrived at St. Vincent's Hospital where I usually worked as a psychiatrist in the HIV/AIDS clinic. The hospital was the second closest to Ground Zero. By the end of the day 600 medical patients had been seen, 150 had been admitted, and four had died. Approximately 100 psychiatric consultations were completed that day. This chapter describes the day, informal consultations and staff reactions, and reflects on the principles and the stressors of disaster psychiatry.

When I reached the lobby of the psychiatry department, the psychiatry disaster plan was chaotically being enacted; people were to be pulled out of the emergency room (ER) if they were screaming or freaking out. I went to the command center and signed in; hundreds of nurses, physicians, and emergency medical technicians were there, many from other, faraway hospitals. We didn't know if 200 or 2,000 people might come in the next hour. I heard a woman in the hallway screaming and crying. Three psychiatrists rushed out. Later I heard that she kept saying, "My skin is burning, I have to get out of the building, the building is falling." Acute psychotic reactions to stress are rare but expected. The head of the psychiatry department was rushing around with packages of antipsychotic medication that could be used to sedate people who became aggressive. He repeatedly told the psychiatry residents and senior psychiatrists, "Just take names, we need to document, but we don't have time to register people." This sudden freeing of administrative duty made me feel giddy but terrified as I pictured waves of people coming in. We discussed how many beds we could make available on different floors and who would be assigned to the emergency room, the wards, and the triage units being set up in the boardroom and gymnasium.

Many months later, I realize that the woman's scream will never leave me: I have never heard such a primitive eruption of terror—not a human scream, but somewhere between the sound of an infant and the sound of an animal, a sound of pure fear. For me, the scream is linked to the image I had in that moment of several hundred people flooding the psychiatry department in similar states of deranged terror, of the possibility that a mob of screaming people could fill the lobby at any moment, diverted from the ER because they were not physically injured but were too distressed or disturbed to be on the street. Thankfully, the mob of terror never materialized. Many hundreds of people came in the weeks and months to follow, but the department of psychiatry was able to set up a new service for the psychiatric needs of September 11 survivors, direct and indirect. On that day it felt disorganized with all the repetition; later I realized that response to a disaster means having a strong but flexible plan that changes to accommodate new and shifting information about numbers of psychiatric casualties expected as the disaster evolves.

I went to the ER to see if we could control people who were disruptive or who needed sedation to cooperate with medical intervention. The ER was controlled pandemonium; oxygen tanks hit the floor as wheelchairs and stretchers competed for corridor space. People were covered in white dust and yellow, papery chunks. Firefighters were on stretchers with oxygen masks. Many people had cuts on their faces, and all had reddened watery eyes from the flood of dust that followed the building collapses.

I was called urgently to the dialysis and the endoscopy units by the ER triage nurse; someone was out of control and needed sedation. I found the dialysis unit but couldn't locate the patient, so I left my pager number. The dialysis floor had become an overflow ward. I rushed to the endoscopy unit using a stairwell crowded with nurses marching downstairs en masse. I arrived to see other white-powder–encrusted people vomiting into plastic bowls, coughing and gasping.

A young man with brown hair bleached white by the cement dust, and eyes wide open with fear was staring at me. The triage nurse said, "He's okay now but leave your beeper number." I saw that the eight beds were soon full and I could do nothing at that point. I began to wonder if people had ingested toxic material and pictured them vomiting up blood, but that did not materialize. Much later I wondered if the nurse paged me because she saw his panic and anticipated him pulling off his oxygen mask in between episodes of vomiting, or whether she was thinking he would escalate from simply banging his fists on the bed to actually hitting out at someone because he was so distressed.

I went by the ER again in time to see a firefighter wearing an oxygen mask try to jump off his stretcher. I stopped him, and he sat back down. He said, "I gotta go back down there. I have guys down there. I gotta go back in."

I looked at the oxygen tank, set to the maximum setting. I looked at his chest and saw his respiratory rate must be pretty high, and I yelled across the noise: "You can't go back. You're on oxygen. You won't be able to breathe without it." He put his face close to mine, stared for a long moment, disbelieving. Then I said, "I'm a doctor. I'm sorry, you can't go." He looked down at the floor, and then muttered a request for water, his voice muffled through his oxygen mask. I agreed to get him water, and a nearby x-ray technician handed me a little paper cup of ice water. I saw that the path to the sink was crowded with rushing people—police, nurses, patients. I just gave him the water. I took some ice in my hand and wet his forehead, which was very hot from a first-degree burn. I asked if he was NPO (nothing by mouth) meaning that he can't drink water because he was going to have an endoscopy or bronchoscopy (a procedure to put a tube in his stomach or lungs). Luckily, he wasn't, so I gave him the water. I asked if he was okay, and he nodded slowly, as though unsure. His face and hair was covered in fine white powder, making his blue eyes look too intensely blue to be real, like the blue painted on Dutch chinaware; the powdered white-gray hair didn't match his young face. He told me he was trapped after the first tower collapsed and was pulled out of the rubble by another firefighter. He had lost his oxygen mask for 10 minutes and had inhaled and swallowed so much smoke that he couldn't breathe.

He asked me to call his wife, and I took his number and said that I would do my best, but the phones were down. I walked off and saw a man in the suture room who was having a huge diagonal gash on his back sewn up. It was a glass injury, a very straight cut. Behind a curtain I glimpsed a patient's arm, very red and oozing, a severe burn being dressed by a nurse. On my way to the next ward, I stopped by the registration department and tried the phones. They were all down. I ordered the secretary to keep trying to call the firefighter's wife to tell her he was alive and at the hospital. She was so nervous, I had to repeat the instructions three times.

The firefighter trying to jump off the stretcher haunted me. Was he "crazy" to want to go back in? Or is it normal for someone in his job to try and rescue the other men in his company, in which case, he is reacting normally to an abnormal situation.

Telling the firefighter that he can't leave is a very brief "capacity assessment" of his ability to appreciate that, at that moment, he needed to comply with medical treatment and that he couldn't let either the demands of his job or the strength of his feelings further endanger him by leaving the ER until he no longer required oxygen to breathe.

I walked back from the main building to the AIDS clinic across the street just to take a break from the ER. The street had been blocked off by police, and a crowd of 100 or so people, and 20 or 30 journalists with both television and still cameras, were behind steel barriers, all turned toward the ER. I walked across the street and saw that one of the World Trade Center buildings was gone; in its place was a cloud of sooty, gray smoke. I kept looking for the building anyway.

My clinic was deserted, so I walked back to the main building, and went up to the seventh floor, where the old gymnasium was being hastily converted into a 30-stretcher MASH-type unit to treat smoke inhalation and lacerations. I told my friend from the HIV clinic, now in charge of this unit, that I was assigning myself to it for a while to help keep order as shocked patients may try to run away from the hospital. She asked me to see an elderly woman who was distressed. She was wrapped in blankets, shivering, with many scalp lacerations. She was staring at the ceiling looking blankly terrified, not reacting to people around her. I asked her if she was okay, and she said, in a heavy Eastern European accent, "We got trampled, and I don't know where is my husband and if he is alive." The two had been shopping on Broadway. I told her the phones were down, but we would try to get her family on the phone. I told her she was safe now, but that she couldn't leave because she needed a CAT scan to rule out internal head injury.

I walked onto the patio, to get some air and a glass of water and observe that dusty businessmen, still holding their briefcases, are sipping grape juice, speaking in solemn tones. I saw a doctor I know, a heavyset Catholic woman who doesn't bill for services for the elderly poor because the paperwork takes too long. She was sitting close to a female emergency medical technician. Both were crying. I felt unsettled by this, seeing another physician in tears. Was she unable to work? Had a relative of hers died? Later I heard that her brother had been missing for a few hours, but was later located.

Miraculously, my cell phone, on which I have been hitting redial, started to work, and I was able to get the elderly woman's family. Her daughter said that her husband was found, wandering on the Lower East Side. I ran into the ward and told her that her husband was alive, and I put the cell phone to her nonbloody ear so that she could hear the news directly from her daughter. She cried a lot and repeated thank you, again and again. Her face was full of emotion and color, she made eye contact with me and the nurse and looked suddenly normal, speaking about her family and how happy she would be when she was back home.

I realized that the emotional trauma caused by not knowing if her husband was dead or alive was far more important to her than any physical trauma. This didn't feel like a psychiatric intervention, but it was. The staff had been concerned about her going into shock or having a decreased level of awareness because of a closed head injury; in fact, she was acutely anxious. Whereas for some patients fear and threat are indeed the essence of a trauma, for others the traumatic element includes a major element of loss, or of threatened loss. After hearing that her husband was alive, the patient was visibly relieved. She requested food and water and was cooperative in getting an IV and waiting for her CAT scan of the head. The practical hierarchy of securing safety, addressing medical injury, and securing connection to the patient's social supports before offering reassurance or psychiatric intervention are typical principles of disaster work.

An hour later, in the early afternoon, things had slowed down. No new patients were arriving. Staff nurses and physicians were huddled around a single working computer viewing CNN on the Internet. We read about the plane that had hit the Pentagon. Rumors flourished, another plane was possibly headed for the Supreme Court. All planes had been diverted to Canada. "Is it a war?" I asked my friend Tony, a handsome Cuban AIDS doctor. "Could be World War Three, could be nuclear," he said, in a who-the-hell-knows friendly tone. He walked off singing the South Park Cartoon song about "Blame Canada!"

My pager went off; it was the overflow unit located in dialysis. They wanted me to see a distressed woman. She was crying, on oxygen, and had a badly sprained ankle, but was otherwise okay; she told me she was on the 42nd floor of the World Trade Center, and didn't know if her boss got out. She said it took an hour to get down the stairs and that she was worried two of her friends who were overweight didn't make it.

She told me she had spoken to her husband and son and that her husband was upset that he couldn't get to the hospital. All bridges and tunnels were shut, essentially cutting Manhattan off. She said her son was a volunteer firefighter and he had been called in. She said her husband didn't want him to go, but she said he's an adult, and its his decision. She reasoned that a firefighter had pulled her out of the World Trade Center and saved her, so her son should go in and save others.

I was feeling numb as she told me this. The TV in the background was talking about the Pentagon. I told her both WTC buildings were down, and that unless her son was a bomb disposal expert or a gas mains guy I doubted he would be there. I had heard the FBI had the whole area sealed off because they didn't know if there were bombs. This calmed her a little, and she said she just wanted to walk up to Pennsylvania Station. I told her that was a bad plan. If she went "absent without leave" with all the phones out, her family couldn't contact her, and they would be worried sick. She said she knew she needed crutches, but she felt she had the energy to walk without them. I reminded her that the ankle was badly sprained. She reluctantly agreed to stay.

I offered her some medication to help her anxiety, but she declined. I gave her my number, and she said, "I'm okay, I'm just a talker." She felt odd, being alive and alone, not knowing where her coworkers were or if they were dead. I told her it was normal to feel this because she was in shock. She responded that she was glad to talk and that she would call me when it was all over. She asked me if they will keep on bombing the United States. "What's to stop the evil from keeping on going and going?" I said I didn't think that was happening. I thought to myself, "I hope that's not happening. That can't be happening. Nobody is that strong," but as she asked me this, I realized that I had no factual answer to her question, only one based on faith, disbelief, and hope.

My medical student came over and asked me a question. I said goodbye to the injured woman, and we went to the other end of the unit and join the medical staff of this half-empty unit watching a tiny TV. We saw repeated footage of the building coming down and shots of the Pentagon. We shook our heads realizing that the firefighters who went in after Tower 1 was evacuated were probably all crushed. "The building pancaked," one doctor said, shaking his head. He stared at the floor, adding quietly, "I don't think we will get many patients out of that."

I went back to the ER and realized I was thirsty. There were no patients to see, so I went outside, feeling a bit dizzy. Outside on the sidewalk were probably 100 doctors, sitting on chairs, waiting. Old commode chairs were shrouded with white sheets. Makeshift wheelchairs and stretchers were lined up on the street. But the many doctors were sitting down, waiting. There were no more patients coming. This felt strange; I felt that minutes were turning into hours, that my sense of time must be slowing down. I wondered if I was experiencing dissociation, an acute anxiety reaction to stress, the feeling that oneself or one's reality isn't real any more.

Little tables had been set up, a command center of sorts. People were being let in from behind barricades to ask if their loved ones were in the hospital. Three people sat in the blazing sun shuffling through handwritten and typed papers of about 300 names, many not alphabetized. They asked me where the new lists were. I said, "I don't know. Ask inside at the family support station." This was the name for the social work center that had been hastily set up in a staff room of the hospital. People were walking to the hospital to check on relatives. I had heard on TV that 1,500 people were evacuated off the island on ferry, to Jersey, and that 600 were in local hospitals, including ours. In the next weeks, 6,000 relatives came to the family center, checking lists of the dead, searching for missing relatives and putting up "missing" posters with photos of their missing dead.

I walked over to a group of men in black, the priests. I felt akin to them, with talk as my only salve in this crazy situation. One asked another, "Are you a brother?" and a young man in white collar said, "No, I'm an Episcopalian." The other two priests said, "Ah well," and touched his shoulder and shook his hand. They said, "Welcome aboard" or "Thank you for coming." I said, "I'm a psychiatrist" and they opened their little raven black circle for me. I said to a man with a purple narrow ribbon draped around his suit like a sacred scarf, "A woman asked me if the evil will stop, and I didn't know what to say." One priest said, "They choose evil." Another said, "We don't know," and another said, "It will stop." One joked with me about us being in the same service, and "What was that, wounded healers?" I smiled, and then, or maybe later, he told me he was going to the actual disaster site to give services, unction perhaps, and do what was needed for people. I was confused and then I realized that the people he meant would be the dying or the dead. I walked away. At that moment I felt so useless as a physician, that I admired the priest's ability to do something for the victims, an hour ago alive, now probably dead, but still alive in his view that the soul of the person merits his care. At that moment I was unable to fathom the idea of thousands of dead people underneath the massive dark smoke cloud that glowered at the bottom of Manhattan.

The discussion of theology seemed at that moment to be the purview of the special world of the priests; however, in the months that followed, each of the patients I treated had to come to some personal reckoning of the experience of sudden random senseless and violent death on a large scale, and how this "evil" could be understood and countered or contained.

I sat down on the curb to drink water and sat next to a doctor, who asked me if I thought they would bomb the hospital, too. I thought for a second and said, "No, we're small fish. They got what they wanted, the WTC, the Pentagon, nobody cares about us." He said that in Israel they bomb the hospitals, too. I said, "No, I can't believe that, I have to believe it's safe in here, I have to believe that." He was an eye specialist and said he was going to cancel his flights for conferences, just in case. I told him that I used to have a schizophrenia patient who stared at the sun and burned his retina. He said, "Oh yes, I've seen that, too. They say they do it because it gives them power." I replied, "Why can't you stare at the moon instead?" We laughed; the camaraderie of disaster made friends of us all. We stared southward down Sixth Avenue at the massive billowing smoke where the WTC used to be. We fell silent. Many months later, I reflected that ophthalmologists are not usually so friendly to psychiatrists but that perhaps my being a psychiatrist allowed him to share with me, and me with him, some normal reactions to disaster—namely, disbelief, anxiety, fear, anger, and sadness.

I wandered over to the psychiatry floor. Everything was under control, and the director wanted me back at 6:00 p.m. to meet the residents and advise them about doing consultations for medical patients. I felt I didn't have any expertise really but then realized he was just overwhelmed and wanted me to teach the residents what to do in a way that was friendly and clear. Later people told me that AIDS is a chronic disaster and that psychiatry for medical patients was something they felt was closely related to disaster psychiatry.

I went home for an hour's break and on the way noted the silent streets, closed shops, and people wandering aimlessly. Back at the hospital, just when I thought that my life could not be more like a disaster movie, I went through the ER. It was no longer crowded with patients but with a swirling, walking mass of staff in white coats, in surgical gowns, in yellow patient gowns worn backward like cardigans. I saw a group of men walking fast, and in the middle Mayor Giuliani, a small, taut man, but all his sharp edges gone. His usual gray face was filled with color, a light coffee brown; he looked healthier than on TV. His voice, too, was not sharp and high-pitched, but calm and genuine. He kept saying "Thank you, thank you" and shaking hands with medical staff, moving very fast, but seeming quite real. I moved against the wall to avoid his security men with the ear microphones, and I watched him go into the street. A couple of hours later, I stood in the psychiatry resident's lounge listening to Mayor Giuliani on TV (now looking like his normal, unreal television self) appealing for civil order and public calm, saying that hatred caused this tragedy, and to respond to hatred with violence is not going to make things better. I marveled at his ability to both acknowledge and contain the bewildered rage of the city.

I met with the psychiatry residents. The head of the department spoke about logistical issues, support groups and new roles for everyone in the next hours and days. I spoke last, discussing psychiatry with the medically ill. I said, "This is so weird because we are helping people with trauma, but we are in it, too." I saw that they looked stunned from watching TV all day. I said that it was important that we observe ourselves psychologically and stay grounded, that it was important not to dissociate. Only in this way could we be of help. I used the example of the woman whose son was a volunteer firefighter to illustrate the consultation principles of disaster psychiatry, EER—express emotion, educate, reorganize. The principles are found on the American Psychiatric Association web site on disaster psychiatry (www. psych.org). First, allow the patient to tell his or her story, because emotional expression is part of the treatment for acute trauma. Listen attentively and without judgment. Summarize back to the patient what was said. Then educate about normal responses to trauma, which are numbing, detachment, derealization (feeling like you are in a movie) and fear, or depersonalization (not feeling real). Finally, cognitively reorganize the event. For example, I described how I had told the patient, "It's not a good idea to walk unaccompanied to a place where there may be no train when your ankle is injured and the phones are down." I noted how anxiety impairs our judgment.

At the time, I was thinking that I had heard how a firefighter had carried the body of his chief out of the wreckage and that the captain had been decapitated. I was thinking that someone had told me there were body parts on the street. I was thinking that I had been told there were people with melting skin and that a friend of a friend who went to help medically ended up being the morgue man and counted 400 bodies, but I didn't tell the residents any of this.

I explained how to write a note, simplifying possible diagnoses. I said, "Decide if it's anxiety, and treat with talking and education; if it's extreme, then medicate. If, more uncommonly, the person is psychotic, paranoid, or aggressive, or has an underlying major mental illness and has decompensated, admit the person to the hospital." I added that we have the skills to help people, it's just that the situation is different. I explained that they needed to reassure patients about their medical concerns several times, because anxious people don't retain information. I explained about acute bereavement, that for people who can't sleep or can't calm down, benzodiazepines or other sleeping medication can be useful. I explained how to pull a grieving person away from a medical situation where he or she may have a negative effect on staff trying to care for other injured people. Whatever I said seemed to make sense, because people were nodding. The director then spoke about the tradition of shell shock and combat psychiatry. He handed out papers to the 30 residents about disaster psychiatry and announced that we would be running support groups the next day, several times a day.

Finally, I left my pager number with the chief of the 18 psychiatry residents who were staying overnight and told them to go talk to the staff out on the sidewalk. I walked out again, and it was nighttime. Outside, I was looking at a movie set of a disaster, only it was real—big lights had been set up, groups of police were standing around chatting quietly, doctors were sitting in the chairs on cell phones like extras on a movie set waiting to be called to action, and two National Guardsmen walked by in camouflage combat gear with large guns. The media people were still pressing at the orange barricades, waiting for something to happen. An ambulance pulled up, the first in several hours, and people all stood up attempting to do something. The powerlessness of our situation—doctors without patients—made us all dazed. We were told to go home, or to relieve nurses if we could because they had been there 12 hours. Their replacements couldn't get into the city.

Secondary Trauma and Compassion Stress

In the months after September 11, St. Vincent's Hospital rushed to create a psychiatric service in response to the event. I supervised a group of social workers who went into individual firehouses to do outreach to the New York City Fire Department (FDNY). We struggled with the sense that not enough could be done in the time available, that mere psychoeducation seemed too little, and that we would never win the battle against an entrenched firefighter culture that resisted talking about feelings, that rejected the public image of "hero" and sought to mourn their 343 dead and cope with threats of bioterrorism—or another 9/11. I ran the group with Gerald Martone, a nurse who worked with the International Rescue Committee. He taught me to reorient my perspective to one appropriate following a disaster. This meant focusing on psychoeducation as the right goal, mobilizing the firefighters' own strong group support and family and community resources, facilitating emotional expression, and subtly doing outreach to those at high risk via the FDNY counselors. This was different from nondisaster work, in which one might have looked for symptoms to diagnose or treat or concentrated on explicit case finding.

Additionally, I volunteered five hours a week at the counseling unit of the FDNY to see individual patients, briefly ran a psychiatry residents' support group, gave grand rounds to my own department on acute stress disorder and posttraumatic stress disorder (PTSD), and treated and wrote an article about the unique responses of the AIDS clinic patients to the 2,800 deaths associated with the disaster.

Doing all this felt energizing and was a relief from the sense of powerlessness on September 11. My own therapist commented that I seemed too energetic. We discussed whether my behavior was either totally appropriate to the scale of the disaster or was a "manic defense" against my own feelings toward it. Like any self-reflective psychiatrist, I sought an explanation for my feelings and behavior. Altruism is a defense, as is humor. Norwood and Ursano (2002) write that "as a member of the impacted community, the local psychiatrist is also affected by the trauma."

Danieli and colleagues (2002) have coined the term *overdedication* to describe relief workers who continue their efforts until the point of exhaustion. I recall needing less sleep and feeling full of vitality, perhaps omnipotently so at times, in endeavoring to do as much as possible in trying to rescue the rescuers, at least psychologically. Innumerable colleagues, nurses, residents and patients in my normal job decided that I was the place to download their 9/11 reactions. At the time, this felt perfectly normal. Six months later, however, I felt out of step with my colleagues, who were beginning to talk of "moving on" and getting on with life; I felt angry and irritable, alienated from people not still actively involved with making sense of the event or helping either the "heroes" or the "victims" of September 11. Individual firefighters described horrific scenes they had encountered that were so intense, I spent hours afterward with intrusive and anxious thoughts about the details I had heard. A colleague and my therapist were invaluable in helping me process these thoughts, which allowed me to contain the emotions of extreme horror and wild grief. After about six months of this work, I recognized that I was exhausted, and with a great deal of regret and some guilt, I stopped taking new 9/11 patients. The FDNY had hired a large staff in the meantime. The decision to stop taking new patients deepened my ability to attend to the patients I had already undertaken and renewed my compassion for their particular struggles to make sense of the disaster—not to "move on" but to "move with" the disaster as part of their lives.

Was I merely one of the 44 percent of New Yorkers described by Silver, Holman, and McIntosh (2002) who felt "substantial stress" after the attacks, in contrast to the 17 percent of Americans outside the city? By self-diagnosis, I was not one of the 7.5 percent of New York City residents with PTSD, and luckily not one of the 20 percent living below Canal Street with PTSD described by Galea et al. (2002). Certainly I was like the 28 percent of Manhattan residents who, like those surveyed by Vlahov et al. (2002), reported increased alcohol use. There are no formal studies of disaster psychiatrists; however, parallels can be drawn between disaster psychiatry and the role of humanitarian workers and peacekeepers who are aware of the mental health dangers inherent in their work. Even those near to disasters are affected by them: Feinstein et al. (2002) found that war journalists have a lifetime prevalence of PTSD of 28.6 percent, professional firefighters in a pre–September 11 sample had a PTSD rate of approximately 29 percent.

These negative effects are described variously as burnout (Freudenberger and Robbins, 1979), secondary traumatic stress (Stamm, 1995; Shalev, 2002), compassion fatigue (Figley, 1985), or vicarious traumatization (Pearlman and Saakvitne, 1995). All of these terms are borrowed from work with victims of violence, rape or sexual abuse, and the severely mentally ill and may be applicable to disaster psychiatry. I now describe each term and explore its relevance to disaster psychiatry.

Burnout was described by Freudenberger and Robbins (1979) and refers to cumulative psychological strain that results in being emotionally drained, depressed, cynical, losing the ability for compassion, and having an overwhelming sense of discouragement.

This is similar to compassion fatigue, which Figley (1985) described as a state of severe biological and emotional exhaustion and dysfunction resulting from prolonged exposure to work with trauma survivors.

Vicarious traumatization (Pearlman and Saakvitne, 1995) describes a permanently transformative change in the mental health worker that detrimentally affects existential aspects of the worker, such as his or her relationship to meaning and hope, connectedness, and self-capacities (e.g., tolerance for a range of emotional reactions in self and others and ability to see oneself as grounded). Pearlman and Saakvitne note that the vicariously traumatized worker may become judgmental, cynical, angry, and develop rescue fantasies; become overinvolved; or develop overly rigid boundaries, avoiding work and social contacts.

Burnout, compassion fatigue, and vicarious traumatization all imply that a traumatic event has overwhelmed the victim and the therapist and that the event has caused irrevocable alterations in both. In contrast, secondary traumatic stress symptoms and compassion stress suggest that although the trauma is substantial, the victim and the therapist can build capacities to work through and repair at least some of the psychological damage of trauma and that the therapist can still work effectively.

Secondary traumatic stress symptoms (Stamm, 1995) are subclinical or clinical signs of PTSD in the therapist that mirror those experienced by patients. Symptoms include intrusive images and thoughts, avoidance or emotional numbing, anxiety, hyperarousal, and depression. Danieli (1981;

Danieli, Rodley, and Weisaeth, 1996) found empirical validation for some of the following themes in Holocaust therapists: guilt, rage, dread and horror, grief and mourning, shame, inability to contain intense emotions, and utilization of defenses such as numbing, denial, or avoidance. Therapists who worked with Vietnam veterans studied by Lindy (1998) suffered nightmares, intrusive images, reenactments, amnesia, estrangement, alienation, irritability, psychophysiologic reactions, and survivor guilt.

Compassion stress is a nonclinical, nonpathological way to characterize the stress of helping trauma survivors and is seen as a natural outcome of the work. This includes feelings of helplessness, confusion, isolation, and secondary traumatic stress symptoms.

In the disaster literature, most writing warns workers to attend to their own needs for sleep and respite and the importance of connecting to friends and family. Arieh Shalev (2002), an Israeli writing about disaster, noted that those who participate in rescue efforts are also at risk for developing stress responses. Excessive self-exposure (e.g., being unable to disengage from work), irritability, inability to relax, and difficulties communicating with others are warning signs. Monitoring rescuer's exposure, securing and ordering resting periods, relieving overburdened workers, and conducting debriefings may help reduce the effect of traumatic stressors on rescuers.

Beyond merely ensuring the therapist's mental survival, the longer term recovery from disaster depends on the ongoing ability of the therapist and patient to make sense of the experience. Whether these changes are ultimately destructive to the helper and to the therapeutic process depends in large part on the extent to which the therapist is able to engage in a parallel process to that of the victim-client: the process of integrating and transforming these experiences of horror or violation. McCann and Pearlman (1990) write that trauma victims must reevaluate their assumptions about basic personal safety and question prior beliefs in their personal invulnerability. Epstein (1989) writes that trauma disrupts four basic assumptions: that the world is benign, that the world is meaningful, that the self is worthy, and that people are trustworthy.

Treating victims of disaster and the emotional trauma that can result seems not only to require a knowledge of the psychology of trauma, but also a framework for understanding disaster. The specific disaster that occurred in New York on September 11 cannot be considered quite the same as an earthquake or a rape; it requires additional thinking through as an act of terror, necessitating an exploration of the nature of terrorism. Holloway and Fullerton (1994) write that feelings of anger, hatred and hostility are common in victims of politically motivated terrorism or trauma, in a way that they are not in victims of natural disasters; this necessitates anger expression and management as part of the treatment.

Making sense of September 11 has preoccupied the political, intellectual, and artistic life of the country since the event and raises the question of whether one's actions or beliefs or relationships need to change in the context of exposure to this historical event. Additionally, there is the need to address how to tolerate the threat of further terrorism.

Making sense of disaster, whether natural or man-made would seem to require both the patient and the therapist to consider their assumptions about a number of important topics, such as personal safety, death, death anxiety, attachment, and loss, to name just a few. It is crucial to work backward from the disaster to understand who the patient was before the disaster, to understand his or her worldview and current life circumstances, and to factor in any previous trauma. Only in this way can the therapist understand how the disaster may change the patient and how to mobilize his or her resources for recovery.

Disaster victims and workers both exist within the meaning framework assigned to September 11 by society and by the media; they must both struggle to understand themselves in categories richer than simply "hero," "helper," or "victim." Disaster psychiatry is unique in that some aspects of the event are shared by both the victim and the psychiatrist; by using self-reflection, meaning can be created that includes both the victim's experience and the psychiatrist's response; further meaning may arise from the therapist–patient encounter. Robert Jay Lifton (2002), in a lecture given at Cornell Medical School on the year anniversary of September 11, suggested that two responses to the disaster are possible: one can close down, become numb, and hope for revenge through war; or one can open outward, seek illumination, and use the death immersion experience to learn more about life and death.

Acknowledgments

I thank Malachy Corrigan, director of the FDNY Counseling Unit, Dr. Spencer Eth and Dr. David Cordon of St. Vincent's Hospital, Gerry Martone of the International Rescue Committee, and the late Dr. Lisa Chertkov, who introduced me to the concept of disaster psychiatry.

References

Danieli, Y. (1981), Therapist's difficulties in treating survivors of the Holocaust and their children. *Diss. Abstr. Int.*, 42:4947–B.

_____ ed. (2002), *Sharing the Front Line and the Back Hills: International Protectors and Providers: Peacekeepers, Humanitarian Workers, and the Media in the Midst of Crisis*. New York: United Nations Press/ Baywood.

_____ Rodley, N. & Weisaeth, L., eds. (1996), *International Responses to Traumatic Stress*. New York: Baywood.

Epstein, S. (1989), The self-concept, the traumatic neurosis, and the structure of the personality. In: *Perspectives on Personality, Vol. 3*, ed. D. Ozer, J. Healy & A. Stewart. CT: JAL Press.

Feinstein, A., Owen, J. & Blair, N. (2002), A hazardous profession: War, journalists and psychopathology. *Amer. J. Psychiat.*, 159:1570–1575.

Figley, C. (1985), *Trauma and Its Wake: The Study and Treatment of Post-Traumatic Stress Disorder*. New York: Brunner/Mazel.

Freudenberger, H. & Robbins, A. (1979), The hazards of being a psychoanalyst. *Psychoanal. Rev.*, 66:275–296.

Galea, S., Ahern, J., Resnick, H., Kilpatrick D., Bucuvalas, M., Gold, J. & Vlahov, D. (2002), Psychological sequelae of the September 11 terrorist attacks in New York City. *New Engl. J. Med.*, 346:982–987.

Holloway, H. & Fullerton, C. (1994), The psychology of terror and its aftermath. In: *Individual and Community Responses to Trauma and Disaster: The Structure of Human Chaos*, ed. R. Ursano, B. McCaughey & C. Fullerton. London: Cambridge University Press.

Jones, K. (2001), World Trade Center disaster: Reactions and recovery in an HIV clinic near Ground Zero. *AIDS Reader*, 11:541–554.

Lindy, J. (1998), *Vietnam: A Casebook*. New York: Brunner/Mazel.

McCann, L. & Pearlman, L. (1990), Vicarious traumatization: A framework for understanding the psychological effects of working with victims. *J. Traumatic Stress*, 3:131–149.

Norwood, A., Ursano, R. & Fullerton, C. (2001), Principles of disaster psychiatry: Principles and practice. Available at: http://www.psych.org/pract_of_psych/principles_and_practice3201.cfm (Web site of the American Psychiatric Association).

Pearlman, L. & Saakvitne, K. (1995), *Trauma and the Therapist: Countertransference and Vicarious Traumatization in Psychotherapy with Incest Survivors*. New York: Norton.

Schuster, M., Stein, B., Jaycox, L., Collins, R., Marshall, G., Elliott, M., Zhou, A., Kanouse, D., Morrison, J. & Berry, S. (2001), A national survey of stress reactions after the September 11, 2001, terrorist attacks. *New Engl. J. Med.*, 345:1507–1512.

Shalev, A. (2002), Treating survivors in the immediate aftermath of traumatic events. In: *Treating Trauma Survivors with PTSD,* ed. R. Yehuda. Washington, DC: American Psychiatric Publishing.

Silver, R., Holman, E., McIntosh, D., Poulin, M. & Gil-Rivas, V. (2002), Nationwide longitudinal study of psychological responses to September 11. *JAMA,* 288:1235–1244.

Stamm, B., ed. (1995), *Secondary Traumatic Stress: Self-Care Issues for Clinicians, Researchers, and Educators.* Lutherville, MD: Sidran Press.

Vlahov, D., Galea, S., Resnick, H., Ahern, J., Boscarino, J., Bucuvalas, M., Gold, J. & Kilpatrick, D. (2002), Increased use of cigarettes, alcohol, and marijuana among Manhattan, New York, residents after the September 11 terrorist attacks. *Amer. J. Epidemiol.,* 155:988–996.

II

Disaster Psychiatrists in Training

In many respects most, if not all, psychiatrists are "psychiatrists in training" when faced with disaster. The circumstances are humbling by their very nature, and many professionals are often thrust into disaster mental health work by chance, not forethought or planning. In this section, resident psychiatrists share their experiences responding to the events of 9/11 in New York City. In their professional youthfulness, their honesty about their uncertainty and inexperience in the face of the events of that day and its aftermath can speak for the entire field of disaster mental health.

At a time when these psychiatry residents were just becoming familiar with their role as both physicians and psychiatrists, they were asked to call on their nascent professional skills in a situation in which many of their supervisors and role models were on unfamiliar clinical and organizational territory. In this alone lies an important lesson for the future of disaster mental health—the need for better training, didactics, and orientation in disaster work for both practicing and future psychiatrists. Learning "on the job" is inherent to medical and psychiatric training but not to the unfortunate extent that trauma psychiatry, disaster psychiatry, and grief work are neglected in most training programs.

At the same time, these young psychiatrists clearly acquired invaluable professional and personal experience by participating in the 9/11 response. The essays in this section suggest that trainees can and should be involved in future disaster responses, both for all that their energy and curiosity may contribute to the recovery of survivors and for all these professionals may gain in their own development. To the extent that disaster mental health planning occurs in the United States and may perhaps have been given a boost by the lessons learned from 9/11, it should be integrated into psychiatric residency programs.

Within the essays of these psychiatrists lie a number of keen observations that capture many of the key elements of disaster psychiatry. Outreach and community-based work are central to effective mental health interventions in the immediate aftermath of disaster—expecting people to seek out psychiatrists in traditional treatment settings like New York's Bellevue Hospital during this time is futile. At the same time, the psychiatric diagnostic system seems impotent and unhelpful amid the mass suffering of a disaster's immediate aftermath. Whether this reflects the inadequacy or irrelevancy of psychiatric diagnosis in the acute aftermath of trauma and disaster remains to be determined. On the other hand, the mental health impact of disasters evolves over time and in clear stages, beginning with seemingly unbounded, unnameable, and amorphous suffering and leading to more traditional, disorder-based problems and interventions in the months and perhaps years thereafter.

Finally, these young professionals clearly felt a not uncommon tension for disaster mental health professionals and for disaster responders in general—that between heroic benevolence and the personal limitations on what they can and should contribute to their community's recovery.

Thankfully, the following essays reflect not the limitations of psychiatry in the face of disaster but its great potential for mitigating the fallout of catastrophic events. This potential should be cultivated in both residency and postresidency training programs for the good of all.

5

Defining the Psychiatrist's Role with Heroes and Tragedies

Eraka Bath

My experience with disaster psychiatry began on the morning of September 11 as I woke in my usual hurried rush to get out of the house and be on time for my first patients. September had been an interesting month. I was in the third month of my third year of adult general psychiatry training, which meant loads of intensive outpatient work. As of July 1, I had been assigned an office, voice mail, a group to colead, and a 50-patient caseload. Needless to say, the learning curve was steep. That morning, before heading out of my building on 15th Street, I remember listening to National Public Radio and faintly overhearing something having to do with the Twin Towers. I was pleased to wake Alex, my then-boyfriend, now husband, out of his usual and privileged artist-hours post–9:00 a.m. reverie and set on my way. Although I noted the throngs of people clogging the sidewalks, the extent of the disaster was not yet apparent to me.

Arriving at the hospital was another situation entirely. Excited and worried voices were discussing the logistics of what had happened when the second plane hit. I immediately called Alex to bring over a pair of scrubs and sneakers for me, anticipating what might unfold. Although the hospital's disaster procedure was running per protocol, it felt like no one really knew what was going on, nor what was really needed in that first hour. A round-up call was in effect for all physicians in the hospital to report to the doctors' lounge, where one would then be directed to their respective call of duty. This is not to say that as a hospital we were not organized, but the humbling reflection that this event was unprecedented and unlike any other had become clear. By this time, almost everyone was floating theories on who did it and why, and news and updates continually trickled in dribbles and drabs: other missing flights, the destruction at the Pentagon, the Trade Center towers collapsing, alleged footage of cheering Palestinians. The fragmented information and speculative attempts to piece it together created an eerie ambience of uncertainty and vulnerability. What next? Is it over? Are we safe? These questions and many more loomed in my head as I tried to be helpful.

I now realize in retrospect how working in a disaster setting sometimes requires what I feel is a "dissociative" posturing—that is, distancing the self enough from a sense of overwhelm so that one can create the illusion of calm and do what needs to be done. The magnitude of what had happened that day made it almost impossible to act and react in the same moment. It was unlike any other clinical challenge ever demanded from me. I remember family members and friends who had been frantic and worried trying to reach me and responding to them in an almost affectless controlled and collected manner. At times I was inappropriately upbeat, focusing on what I thought was the job at hand. Unconsciously, this defense of minimization was likely protective in these early moments—could I have been an effective caregiver if I had let my spirit take in the full scale of this horror?

My decision to follow the "action" stemmed both from my own anxiety about being helpful and useful and also from not wanting to be mired in the logistical mayhem of the ad hoc bureaucracy. I found myself first lugging additional medical equipment from central supply to the top floor of the Reiss, St. Vincent's psychiatric facility, where a makeshift ward had been set up for potential victims. Then onto the ER, where I would wait for a chance to talk to someone besides my colleagues or other staff. I ended up assigned to an intoxicated man whose clinical presentation had nothing to do with the disaster and feeling an exaggerated frustration that I wasn't seeing any of the "real victims." Needless to say, the already busy emergency room became more bustling by 10:00 a.m., but primarily with the walking wounded and families in search of loved ones. By the late afternoon, it had become increasingly clear that the magnitude of the disaster resulted in an overall paucity of survivors. There was a "hurry-up-and-wait" quality to the entire day. En masse we would rush to the walk-in clinic, to the ER, then back to the makeshift trauma ward on the seventh floor, then outside to the ER bay to witness the media frenzy and the hoards of volunteers. I think what impressed me the most was this endless waiting. Like most physicians, the narcissistic urge to heal and help by any means necessary became a source of burgeoning anxiety with its own kinetic whirlwind, particularly as my best intentions seemed useless because of the nature of the destruction.

At one point around 4:00 p.m., a few colleagues and I noticed that there were select police-escorted convoys taking doctors down to the site. Although our administrators had instructed us not to go anywhere near the site, this warning felt paternalistic and out of touch with reality. I think also the anticipatory anxiety had gotten the better of us, and at that point we became privy to a syndrome of hypervigilant, heroism overdrive. The rescue fantasy scenario was in full effect. Our logic being that if we could be right there, close to the victims, maybe then we could help someone. Maybe then we could triage for signs of acute stress disorder or offer supportive therapy. We were fueled by each other's sense of doctorly duty as we felt it incumbent to tread into the belly of the beast to do our jobs. These unconscious drives toward duty were further buttressed by a host of rationalizations, intellectualizations, and justifications. And so the four of us jumped in the van and were shuttled into the vortex. It was horrific. We arrived just as Building 7 fell, and the clouds of dust were oppressive. We all began coughing immediately and experiencing the occult attack of particulate matter in our eyes, nose, and throats. We were quickly handed goggles and masks, for it would have been impossible to navigate the carnage without them. It was bewildering to be in the midst of these endless piles of paper, many shredded to dust, yet many intact when there were so few survivors. If something as frail as a piece of paper or a photo could survive the onslaught and heat, why not more people?

Our rush to "really do something" was in vain. No sooner had we arrived at the high school where the makeshift triage center had been set up, than we found ourselves amid another entourage of well-meaning physicians pumped by the same adrenaline, also seduced by the fantasy of rescue and the righteousness of doctorly duty. In fact, many doctors, nurses, and other health care personnel had situated themselves at the site from hospitals all across the city. The harrowing emptiness of the triage unit further amplified everyone's awareness of their limitations: It was up and running, but there were no patients. And since there was no one to help, folks began to help themselves. Munching the free cookies and drinking the donated bottled water was both gratifying and self-soothing. I suddenly began to feel foolish, painfully aware of the hubris of my thinking that being there could have an impact on anyone. My zealousness and naivete started to collide as I struggled with the profound sense of inadequacy and hopelessness I felt in that moment. I also felt embarrassed by my own voyeuristic curiosity. The need to see and experience the destruction with my own eyes felt cheap and sickening. I just wanted to go home at that point, as I realized that I might be waiting around forever. It was getting dark, and I was getting scared.

I went back to the hospital and arrived late for the debriefing organized by my department's administrators. There was no new information to be passed on to us, and I became irritated at the perfunctory administrative micromanagement and self-appointed trauma-expert soapbox-style debriefings. In retrospect, who could really absorb the onslaught of carefully xeroxed packets of useful articles and disaster outreach tips?

I retreated home into ceaseless TV watching, a dangerous zone given the potential risk repeated visualization of violent and disturbing images can have on the development of posttraumatic and acute stress symptomatology.

The next days seamlessly fused as I would report to the hospital and then get sent home because I wasn't really needed.

On the third day after the disaster, the family crisis center opened at the New School around the corner. Many of our supervisors remained at the hospital without sleep for two nights to get things set up. I and other psychiatry residents mobilized at the chance to finally participate and heal. The ratio of treatment providers to those who needed counseling was staggeringly high. The counseling unit was a subterranean labyrinth of treatment providers stationed adjacent to each other with desks and tons of chairs. We were supplied with some pamphlets regarding posttraumatic stress disorder (PTSD) and large, stapled copies of hospital lists of the few identified and unidentified folks who had presented to ER and medical and surgical units from as far away as New Jersey.

We would meet briefly with the families, then get a brief description of their loved ones—where they worked, or when they had last called home, and then comb these lists for possible signs of life. Of the dozens of family members and significant others I interviewed, I did not have one match. I remember looking around desperately at my colleagues whose faces conveyed a sense of depletion and futility. No one I knew had found any matches either. In reality, by that point, most people who knew anyone in the buildings had already contacted them by phone, were with them at home, or had found them in the hospital. We then became the designated bearers of bad news—it was as if I were Dr. Death or an oncologist. After the first 20 or so people who came in looking for loved ones, I began to notice certain patterns. For example, anyone above the 89th floor, anyone from Cantor Fitzgerald, or employees of Windows on the World were not likely to have survived.

I was also struck by the diversity of those affected. From Easthampton aristocracy to the relatives of undocumented workers, the affliction was universal and represented a true microcosm of New York City. A small-boned indigenous woman from Nicaragua was accompanied by a British young man who had found her wandering the streets and decided to act as her Spanish interpreter. At the same time she was fearful about the loss of her brother, she was also cautious about her illegal immigration status being discovered.

For me, these were probably the most difficult moments in my disaster work, and these were the first moments of disaster work I had ever had. Never before had I delivered so much bad news. Occupying that role so suddenly with little training felt both awkward and unsettling. I recall trying to do anything to delay the anxiety of dropping that bomb—the "No, I don't see the name here" and the ingratiating efforts to look through multiple lists several times over. Possibly, this was a way to assuage my own fallen super-ego and sense of disappointment. I somehow felt responsible for their losses and wanted to do right by them. Those were uncomfortable moments at best. I wanted to say something that was not death and disaster, like "It is going to be alright" or "More lists are coming later." I struggled with trying to deliver the news honestly without the nervous editorializing chatter that unconsciously eased anxiety and made me feel better. I had a hard time feeling like I was doing something of value and again felt a sense of failure for not being able to do more. It was a narcissistic blow not to be able to have that golden moment in the sun that we all relish in medicine—making a person feel better or giving them hope.

It was the family crisis center that finally broke my affect of stoic dutifulness. I remember a very regal, well-coiffed, suited woman inquiring about her investment-banker son. He was unfortunately located in the no-man's-land of Cantor Fitzgerald, but I searched the list anyway. She thanked me and thanked all the volunteers for "all the hard work" and "all the help." As far as I was concerned, this postmortem do-goodism was overrated and draining and begat more grief than ever. The truth was, I felt like a fraud and was ashamed by my sense of inadequacy. I felt like I wasn't doing anything. Taking extra time to look through the lists, or providing information for other crisis centers felt paltry at best. At the same time, I was confronted with my own humanity as a physician, and I was no Dr. Feelgood, in body or spirit. That's when I remember taking a break. I went out and sat on a nearby stoop, with my social-worker colleague. An occasional smoker (when on call or stressed at work), I bummed a smoke and began to cry non-stop. I cried for the dead, for the bereaving, for the dead to come, for my sense of not doing enough. I cried for feeling tired and beleaguered and feeling scared for my Middle-Eastern–looking partner. I cried for what might happen to the stability of our country and the world, race relations and hate crimes.

The next phase of my involvement with disaster psychiatry was working with outpatients. Because of all the media attention my hospital received, people were flocking in droves to the walk-in clinic for both disaster- and nondisaster-related traumas. There was a massive and powerful positive transference to St. Vincent's Hospital. People would reference the images they had seen on TV with a reverence later reserved for New York fire (FDNY) and police (NYPD) departments, saying that they saw how much the hospital was "really going out of its way for the community" and how they really wanted to be a part of it. The first two months immediately following the disaster, my colleagues and I experienced an overall 20-percent increase in our casework, and the clients with premorbid psychopathology required more intensive management.

Typically following disaster or trauma settings, many people experience an exacerbation of their conditions. Those with substance dependence use more drugs or are more likely to relapse from sobriety, those with psychosis become more delusional and paranoid, the anxiety ridden become more worried and more agoraphobic and the PTSD sufferers more traumatized. Many of our regular patients were more vulnerable than ever and required additional support to prevent hospitalization. Some were always precariously perched, and this was the precipitating stressor that pushed them toward decompensation.

During that time, I treated many mental health consumers with a variety of psychopathologies—from dysthymia (persistence of depressed mood of at least two years) to chronic paranoid schizophrenia—and almost all were affected by the disaster regardless of their geographic locale at the time of the attacks or their connection to a deceased loved one. A colleague of mine had a client with schizoaffective disorder who worked at the airport and had chronic paranoid delusions and fears of Armageddon. He pleaded with her to write a letter to the president proclaiming his innocence and noninvolvement with the attacks. Another client with a significantly long refractory period had psychotic delusions that worsened so much he required two hospitalizations by January's end. The patients with traumatic histories and PTSD were particularly sensitized, and the attacks became generalized to previous traumatic experiences, bringing about flashbacks, anxiety, altered sleep, and intrusive thoughts. Some of my higher functioning psychotherapy and neurotic clients struggled with the existential angst evoked by these events. At times, I had to temper my own fears and uncertainties about the state of the nation while offering reassurance and support. In different moments, I too felt nervous when taking the subway or crossing bridges, and sometimes not acknowledging that in order to be therapeutic felt phony. Of course, these concerns did not place limitations on my activities, but I also felt a pressure to repress them in my role as physician.

By October, St. Vincent's Hospital had formed a liaison with FDNY Counseling. The arrangement called for the resident physician volunteers to give counseling or medication management for the bereaved and others affected by the disaster. I worked on Friday afternoons and would meet with clients to assess their needs. Some required medication management, in addition to supportive psychotherapy. Many needed referrals to outpatient treatment centers nearer to their homes, whereas some clients utilized services at both the St. Vincent's outpatient clinic and the counseling center. I ended up working closely with a handful of individuals who had various levels of exposure to the trauma. Even for those with seemingly disparate connections to the disaster, September 11 had unearthed previously unresolved conflicts or provided the stress diathesis for the development of more serious psychopathology. Some clients who had other stressors unrelated to the disaster—for example, marital stress, substance use, familial discord, or medical illness—might not have presented at the time they did were it not for the crisis. On some levels, it enabled those who had long put off seeking services to utilize them without as much stigma, although there were still a lot of barriers to accessing treatment.

Certain populations are more put off by mental health care than others, and I observed that within the heroic code of ethics and conduct that govern the socialization process of many firefighters, there are limits to the degree that one expresses certain emotions. Furthermore, the collective conscious for what constitutes "strong" behavior is well defined and sometimes myopic. There is also a gendered paradigm of the male superhero to contend with, and it can be too limiting to accommodate the emotional spillage of those who were deeply affected by the trauma. Many firefighters (I was most often treating men) had difficulty negotiating the pain they experienced and society's need for them to "be tough and strong." Some who were more able to be in touch with their grief and sadness, felt "lame" or "soft" for acknowledging these thoughts and guilty for having survived the attacks. Many were stricken with rumination of self-doubt, wondering if they had done enough despite having indisputably engaged in heroic feats and rescue efforts. Some felt that because they were alive or had been off duty on the day of the disaster, their work efforts and subsequent development of traumatic symptomatology related to exposure were indicative of a weakness of character. They would say things such as, "Well, this guy was in the building when it fell, and he's okay, so why am I like this when I only worked on the site for a few weeks?"

There was profound survivor's guilt in many firefighters, and it manifest in numerous ways. Some men had to be ordered to leave the rescue and recovery site and return home to their wives and children because their dedication to the job had crossed into a pathological overdrive. There were others who felt they had to work overtime to compensate for not having been at work on September 11 or not having lost any coworkers. Many felt compelled to expose themselves to the carnage just so they could "understand and relate to" what had happened. My colleague and I would sometimes accidentally stumble on cases while chatting with many of the men during their coffee breaks. It felt safer for them to approach us with the casual distance afforded by idle banter over the coffee pot. Many people presented two months or more after the tragedy (as is consistent with PTSD) after endless sleepless nights or depressive symptoms. It was surprising how long people would cope with certain problems out of fear of meeting with a mental health provider. They grappled with what that might say about them, even when the problem was clearly causing social and occupational dysfunction. The social stigma of having psychological difficulties is a potent barrier to seeking mental health treatment. Diagnoses among these individuals were a confluence of concentric circles, overlapping many spectrums of disorders, and, as is often the case in psychiatry, not easily narrowed down to one *DSM-IV* diagnostic code.

FDNY Counseling was overwhelmed early on, and many of its longtime employees began logging in hour upon hour to organize treatment and care. Never before had they had so many new clients, and now they were also serving higher numbers of family members, FDNY retirees, and support staff. Our role developed into offering both psychoeducation about PTSD to employees and clinical treatment to firefighters.

After meeting with clients at the counseling center, those who required medication would enroll as outpatients and see me in the clinic at St. Vincent's Hospital. It was difficult establishing the therapeutic framework and treatment plan for these individuals. My superego, that part of the mind that strives toward moral fortitude and righteousness (among other things), was already overactive. My training program added to this quandary by encouraging residents to be perennially available to the FDNY clients. This was difficult because I had just begun to understand the clinical importance of establishing therapeutic boundaries and was becoming more comfortable at enforcing them.

On some levels, we all wanted to extend ourselves for these clients, both out of our own feelings of guilt and the powerful countertransference they evoked. Were they really different patients? Were they more deserving of after hours appointments, refills over the phone, frequent last minute cancellations and rescheduling, longer than scheduled appointments? The pressure that came along with treating "America's Finest" while maintaining the same frame as we did for other clients at times felt strident, so I went with what felt most correct and clinically therapeutic. It was difficult to negotiate, however, and I felt awkward setting limits because of the nature of the trauma they experienced and its ramifications for their lives. There was unfortunately little preparation for how we were to navigate these issues in our clinical work with these individuals. Many clients who would come to the clinic for medication management, for example, also had outside therapists for supportive psychotherapy but would also frequently have "mini-therapy" sessions with the resident-examiners. Was this okay? With other clients, we were taught that our rapport was much more circumscribed. In the era of managed care and for-profit medicine, we functioned more as pill dispensers with the necessary discussion that accompanies it, and some supportive psychotherapy sprinkled in for good measure. When working with these individuals, my countertransference made it harder to keep to the scheduled appointment hour; occasionally I would let some clients in the midst of distress continue their session. My countertransference at times made me feel I was cutting them off, as opposed to keeping to the sanctioned time limit. I wanted them to be able to tell their stories and express their fears openly, because I was aware of the multiple barriers that precluded them from doing so under predisaster conditions. Because my lack of experience may have made it difficult for me to steer the session in such a way that clients weren't in a hysterical heap by the end of their session, I felt I needed to allow extra time for them to compose and reconstitute themselves.

In the long run, stepping out of bounds proved to be clinically appropriate, however. My approach enabled me to become part of a multi-disciplinary team, which I suspect benefited the patients more and made their treatment regimen more efficacious and meaningful. I learned a lot from the on-staff FDNY counselors, and we would consistently interact to develop treatment plans much like an inpatient psychiatry service. Rather than duplicating efforts, having many treatment providers working in concert buttressed the clients support system and ego strength. They were also invaluable sources of collateral information who helped me further elucidate some of the psychiatric symptoms and treatment issues I may have missed.

The work was rewarding and difficult at the same time, and I became overwhelmed and exhausted from it by April 2002. Because I had already developed a consistent group of clients related to the FDNY whom I was seeing at the clinic, I eventually became weary of my weekly foray to the counseling unit. The coming of springtime perhaps lifted the heavy pall of doom from my shoulders, and I wanted to be unencumbered from pain and discontent of any sort. It was interesting because at that point the few residents who had been consistently working at the counseling center also dropped out of the picture with regards to triaging new cases and holding weekly open office hours. I was burnt out from the doldrums and requirements of third year, not to mention taking on five clients from the counseling unit with whom I met regularly. The freeing of my Friday afternoons suddenly felt liberating. Awareness of my limitations enabled the dutiful doctor superego to loosen.

I noticed that many providers had overactive superegos during the months that followed the disaster. Medicine has long been a hierarchy and a competitive arena for one-upmanship. There were many "disaster junkie" providers who never tired of volunteering exhausting hours, even though they began to quietly decompensate and exhibit maladaptive coping skills in other spheres, suggesting some vicarious traumatization.

What was it about this work that inspired such fervent dedication? One of my theories around why superegos are stimulated in providers at the time of disasters is the sense of called-on duty. Medical training often requires a diligence and commitment to help and heal. On many levels, disasters and crises exemplify that challenge, and doing any less feels cheap and negligent. In fact, the ways the superegos of the medical providers were stimulated were similar to those of the firefighters. The dutiful doctor resonated with the superhero in many ways. Many felt that to do enough, they had to do more. And more would never be enough, because the regulatory capacity of the self to set limits did not rise to the occasion. The sense of chaos in the aftermath of the September 11 tragedy likely reverberated in internal chaos, stimulating many superegos to seek a control and mastery that was beyond the reach of normal ego functioning. The overdrive of endless working, giving, and volunteering likely served as a way to master the anxiety of helplessness evoked by the uncertainty of these events. Among the most important lessons I learned working in the disaster psychiatry sphere was the importance of establishing limits for oneself. It is critical to the disaster worker's livelihood and can aid in the safeguarding and prevention of vicarious traumatization. It also helps regulate narcissism and the overactive superegos that become stimulated in many providers during times of crisis.

In the end, I am proud to have participated in such dynamic work. I was able to accept my limitations humbly while feeling that I engaged meaningfully in therapeutic work with my clients. This experience facilitated considerable personal and professional growth and highlighted the need to institute disaster psychiatry and trauma training into the general psychiatry residency training program.

6

You Are Alive

Hope and Help After September 11, 2001

Diana R. Graham

In the weeks after September 11, 2001, I walked the outer reaches of my Manhattan neighborhood—Gramercy Park, Union Square, Greenwich Village—taking photos and reading signs. Flyers, posters, graffiti were everywhere, with messages of every variety. Hundreds of the now famous "Missing" flyers cried out from every brick wall and bus kiosk, sporting photos of men in police uniforms and wedding tuxedos, women with laughing children in their laps. Other messages came fast and furious. Hopeful: "Our spirit is strong—we will rebuild." Wary: "Indiscriminant killing is un-American," "Safety begins at home—protect your Arab and Muslim neighbors." Probing: "Jesus, Gandhi, MLK, and Buddha say love, Bush says war—who will you follow?" And mysterious: "You Are Alive."

I do not remember if I saw that last giant graffiti message with my own eyes or in a photo, but it has stayed with me. It is vivid in my mind. Four-foot-tall white, spray-painted letters, stark and unadorned on a red brick wall. I imagine I must have walked by and stopped to ponder. I think about its meaning at odd moments—in the shower, on the subway. Is it an accusation: You are alive, others are not? A wake-up call: You are alive, damn it, stop grieving and get busy? A reminder: You are alive, don't take anything for granted?

In the weeks after 9/11 I felt, in many ways, more alive than at any other time in my life. Each day was full of one intense event after another, moments that were seared into my memory, my body and senses humming with adrenaline. But at the same time, "You Are Alive" might have been a necessary reminder; aspects of death were all around as I numbly watched yet another truck full of human remains pull up in front of the medical examiner's office next to the hospital where I work, as the smell of the burning Towers drifted in and out of my living room day after day. My colleagues and friends and I moved through our days as if we had walked into a Salvador Dali painting.

And as I write this 14 months later, "You Are Alive" is in many ways just as surprising and jarring as it was in the Fall of 2001. Here I am, reading, writing, reflecting, working, living. Life goes on, in ways that were impossible to contemplate when that unknown public poet left those three provocative words on that wall so many weeks ago.

On the night of September 10, 2001, I was an unhappy third-year psychiatry resident, typing "alternative physician careers" into Internet search engines, hoping for inspiration. The grind of residency—10- to 12-hour days shuttling between as many as three or four hospitals and clinics, spending hour after hour doing inpatient consults, attending classes, endless nights in emergency rooms—was taking its toll. The transition from second to third year was proving difficult. My classmates and I were less closely supervised than in the past, and engaged in many aspects of outpatient care in which we had little experience. Suddenly we were "therapists," working one-on-one with distressed and often difficult patients, facing situations in which we often were at a loss as to what to do, terrified of making mistakes. I was exhausted, and my confidence in my professional abilities was low.

On the morning of the 11th, I trudged up to 125th Street in Harlem, where I was spending each Tuesday working in a state-run clinic for people with serious, chronic mental illness. It was one of my less taxing, but also less interesting or inspiring tasks. Blissfully unaware that this was anything other than a normal workday, I got off the subway around 9:15 a.m., later realizing in horror that I had been underground on the Number 6 train as the attacks were taking place. My mother paged me a few minutes later. My first thought at receiving her unusual early-morning call was that one of my grandparents must have died. When I finally found a working phone, I listened with some detachment to what she was describing as she sat in her Midwest living room watching footage of the burning Twin Towers on CNN. At first I assumed that she must have gotten the facts wrong. The scene sounded completely impossible.

I finally made it to the clinic and met up with my fellow residents, only to be evacuated moments later, as all government buildings were closed for the day. We were at something of a loss. As psychiatry trainees, we had no kind of disaster protocol, no clue what to do or how we might be useful. Our instincts pointed us all in the same direction—back to Bellevue Hospital, our mother ship, what I had, until then, always referred to as the Ground Zero of psychiatry. Bellevue is also a major emergency trauma center, and where our residency director and most of our supervisors and instructors work.

Our first challenge was merely to get there. We were 100 blocks away, and the streets of Harlem were filling with emergency vehicles from increasingly distant towns. The names on the sides of the vehicles read Mamaroneck, Scarsdale, and New Rochelle—suburbs I could not find on a map, let alone imagine what their fire engines and ambulances were doing pouring into the city. They made their way south toward the dense cloud that we could see billowing over lower Manhattan. We stopped traffic ourselves, nearly getting run over as we stood paralyzed in the middle of Fifth Avenue, mouths hanging open at our first sight of the Towers spewing smoke six or seven miles to the south.

Even in the chaos of that day, we stayed true to the tenets of medical training, according to which each trainee is expected to teach and supervise those working at levels below her. We had a fourth-year chief resident with us, and she took charge of our increasingly bizarre commute back to Bellevue, herding us through the streets, on and off the bus. She called herself our Mother Hen.

When we finally reached the hospital two hours after setting out, we found that even the people in charge seemed to be making things up as they went along. In retrospect it's hard to believe we thought someone would know what to do, or that anything might take place as usual. We actually phoned the residency office to find out if the Tuesday afternoon lecture classes would go on as scheduled.

The Bellevue psychiatric emergency room, set up to care for minor-injury overflow patients who never materialized, was packed with nearly every resident in the program. Hundreds of staff poured into emergency rooms around the city awaiting mass casualties that never arrived. There were almost no physically injured survivors to treat. After hours of waiting, we were sent home. After a few days of putting everything on hold while we tried to make ourselves useful with "disaster relief work," we returned to something resembling a "regular" clinic schedule, and realized that our existing patients would need help restoring their routines as well.

Although we spend a significant amount of time at Bellevue, as residents affiliated with NYU Medical Center, we treat a large number of NYU students from the undergraduate and graduate populations. During my third year of training, I was spending a half day a week at the student counseling

service, where the presenting problems could include anything from sadness after a breakup, to homesickness, to serious depression and substance
abuse, to the occasional new onset of psychosis.

The tone at the counseling center changed entirely after 9/11. A large
number of campus buildings were below Canal Street, the now decimated
area of lower Manhattan where the Trade Center had stood. Thousands of
students were displaced from their dorms immediately after the attacks, and
hundreds were indefinitely unable to return. The athletic facility became an
emergency shelter. I sat with the students who initially presented at the
counseling center and heard tale after tale of how their typical Tuesday
morning—late for class or daydreaming out the lecture hall window—
turned into a horror film. Suddenly they were watching jets tear into buildings and running for their lives. With each student who came into my office,
I felt like I was watching a movie scene played over and over, with every replay showing a slightly different angle on the events.

The worst off seemed to be students who had feared for their own safety
or, particularly, the safety of those they cared about—unable for hours or
even days to find a boyfriend who worked downtown, or reach Dad at his in-
vestment-banking job. To add insult to injury, many were teenagers on
their own for the first time, immersed in the excitement and uncertainty of
their first semester of classes. All traces of budding independence were
erased in an overwhelming urge to head home. I knew just how they felt. I
wanted to go home to my mother, too.

My residency training program tried to take care of us. In the early weeks,
we had meetings in which each of us would report in turn on the kind of
work we were doing and how it was affecting us. We were urged to take time
off, be with our friends and family, but reminded not to neglect our ongoing
clinical responsibilities. Life had to go on. Read this article about common
emotional responses to disaster, but don't forget your ER shift tonight.

Although I had not done previous disaster work, what struck me about
the experience I was having was how hard it was to tell who the "victims"
were. There were situations in which it was abundantly clear—the secretar-
ies who escaped from the towers, the lone firefighter who lost his entire bri-
gade, the bystanders caught in the dust and debris from the collapses. But
the ripples outward seemed never ending. Lower Manhattan residents from
Tribeca and Battery Park displaced from their homes came to the Bellevue
crisis clinic wheeling suitcases. I heard haunting stories from Brooklynites
who had stood transfixed on the Promenade, where their formerly enviable
view of the Manhattan skyline must have seemed like a torment out of *A
Clockwork Orange* as they witnessed each agonizing moment unfold against

that morning's impossibly clear skies. Friends e-mailed me frantically from hundreds of miles away to ask if I was safe and hoping for news of other Manhattan friends they were unable to reach. My cousin wrote from his semester abroad in Australia to describe how all the Americans at his school sat together and wept in front of the TV. I did not have contact with a single person who could be called unaffected.

My own immediate neighborhood, the 10 blocks around Bellevue Hospital and NYU Medical Center where I live and work, became transformed. The first two family assistance centers were within a few blocks, and their proximity, combined with the presence of several large hospitals and the Office of the Chief Medical Examiner, made the area a magnet. Desperate family members came in droves in the first few days, leaving in their wake "Missing" flyers on every imaginable surface. News trucks double-parked along the avenues. Firemen and police officers populated the streets, most off duty. They returned each night after their shifts to search for colleagues among the remains being unloaded from the trucks wearing a path between the morgue and Ground Zero.

At around midnight on September 12, the smoke plume from the burning WTC site hit the area, setting off fire alarms in Bellevue. Our beleaguered neighborhood firehouse responded. I was on one of the higher floors of the hospital at the time, talking with a hospitalized emergency medical technician who had somehow survived the collapses of both towers, and for a moment I feared for my own safety. I smelled smoke, and it suddenly occurred to me that the hospital might be a target for further attacks. The elevators shut down when the alarm went off, and the stairwells were locked. There was nothing to do but wait for the all clear.

My attention went to a television playing over the patient's bed. The local news was on, and I assumed that if Bellevue were under attack, the station would be carrying the story. Instead, the reporter described an event that had happened a few hours earlier. A bomb threat had caused the evacuation of the Empire State Building and the surrounding blocks. I later learned that my husband-to-be and a friend, walking on their way to try to volunteer at a Red Cross center, had been caught in the crowds fleeing that area. They sprinted for half a mile, terrified for their lives. The ripples in the pond were causing parallel processes of fear all over the city. I began to wonder how I could take care of patients when it seemed disaster might swallow me up at any moment.

But I did. We all did, calling on whatever reserves we had to keep moving. I think the work kept us going. Mental health clinicians were being requested all over the city, and the drive and opportunity to do *something* allowed us to put our focus outside of ourselves. Everyone else seemed envious. People were returning to their routines, but they often found the return to work excruciating. My nonmedical friends told me how lucky I was to be in a position to help in the relief work. They emptied their wallets of contributions, searched their closets for extra clothes to give, bought bottled water, work boots, surgical masks, or whatever item du jour was rumored to be needed. After depositing their donations at the Ground Zero relief collection points, they went about their business. Even doctors in other fields, in the days before anthrax and smallpox gave them so much to occupy their time, were envious. Everyone wanted to talk with us.

One Saturday in October, I was volunteering with Disaster Psychiatry Outreach at the Family Assistance Center at Pier 54, an enormous, mind-boggling facility that provided survivors and victims of the Trade Center attacks with almost every kind of assistance imaginable. It looked very much like a crisply organized convention center, set up in row upon row of tables and display booths. I watched as exhausted columns of people lined up to apply for housing assistance or drop off DNA samples of family members to assist in the identification of remains. On my lunch break, I walked the length of one wall, mesmerized by the wrenching sight of hundreds of teddy bears and letters sent by the children of Oklahoma City.

That afternoon, two women in their early 40s approached the Department of Mental Health table, clutching their pocketbooks, eyes wide. They had fled from one of the towers and wanted to speak to someone. One woman was black, the other South Asian. They were almost exactly the same age, had worked together for years, and both had their periods that day. It was as if they were synchronized. I offered to meet with each woman individually, but they would not be separated. We moved to one of the tastefully furnished faux living room areas in the back, and they took turns describing their escape from the trade center. Since their ordeal they had both developed symptoms of acute stress disorder: they had trouble sleeping, were jumpy and unable to concentrate in their new makeshift offices, felt afraid to let their children out of their sight, and found themselves emotionally numb.

I asked about their workmates. Of the several hundred people in their office, one person was missing, an older woman who was last seen in the towers trying to get in an elevator, despite urgings to head for the stairs. Dozens of images of Cantor Fitzgerald employees flashed through my mind, faces I'd memorized as I walked past the "Missing" flyers each day—and columns of numbers printed daily in the New York Times, listing by floor how many dozens or hundreds were missing from each company.

I called my attention back to the pair in front of me. "Wow, your office was really lucky, then," I said, probably a little too brightly. "Only one person." Their faces shifted.

"Well," one of them began tentatively. "She really was a nice person. We'd known her for years. Everyone liked her." She looked at her lap, uncertain.

I took a breath, horrified with myself. I had practically congratulated them on the death of their friend. I realized in that moment how surreal everything had become. One loss seemed lucky, was nothing in the face of hundreds or thousands feared dead. The numbers had become too large to grasp, even in the context of endless collages of photos and onslaughts of desperate pleas—"Help us find our daddy." "Last seen on the 109th floor, Tower 2." To me, excruciatingly lucky and having lost no one, the numbers were huge and unfathomable. To the women I was sitting with, the loss was very simple: a coworker with a lovely smile who made great coffee each morning.

As I write this over a year later, I can still feel that fist of horror in my gut as I wondered how I could have said such a thing. I finished the evaluation, eventually separating the women and speaking to each privately. They left with some educational materials and a few days' worth of sleep medication. Both women thanked me as we said goodbye. But I went on to replay that moment over and over, worrying that I had done more harm than good.

My mistake threw into relief the scale of what was happening around me. I approached disaster work with a bit of franticness. There was so much to do, so many to help, so many places to be in at once. Volunteers were needed at the hospitals, the Family Center, the morgue, Ground Zero, the bond trading firms, schools, hotlines. There were survivors, injured, witnesses, rescue workers, family members, each group with different needs and different timetables. But as an individual clinician, my focus had to be on the person in front of me: her story, her needs, her particular losses. The real work was not in the numbers, but in the moments.

Eventually, I realized that it was exactly in those moments that I could be the most helpful. Yes, we as a field, as a city, as a country, as a species, were overwhelmed. But we are fortunate in that there are so many of us. If you don't have those moments in you today, someone else does, and you will have them tomorrow, or next week. There is room to pause, take care of yourself, and come back when ready.

As time stretched on, as "You Are Alive" seemed more a permanent condition than a tenuous one, the urgency and franticness decreased. Over a year later, I am still seeing patients presenting for the first time with

9/11-related symptoms or issues. There is no end to those moments, and each one unfolds in its own time. People of all kinds—patients, colleagues, friends—are forgiving of mistakes, tolerant of shortcomings, and hungry to help and be helped. You *are* alive. I am, too, and we are in this together.

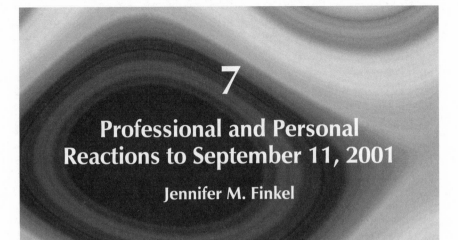

7

Professional and Personal Reactions to September 11, 2001

Jennifer M. Finkel

Before September 11, 2001, I knew very little about disaster psychiatry. I thought disaster psychiatrists dealt with problems in remote areas where hurricanes hit, flashfloods demolished entire villages, and earthquakes shook whole communities. I concluded that disaster psychiatrists dealt with issues in places far away from the comfortable reality I was used to.

I am a born and bred New Yorker and chose New York University and Bellevue Hospital, a major metropolitan hospital and renowned psychiatric center, for my psychiatric residency because I wanted to be exposed to the entire spectrum of psychiatric experiences.

Although the patients were much more challenging than I had originally anticipated, I quickly adapted and felt a sense of satisfaction when I could classify them neatly into psychiatric categories. I learned to describe my patient's symptoms according to guidelines established by the *Diagnostic and Statistical Manual of Mental Disorders* (DSM), the official psychiatric coding system used in the United States. I thought practicing psychiatry consisted of performing a psychiatric interview, interacting with people with psychiatric disorders, and prescribing medications, all of which I learned to do. But one day dramatically changed my perspective of clinical psychiatry.

As a second-year psychiatric resident, I was scheduled for on-call duty in the psychiatric emergency room on a regular basis. The night shift of September 10 had been a particular busy one for me, and I was looking forward to going home to rest after winding up my clinical responsibilities on Bellevue's inpatient psychiatric unit.

When I arrived at the inpatient unit at 8:50 a.m., a nurse told me that one of the twin towers of the World Trade Center was on fire. Dumbstruck, I went to look at the television in the community room and saw Tower 1 ablaze.

Staff and patients stood side by side watching horrifying images that soon would become ingrained in our collective psyche. We were alternately dumbfounded, astonished, and mesmerized. The time was 8:53 a.m. The assistant chief of the inpatient unit, who was also the cofounder and vice president of Disaster Psychiatry Outreach (DPO), asked for volunteers to help counsel victims at the World Trade Center after work. He explained that DPO was an organization of psychiatrists whose primary mission was to aid in disaster relief by providing on-site psychotherapeutic and psychopharmacologic services to victims of disasters.

I agreed to go after work but hoped our supervisor would let us leave sooner. No one, however, could foresee the enormity of the disaster.

At 9:10 a.m., I learned that the second tower had been hit by a plane and that terrorists were the suspected culprits. Within the next 20 minutes, rumors flew, and we didn't know fact from fiction. Two planes were missing, then six, then eight. The Pentagon was attacked. Camp David was attacked. The Sears Tower was attacked. Bellevue lost all phone service.

When I learned that both towers of the World Trade Center collapsed, I panicked for the first time in my life. I wanted to leave, run home, see my family and gather as much information as possible. But the unit chief reminded me and my fellow colleagues about our duties to the patients.

"You must be a doctor today as any other day. Notes must get written, and the labs must be checked," he said. I took a break to collect myself before continuing with my clinical responsibilities. I wondered how my patients would handle the devastating news, given the difficulty I was having.

At 11:00 a.m., the staff met to discuss how best to deal with the disaster. We agreed to keep the unit running and fully staffed to ensure a safe environment for the patients. We also decided to hold an emergency community meeting to provide a nurturing environment for the patients to ask questions, vent their feelings, express their fears and contain their distress. "Would other sites in Manhattan be attacked," they wondered. Could they call their families to check on their safety?

I was surprised how calm most of the patients were at the meeting. One of my patients offered some insight. "Dr. Finkel, I'm used to chaos and disorder. It has been my life for as long as I can remember. I think you're now only getting a taste of what it's been like for me—for all of us," he told me.

For the rest of the day, the residents met with their patients individually and in groups. I became less aware of patient's *DSM* diagnoses as patients with schizophrenia, depression, and bipolar disorder intermingled and focused on the same issue—coping with the emotional toll of the disaster.

The nature of my psychiatric practice had changed. Without warning, a disaster had thrust itself into my life, into my patients' lives, and become a key component of my psychiatric practice. When I left work later that evening, I searched for answers to what had happened. I had been inside all day and had not witnessed much of the chaos that other New Yorkers experienced. I had not seen the televised images of the towers collapsing, or the huge rescue effort that was immediately employed.

I heard of huge hoards of people walking home from work across the city and across the Brooklyn Bridge. I heard of huge lines of people lining up to donate blood, but by the time I left the hospital, the streets were eerily quiet.

When I awoke the next day, New York was transformed. Army vehicles lined the streets; news media vehicles parked in front of the hospital. Posters of missing loved ones were plastered all over the city—on the hospital walls, at bus stations, on lampposts, everywhere. Police barricades were erected in front of Bellevue and security was heightened dramatically overnight. There was no escaping the new reality, and I felt I needed to get involved.

On the evening of September 12, I went to Bellevue's psychiatric emergency room and signed up for extra shifts. The staff expected a huge influx of people seeking psychiatric care and possibly requiring admission. Hospital administrators ensured that beds were available by discharging stable patients.

Surprisingly, no one showed up that night with problems related directly to the attacks. The next evening, I was asked by one of my supervising attending physicians to volunteer next door at the Administration of Child Services (ACS) building, which had had been made into a makeshift resource center for victims and their families.

In the few days right after the attack, people were more concerned about obtaining information than seeking counseling. My colleagues quickly realized that to provide grief counseling, they had to seek out the victims, instead of waiting for them to seek psychiatric care.

One of my attending physicians directed me to the fifth floor of the ACS building, where I wandered through numerous hallways, none of which were marked with directions to the counseling area. I noticed that pamphlets about grief counseling had been distributed to the volunteers. Grief counseling teams, consisting of a social worker, psychologist or psychiatric resident, and an attending physician, had been assigned to work together. After waiting to do grief counseling for three hours, I realized that a single well-marked, centrally located "resource" facility was needed. Outreach was clearly the key, but it needed to be implemented in a more efficient manner.

The following day, September 13, I volunteered at the newly created Bellevue Crisis Center. Contrary to the staff's expectations, no one arrived at the Crisis Center in search of counseling related to the World Trade Center attacks. I walked home that evening wearing a surgical mask to protect myself from the fumes that now wafted heavily in my neighborhood.

I was literally amid the destruction and despair, yet I had not talked to a single person directly affected by the attack. I felt frustrated and enraged by my helpless position.

On Saturday morning, September 15, I went to the 26th Street Armory, located two blocks from my apartment. The armory was organized as the central information center for victims and their families. There were at least 50 stations established at the armory, including for missing persons, the American Red Cross, the fire and police departments, and several corporations.

When I arrived at the armory, I was directed to the DPO station. I met with an attending physician who briefed me about the armory and the work I would be doing for the victims and their families. I was asked by families to look up names of missing persons on master lists kept in debriefing rooms, which were the busiest areas of the armory. The lists contained names of people who were hospitalized, treated, or deceased as a result of September 11.

The debriefing rooms with master lists simplified the process for families who had been going from one hospital to the next in Manhattan to find out whether the persons(s) they were looking for had been treated. As I walked to the debriefing rooms, I noticed the huge lines of people waiting to get into the rooms. I quickly realized that this counseling experience would be unique. Despite my good communication skills, this was the first time I had interacted with people who were so acutely affected by such a devastating and uncertain trauma.

I sought guidance from experienced DPO psychiatrists who gave me reading materials about grief counseling and guided me through the process. They explained that most of the people who would be coming to the debriefing rooms wanted answers, not psychotherapy. My job was to search the master lists and provide a safe environment for victims' families to express the difficult feelings of grief and helplessness.

I was assigned to a team with a social worker and prepared myself emotionally for the work. The first woman who approached me handed me a list of 20 names of missing persons. I slowly sifted through the master list for the name of the first missing person, using my forefinger to guide me through the 30 pages of names. I did not find the first or the second missing person's name.

With each subsequent name that was not on the list, I felt increasingly anxious. Was I going to have to tell this woman that none of the 20 missing persons were on the list? When I finished looking up the name of the last missing person, all I could say was, "I'm so sorry." The woman sighed, and lowered her head on the table.

I said, "I know this must be such a difficult time for you. And it must be impossible to think about yourself when so much is going on. But I just wanted to ask how you are doing." The woman raised her eyes and replied, "You know, I haven't even thought about myself until you just asked."

The woman discussed her personal experience with me, how she had missed work on 9/11 because her three-year-old child had come down with the flu. That morning, she had cancelled her carpool with a friend who was now missing. When she saw what had happened on the news, she described feeling totally numb. The entire first day she sat at home, watching the news and making phone calls.

By the third day, she and several other surviving coworkers divided up the work of making posters and traveling between the different hospitals in an effort to gain some semblance of control. She began to cry when she told me how guilty she felt that most of her coworkers had either perished in the collapse, or were trapped in the rubble. She wept quietly as she said, "I just don't know what else to do. I've been here 20 times checking these lists. Sometimes I wonder why I keep coming. Maybe it's hope that one day, some of these people will turn up. Or maybe, I come to be doing something, anything to help with the way that I feel."

The woman and I spoke for two hours. More than anything else, I listened. At the end of the conversation, the woman thanked me and said, "You know, it really is the little things people do that are helpful." I then handed her referral numbers for counseling services that were available if she wanted to talk further. She took the numbers, leaned over the table and hugged me.

The woman was the first person affected by the World Trade Center disaster with whom I had spoken. Even though I knew that I would probably never see her again, I finally felt some degree of purpose. I realized that the people I would be talking with over the next several weeks were not patients in the traditional sense. I was not going to focus on diagnoses and would not be prescribing medication to treat psychopathology. I would discard the typical boundary lines that separated me from my patients, and instead invite a mutual and even physical expression of emotions.

That evening when I came home, I felt physically and emotionally drained. I had been inundated with disaster psychiatry resources and began reading them over and over at a feverish pace.

I started questioning my own response to the World Trade Center collapse. I even wondered whether my participation at the armory was reexposing myself to the disaster and whether it would lead to my own traumatization. Being a psychiatrist did not make me any less vulnerable to the media coverage, the victims, and the reality of terror. I questioned whether I should return to the armory and struggled with what I perceived as my own selfishness. The next morning, I walked the two blocks to the armory, more prepared than I had been on the previous day.

My responsibilities at the armory on the second morning were very different from those of the prior day. I was asked to assist police officers in the collection of DNA samples from victims' families. Initially, I sensed a bit of resistance from the police officers. "What role does a psychiatrist play in such a process?" I imagined they were asking. I admit that at the time, I was asking myself the same question.

The collection of the DNA was a traumatic process for the victims' families. On one level, it served as a painful acknowledgment that hope for rescue was dwindling. Additionally, the DNA collection process required parents, wives, and husbands to turn over physical and personal evidence of their loved ones. Sadly, the DNA specimens were all that remained of the thousands of people who were still missing. It is impossible to describe the gravity and the intense sadness of the DNA collection process. When I saw the police officers holding back the tears, I honestly felt frightened.

Participating in the DNA collection process was the most difficult experience I had after September 11. The emotions were raw and intense. One couple from Queens who approached my table had spent the initial days desperately trying to locate their son, who had worked in the first tower on one of the higher floors. By September 16, they agreed to submit a hair sample in case it would later be helpful in the identification process. The father, visibly shaken, handed the sample to me rapidly and watched as I carefully sealed and labeled it in the appropriate package. The couple then decided to give their own cheek cell samples as additional DNA evidence. After I demonstrated how to swab their inner cheeks, the father attempted to get the sample. He took out the swab, held it in his hand and trembled so violently that he was unable to obtain the sample. He tried several times, but was unsuccessful. He banged his hand on the table in anger and cried out in frustration, "I can't do it. I'm letting him down, I can't do it."

I reached over and took the father's hand in mine. I tried to empathize with him about how painful, almost inhuman, the DNA collection process must be for him. I explained that feeling intense sadness, even anger, was normal considering the abnormality of the circumstances in which he now found himself. I reminded him that he need not feel ashamed or embarrassed. I assured him that I would remain with him as long as necessary to get the DNA sample.

The father started telling me about his personal experience since the attack. He had felt plagued by guilt ever since he misreported to the police that his son was wearing a watch with a gold band that day, when in fact, he was wearing one with a black band.

"How can I be a good father when I can't even remember what my own son wore?" He broke down in tears. I held his hand firmly and responded, "I am sure your love for your son was felt by him every day. This situation is causing you to focus on things that would ordinarily have seemed trivial." The father nodded and squeezed my hand.

He was still trembling too much to obtain the sample and I asked whether he wanted me to help him, which he appreciated. I obtained the sample and he gratefully thanked me. I then offered to escort him to the counseling room to talk more about how he was dealing with the tragedy. He graciously accepted my offer. While I had questioned what my role would be in the collection of DNA, it became clearer.

After that day at the armory, I felt overwhelmed by the tragedy and the myriad stories I was hearing. Following 9/11, terrorist threats occurred daily in New York City and became an almost inconceivable routine in a new reality. Bomb threats were reported all over Manhattan, at Grand Central Terminal, the Statue of Liberty, and the Empire State Building.

One of the earliest patients afflicted with anthrax was treated at NYU, my institution, and four blocks from my home. I found myself experiencing symptoms that I had discussed with victims' families: I felt more anxious, and had difficulty sleeping and nightmares about planes crashing into buildings. Determined to take the advice I had been giving to others, I stopped watching media coverage, tried to immerse myself in my usual activities, and took some time off from volunteering. I questioned whether it was appropriate for me to provide grief counseling at a time when I was feeling traumatized by the very same disaster affecting the victims. I waited until I felt ready to reimmerse myself in the outreach, and started volunteering at Pier 94 about two months later.

Pier 94 had been transformed into the Family Assistance Center, a more organized version of the armory. The overall feel of the Pier was less chaotic than the armory. The building itself was much larger than the 26th Street Armory, and services were spread out in an organized fashion. Guides familiar with the Pier's setup were available to direct families to the specific services they were seeking. Within minutes, clients were getting help with their specific needs and their wait time was dramatically diminished. Walls and curtains separated the different booths, enabling a much greater degree of privacy. A separate enclosed area was devoted to disaster psychiatry and several private rooms were devoted to counseling.

I was assigned to work with an attending psychiatrist, and cases were presented in a more orderly fashion. I immediately felt more comfortable at the Pier, where my responsibilities were clearly delineated and the structure was more organized than at the armory. I knew that victims' families would also feel more comfortable in the more stable environment.

The two months since September 11 had a major impact on the type of counseling I provided. By this time, most people had already submitted necessary information about missing persons and had applied for financial aid. Debriefing rooms were unnecessary because the master lists were gone. Furthermore, the rescue effort was slowly turning into one of recovery. Many people who visited the Pier specifically came seeking psychotherapy, as the original chaos had dissipated and people once again had time to focus on themselves.

Although the initial trauma was over, Ground Zero remained a perpetual reminder of death and destruction. Additionally, new threats of terror continued, causing people to feel uncertain about their future all the time.

When I started talking to the people who had come to the Pier, I was immediately struck by their eagerness to discuss the symptoms they were having. Symptoms of acute stress disorder and depression were prevalent in this population, and many people seemed frightened by them. The questions I had encountered two months earlier, such as "Is this name on the list?" were now replaced by questions such as, "Doc, am I going crazy?" Obtaining information about symptoms had replaced obtaining information about missing loved ones, a paramount concern two months earlier.

Reassurance at this point was critical and took numerous forms. Providing education about the recovery process helped people understand what they were going through. Normalizing new emotions of anger, disbelief, sadness, anxiety, and fear was key for patients who had never experienced these emotions at such intense levels. For others, using cognitive behavioral techniques to develop a plan for coping was helpful. Coping plans consisted of minimizing exposure to news media, identifying key stressors, spending time with close friends and family, and occasionally beginning therapy at an outpatient clinic.

During this period, some of the more challenging cases seeking disaster psychiatry were people who were peripherally connected to the trauma. They felt "left out" of the monetary aid that was being provided to victims' immediate families. A fiancé of someone who had perished in the attack, described to me almost on a daily basis posttraumatic stress symptoms of increased anxiety, hypervigilance, avoidance, and reexperiencing the trauma through nightmares.

Her primary problem, however, was financial. She and her fiancé had planned to marry in November but had combined their finances for the past three months. She had sought financial aid since September 11 but was denied because she could not prove that she was a direct dependent of the deceased. In this situation, I was unsure of how I could assist. We discussed several options to help with her new financial situation but she did not find any of these options realistic. She requested a letter from me stating that I believed her to be incapable of dealing with her finances, suggesting that she be given the same aid that a direct family member would be given. I felt uncomfortable in this situation and wondered about possible secondary motives, as I had been informed that many people had such intentions.

Nevertheless, I believed this woman was suffering from true symptoms, and I wanted to help her. I knew that my countertransferrance was affecting my judgment, and I discussed this with a supervising attending psychiatrist. At his suggestion, the patient and I agreed that she would ask her previous psychiatrist whom she had seen for two years whether she could write such a letter for her.

The world changed on September 11, and the practice of psychiatry changed along with it. Disaster psychiatry immediately entered mainstream psychiatry and became an integral part of clinical practice. My personal experience with Disaster Psychiatry Outreach post–September 11 has been an invaluable learning experience, albeit a difficult one, as it challenged some of the basic psychiatric tenets to which I had previously adhered. In the disaster psychiatry efforts post–September 11, there were no strict boundaries between victims and counselors, little need for DSM classification, and infrequent use of medication. Psychiatrists were seeking out patients, rather than the reverse.

In addition, psychiatrists' roles were not clearly delineated, and they often served in multiple roles—as counselors, social workers, and even forensic collectors. It was the psychiatrist's primary responsibility, however, to provide a safe environment in which victims' families could voice their concerns and fears. The psychiatrist played an integral role in the disaster response by his or her unique ability to communicate and empathize, rather than in the ability to diagnose and medicate. Acute interventions focused on normalizing a person's response to the trauma rather than pathologizing it.

The disaster of 9/11 differed from all previous disasters in the United States because of the vast number of people who were affected simultaneously. The scope of the impact of September 11 is truly immeasurable because it affected victims' families, emergency rescue personnel, firefighters, police officers, every resident of New York, and even those who witnessed the collapse of the Twin Towers on television.

Although the degree of connection to the trauma might have differed between counselor and patient, never before have the victims of a disaster been so closely linked to those helping them. As such, the realm of disaster psychiatry evolved and expanded in a matter of a few short weeks.

I am humbled by my prior ignorance regarding the importance of disaster psychiatry practices and am continually reminded of its usefulness. The psychological effects of September 11 will be long lasting; as such, disaster psychiatry will continue to play a part of everyday psychiatric practice. I was reminded of this reality on September 11, 2002, when I was in the psychiatric emergency room admitting a high-functioning outpatient with a 10-year history of posttraumatic stress disorder who had acutely decompensated.

Patients will continue to present to clinicians with symptoms directly related to the trauma of September 11, 2001. Anniversaries of that date will forever be linked to the tragedy of that day, and the psychiatric implications of 9/11 will have long-term consequences.

I am fortunate to have worked with Disaster Psychiatry Outreach following September 11, and the knowledge I gained will continue to help me throughout my career. Disaster psychiatry is clearly not a practice that can be overlooked by the general practitioner in psychiatry in this ever-changing, often tumultuous world.

III
International Perspectives

When psychiatrists turn their attention to disasters across the world, an immense range of challenges and experiences naturally come into play. As noted at the start of this book, every disaster is unique. Whereas earlier chapters reflected the range of responses to a single disaster, this section emphasizes the variability of disasters themselves. One may well wonder what the crash of Swissair Flight 111 in Nova Scotia and the chronic disaster of civil turmoil in the Gaza Strip have in common.

This section also reflects the long and daunting history of worldwide events. Many Americans remain ignorant of the frequency of disasters in certain parts of the world. Even when Americans are aware of the serial devastation that occurs in other countries, it is often difficult for any outsider to understand the complex effect of these disasters on the culture, politics, and individual psychologies of a particular populace. Yet the essays in this section manage to convey a hope and optimism that is thankfully found on the other side of all catastrophes. These psychiatrists have attempted to bring their professional knowledge to bear in disasters, despite the often low priority assigned to mental health in overseas relief efforts. In the absence of accepted systems and protocols for disaster psychiatry, they have had to be mental health advocates and innovators under horrific circumstances. In some cases, such systems have begun to grow from the very efforts of the authors.

The questions that frame Raquel Cohen's essay may speak for all of the authors: "What will I find? How can I help?" Trained in the controlled environments of hospitals and medical centers, psychiatrists who venture into the worldwide community at times of disaster are confronted with a very steep learning curve. They must not only acquaint themselves with the physical and psychological impact of the disaster but also with the community that predated the event. One cannot minister to the psyche of a stricken community without knowing its social, political, economic, and cultural rhythms. Inherent in this information gathering is a determination of the local "mental-health–mindedness" and resources. A considerable variable in international disaster mental health is the extent to which Western psychiatry is relevant, accepted, or practical in a given locale. Use of local resources and customs for ministering to the psychological needs of an affected region seems to be an important rule of thumb. Psychiatry practiced in atypical and chaotic situations requires a flexibility of spirit and deed; it frequently must make do with a scarcity of resources that predated the disaster.

These essays are ultimately personal tales of professional endeavors and are marked by very individual motivations for psychiatrists' engagement in the disasters described. A connection to one's birthplace plays a role in several instances. Likewise, many of the authors convey the powerful personal impact of their disaster work, from fear to exhilaration, as they seek to straddle the world atop psychiatry. Far from their families, homes, and offices, they must make do both personally and professionally. In helping to confront the emotions of others in the face of disaster, humanitarians' own emotions are often central to the tale.

This section also raises questions about how we conceive of disasters and the role of disaster psychiatrists when there are prominent political dimensions to the event. Ongoing conflicts such as that portrayed in Dr. Raasoch's chapter are fundamentally different from natural disasters or single-event manmade disasters such as the 9/11 attacks. Here, as in later chapters describing wars (the civil war in El Salvador in Dr. Kessler's chapter and the Vietnam War in Dr. Meyerson's chapter), the psychiatrist is challenged to consider how and when to separate personal feelings, political views, and professional commitment to healing. Although many chapters in this book make a forceful case that disaster psychiatry should include an awareness of system issues and an active advocacy for one's patients, some may question Dr. Raasoch's decisions in Gaza. Nonetheless, his description of his experiences vividly portrays how he thought through his decisions. Thus, the chapter offers valuable insights for anyone who practices disaster psychiatry—since all disasters, including natural disasters, have the potential to become heated political issues.

8

Outreach in Australian Disasters

Beverley Raphael

My interest in disasters and involvement in disaster outreach commenced in work with those experiencing personal disasters such as bereavement, major illness, and the consequence of war. As a young general practitioner, I learned a great deal about people as they struggled to deal with both acute experience (such as tragic deaths of children) or the longer term consequences of, for example, World War II. I was working in a large veterans practice, and the principal had himself survived Changi, the Japanese prisoner-of-war camp at Singapore known for its severity. Many of my patients were women who, with great courage, dealt with terminal breast and gynecologic cancers. They had presented "late"—only being willing to show their bodies to a woman doctor, and even then doing so with shame. There were also the women who survived the horrific backyard abortions of that time, and there were families terrified and overwhelmed by the acute and life-threatening illnesses of their children. I learned during these years of the courage and fighting spirit with which people faced adversity. Being a general practitioner in Australia at the time (1959–1963) involved intensive outreach and home visits, and this has always given me both confidence in and a sensitivity to the meaning of outreach to peoples' own places of home and community and the particular issues of "helping" relationships in such settings.

When I completed my training as a psychiatrist, I undertook a doctoral research study that involved investigating the models of crisis intervention, and testing the effectiveness of such intervention for recently bereaved widows deemed to be at heightened risk of adverse outcomes (Raphael, 1977a). This involved outreach to widows in their homes in the acute period of the early weeks following their loss. It involved the adaptation of psychotherapeutic techniques to this domestic and personal context in response to current and acute stressors. It also involved engagements with a range of clergy, community organizations, and other groups involved in response to those in crises and in helping those recently bereaved. This exploration of crisis was also extended to women having a hysterectomy. More generally this study involved the investigation of intervention for those experiencing major life crises, and the possibilities of preventing psychiatric morbidity, as in the work of Caplan (1964).

On Christmas Eve of 1974, the northern Australian city of Darwin was destroyed by Cyclone Tracey. Many of its inhabitants were evacuated to southern cities, for fear of illness and other threat. No mental health outreach was allowed to this devastated and isolated city, 4,000 miles from the nearest major centers. It was decided that support and outreach should be offered to those evacuated to capital cities around Australia. Because of my experience with crisis intervention, I was asked to train workers in Sydney to assist evacuees in dealing with the crises of the disaster experience.

This program of education and outreach could be implemented only in minimal ways. It became clear that systematic and structural issues were critical to any disaster response. There was no readily available list of survivors and evacuees, nor of their whereabouts in the cities to which they were evacuated. The response to the territory in which Darwin was situated was through the commonwealth and its operational arms such as the defense department. The specific roles of the states and commonwealth and an organizational template for disaster response in such circumstances did not exist. Furthermore, in what was seen as critical to outreach and assistance, mental health was not considered to have any significant acute role, and longer term issues were seen as requiring principally social rather than psychiatric outreach. This was despite the fact that a growing literature was indicating the risk of significant psychiatric morbidity among disaster-affected populations (Kinston and Rosser, 1974). Nor was the opportunity for prevention considered. Although I did provide outreach to a small number of evacuees in Sydney, it seemed that the system was "not ready" for mental health interventions.

In the months following this cyclone, I was asked by the Royal Australian and New Zealand College of Psychiatrists to develop a strategy for psychiatric response in major disasters. To accomplish this, I met with disaster-response leaders such as the head of the response team, Major General Stretton, and the mayor of Darwin, who was involved in the longer term recovery processes. I also met with community organizations, victims, health, police, ambulance, defense, and social-service providers. The ensuing report highlighted the need to create an organizational structure for mental health response that reflected the system of federal and state governments and emergency-response systems, a structure that was accepted and integrated with them (Raphael, 1976). The engagement with this wide range of stakeholders revealed their interest in and awareness of what they called "the human factor." This referred to the psychological aspects of disaster response seen to be so influential that the effectiveness of emergency and recovery response would be significantly influenced by them. As a consequence, the national body responsible for emergency management training held its first seminar on disaster behavior, with involvement of the diverse stakeholders responsible for management at federal and state levels. This collaborative endeavor was a milestone in acceptance of the relevance of mental health issues to disaster management and response, in both the emergency and the longer term. It is also of interest that this meeting, which set in place a new climate of inclusion, took place in late October 1976.

The next major disaster in Australia (the Granville train disaster) occurred in January 1977 when a commuter train crashed into the pylons of an overhead concrete slab bridge, bringing it down on the carriages, killing 83 people and injuring many others. I was involved in developing and implementing both the acute and longer term mental health aspects of disaster response following this event (Raphael, 1977b, 1979–1980). There was much more to learn; now psychiatric outreach and mental health interventions had the beginnings of an accepted place in the structure of response. A team was set up in the city morgue, and we worked with families when they came in to identify their deceased loved ones. We (my team) sat with family members while they waited at the morgue, went in to share the viewing of their family member if they so wished, and supported them afterward at this site. I found that these family members had great courage and a great need to see their loved one, even if the body had been mutilated. Seeing part of the person's face or hand and to be able to touch if they wished reassured the family members.

I then drew together a group of people whom I knew to be trained, experienced, and sensitive for the task of follow-up outreach to the bereaved in their own homes and communities. There was the first-week period of outreach to families at the morgue, organization of follow-up outreach to those who had been in the disaster and those bereaved, and the establishment of collaboration with welfare and other agencies for the longer term recovery phase.

It was at this time that I came to understand personally the meaning of the "counterdisaster" syndrome of overinvolvement and a sense of urgency that disaster workers experience, combined with the inability, but overwhelming need, to step down. I had had extensive experience, in many other settings, dealing with those who had been bereaved and psychologically traumatized, for instance, when a family member died in horrific circumstances.

On the fourth day following the disaster, I lay awake, feeling overwhelmed in knowing what was needed for the families of those who died in such highly traumatic ways and that there were not enough skilled people available to handle their current mental health needs and those that would arise in the months ahead.

Nevertheless I, and a number of others, did provide outreach to families in their own homes. These were complex bereavements, including many deaths of adult children. The losses were found to be associated with complex grief that was difficult to resolve. I also conducted a group for widows in one community, and learned here of their complex grief, their struggles to meet the needs of their children, and the way in which the suddenness of the deaths had sometimes cut across the ambivalence of everyday life, leaving them to come to terms with the unresolved anger of the morning their husbands or loved ones had caught this train. Many encountered the stigma of being "investigated" to make sure they were not cohabiting with other men before they would be given "deserved" compensation. These women were angry, too, that I had seen their husbands' bodies when, in terms of the culture of the day, they as women had been protected from so doing; I thought often and long about the rows of grey cold bodies in the morgue.

I felt in this outreach both the traumatic circumstances and the overwhelming nature of such sudden deaths, so many deaths, and the complexity that I and other workers faced in delivering the sophisticated and sensitive bereavement interventions that were needed. This was also one of the first disasters in which any longer term evaluation of interventions was attempted (Singh and Raphael, 1981). We found that parents, particularly mothers, were at highest risk; that not seeing the body was associated with poorer outcomes; and that some limited benefit seemed to result from the interventions when perceived as helpful and needed.

Outreach to workers and some attempt to assess their needs also took place, providing fascinating insights. I held my first "psychological debriefing" with a volunteer rescue team, the members of which had been courageous in their endeavors to save those trapped under the slab. This outreach was about 10 days after the disaster, and the team members had had to deal with a large number of other traumatic incidents during that time (e.g., major motor vehicle accidents). We sat on the floor, I shared a beer with them at their request, and they told me of their experience. This, like other postdisaster outreach, symbolizes the sensitivities and complexities of using psychodynamic and psychotherapeutic principles to assess need and to provide an appropriate response. There is no ethical agreement for "treatment," yet there is a seeking of effective help for perceived risk and needs. People do not come for treatment; you contact them. They are not patients unless they agree to be. You assess for prevention and perhaps intervention; this is different from treating those who are ill. The translation of the understanding of group dynamics and the principles of psychodynamically informed interventions into outreach programs represents significant challenges, particularly in physical and social environments that are far removed from the psychiatrist's office.

The uncertain and acute nature of the postdisaster environment, the lack of a "patient" label for those to whom outreach is offered, and the mental health worker's or psychiatrist's identification with those affected that occurs in disasters can all compromise attempts at intervention. These factors may lead to feelings of helplessness and preoccupation with structured approaches to reassure oneself in the face of distress and chaos, to excessive empathic involvement, or to numbing, automatic, or withdrawal responses. Nevertheless, engagement with disaster-affected persons also helps one to recognize the powerful forces of resilience in almost every case. There are also new things to be learned. For instance, in a survey of almost 100 workers of every persuasion who had been involved, we found that, although distressed and at times uncertain and frustrated in their roles, a great many felt positive about their involvement. Their experiences had made them reevaluate their lives, recognize the importance of their families, and place more value on their relationships with their loved ones (Raphael et al., 1983).

Although I was subsequently involved with a number of disasters, my next major experience was as a consultant to the South Australian government, assisting them in the development of their mental health response following the Ash Wednesday bushfires in 1983 (Raphael, 1984a). These fires had destroyed homes and communities and caused more than 70 deaths. This provided an additional learning experience in the role of the psychiatrist providing outreach as a disaster consultant to a system in another state. This is a different form of outreach that involves engaging politicians, the media, community leaders, and others to ensure an understanding of and commitment to the mental health needs that arise for disaster-affected populations (Raphael, 1983a).

This form of outreach also involves recognizing the strengths of affected communities and building on their capacity both to determine their own recovery and to develop the skills and resources to assess and respond to mental health needs. To assist with this, I took a young academic (Sandy McFarlane) with me. He subsequently provided outreach and undertook research on the impact on those affected; indeed, he became an expert in the field (McFarlane and Raphael, 1984).

Outreach also requires an understanding of the social processes of reaction and response following disaster—for instance, the lowering of traditional boundaries, the affiliation behaviors, and the intensity of the experience of being involved in and responding to disaster. This is sometimes called the "honeymoon phase" and is often followed by a phase of "disillusionment." In the former there are feelings of shared closeness and heightened arousal in the early days of response and an urgent need to do everything possible to assist those affected. Disillusionment may follow, however. As time passed following the Ash Wednesday bushfires the barriers to effect action seemed to increase, as did frustration and irritability, and there were feelings among most teams that others, themselves, and the government were not helping as they should. Irritability, frustration, and confrontation with anger, grief, and the complexities of recovery seemed to weigh down everyone.

During the honeymoon period, there is a rush to make everything right again. Community leaders and politicians may make promises they cannot keep in their wish to undo what has happened, to make restitution and so forth. This type of outreach may involve educating and supporting leaders, often in subtle ways, to assist them in understanding and dealing with both their own and others' reactions in the emergency and early recovery phases. Social constructs are also helpful in understanding the emergency response that evolves—the "emergency organization" and, later, the "recovery organization."

In my experience, one can view the postdisaster response through two systems. First, there are the social response systems as described earlier as well as other social responses such as the search for shared meaning and for socially constructed interpretations of how and why the event occurred and what can be done to prevent its recurrence. The second system is the psychodynamic perspective, the psychological responses of the individuals affected and how these may indicate their adaptations to trauma, loss, and dislocation. Within the psychodynamic system, a tension exists among such themes. The normal reactive processes do not mean that those exposed will inevitably develop psychiatric morbidity; the majority will not. So, in providing psychiatric outreach and consultancy, an understanding of these complex and interacting explanatory systems is essential to interpret the responses of those directly affected, to be aware of one's own responses, and to provide guidance and advice regarding appropriate actions that will do no harm. This is with the aim of providing interventions that are humanitarian and compassionate and that respond in effective ways to identified risk and need.

Enhancing the understanding of mental health aspects pre- and post-disaster is critical to providing appropriate and effective psychiatric outreach. For instance, the people affected by the bushfires had frequently denied the possible threat, and those who had experienced more guilt in the fires' aftermath frequently projected their anger and envy onto others who had not been as badly affected. Denial of threat and warning may be associated with greater "shock" and risk of morbidity.

Developing a coherent research approach is central to this. A number of international collaborative workshops were held to further this aim and provided a draft methodology to guide future research in this field (Raphael, Lundin, and Weisaeth, 1989). These research workshops were held in Australia and Norway and in association with international academic conferences. All participants had had experience in disaster research including oil rig, transport, fire, and nuclear disasters.

Australia is subject to many natural disasters, especially bushfires, drought, storms and cyclones, and floods. Although earthquakes have occurred, the earthquake that struck the eastern coastal city of Newcastle in late 1989 was alien and shocking, taking people by complete surprise. The ensuing psychiatric consultancy focused on the strengths of the people in this coal and steel city, which had been through many tough times. My role involved consulting with the mayor of Newcastle and providing advice. It also required engaging mental health providers, providing advice on models of outreach, and stimulating the interests of researchers who subsequently produced a series of excellent studies on the impact of this disaster over time (Carr et al., 1995, 1997a, b; Kenardy and Carr, 2000). These studies attested to the morbidity that could develop but also showed that debriefing had not been effective in preventing psychopathology and may even have made it worse. Again the social and psychological processes could be evaluated and taken into account. Indeed, a review of newspaper headlines of the major city newspaper over the weeks following the disaster reflected the honeymoon and disillusionment phases and the gradual recovery processes.

Initially the headlines reported on all the great things that were happening and the positive responses of the community and showed politicians visiting the disaster sites. As the days progressed, headlines started to speak of anger, who was to blame, what was not happening, and multiple problems.

Disasters that are "man-made" carry additional impact in a psychological sense in that the questions of causation and blame are more prominent. Transport accidents may constitute a disaster when multiple deaths and horror of circumstance are prominent, but even the high number of motor vehicle accidents affecting smaller numbers of individuals have the impact of a personal disaster (Raphael, 1981). Providing outreach in all these circumstances is difficult because people are often together coincidentally and come from diverse regions or even countries. This is less an issue with commuter trains, as in the Granville incident, but more prominent in cases such as tourist buses, airplanes, and so forth. People disperse to their homes, often in distant settings, in what has been called a centrifugal type of disaster.

Ensuring follow-up and care in such settings is difficult. When communities and affected groups organize themselves into self-help, mutual support, or advocacy groups, however, an opportunity is afforded to assist with education, advice, and care through outreach participation and consultation regarding the psychiatric problems that may arise.

The spectrum of human involvement in the causation of disaster etiology ranges from simple mistakes, to negligence, to active human malevolence—for instance, mass shootings or similar violence. In the past decade or so, there have been a number of such episodes in Australia, the most notable being the 1996 shooting at Port Arthur in Tasmania. This small state had a significant mental health response to the incident and its follow-up. Although only peripherally involved, I was asked to visit and provide advice on the development of a memorial at the site of the shooting (a tourist venue because of its ruins and violent past as a convict prison in the early history of Australia). This outreach request, coming as it did more than a year later, highlighted the different needs of affected populations. Those who were psychologically traumatized wanted no, or few, reminders of the event; the bereaved, however, wished for a place to visit, a memorial to help them mourn their loved ones. A similar issue has emerged in relation to Ground Zero in the wake of the bombing of the World Trade Center.

This disaster also highlighted the particular stress involved in coping with the knowledge that another human being with intent, either general or specific, deliberately caused death and destruction. The struggle to come to terms with this darker side of human nature, this perpetrated violence and malevolence, is complex; it frequently leads to perceptions of the "evil" in the other and the "innocence" of the self. Victims can become preoccupied with why or how a person or persons can kill others—others they do not know—who were on holiday, as in the Bali bombing incident. They saw the perpetrators as "evil," because they could not see themselves as violent or perpetrating such killing actions, highlighting the dynamics of splitting in such circumstances. Even though there had been other such violence after the Port Arthur incident and before that in Bali, there was a popular and frequent theme for communities and individuals involved in these two events: "We have lost our innocence."

Before the 2000 Olympics in Sydney, the extensive preparation included development of operational plans and standard operating procedures to deal with any disaster or terrorist attack that might occur. Mental health is an established part of the response system under the health disaster plan, and the mental health controller is alerted to act when there is a potential threat or the health disaster plan is activated. There is a general health disaster controller, a public health controller, and a mental health controller, and each sector has standard operating procedures. This plan is then reflected down to regional levels when the organizational and response structure is replicated.

An evidence-based manual was developed (New South Wales Health Department, 2000), and mental health staff members were trained to respond. This organizational structure has continued and is activated centrally and regionally in response to diverse major and minor disasters: Sydney hailstorms, Sydney bushfires, the World Trade Organization meeting, New Year's Eve at Sydney Harbor, and so forth. It has been invaluable in establishing and strengthening mental health's role as a key component in effective response to disaster.

I have, in the past, been involved in outreach in many disasters to which the response has been less formal. There is no doubt in my mind about the value of such a standardized structure of operational approach. I am now the mental health controller for the state of New South Wales and for Sydney. The work done in preparation for the 2000 Olympics helped us contribute to the consensus conference process in the United States resulting in the Guidelines for Early Intervention following Mass Violence (Consensus Workshop on Mass Violence and Early Intervention, 2001). These guidelines are now also applied in Australia.

The threat of human malevolence can be pervasive and continuing, as with mass violence, or it can be unpredictable, as with terrorism. On October 12, 2002, Australians faced the experience of a terrorist bombing at a popular tourist resort in Bali, close to Australian shores. Many young Australians were killed, and many others injured and shocked. They had not known an experience like this before. Again our "innocence" was lost, but universally those returning on Qantas flights (an Australian icon), spoke of the sense of safety and security experienced with their "feet on Australian ground" again. The state-based mental health services provided systematic outreach ranging from meeting returning planes and providing support for returning families, to assisting the bereaved when the bodies of the deceased were returned home, to establishing guidelines for media communication and supportive themes for public dissemination and providing outreach bereavement and trauma counseling for those at high risk over the following weeks. Such efforts included setting up a counseling help line, providing outreach to organizations such as football clubs that had lost several members, offering public information about coping and sources of help, and advising mental health providers about the potential presentations of those with heightened anxiety or the incorporation of terrorist themes into their delusional systems. This work is ongoing and has posed different challenges, particularly with the pressures on mental health staff who are already heavily committed and the additional impact of dealing with the potential of an ongoing threat.

There are also anxieties about the heightened risk of a terrorist attack on Australian soil and the complex challenges of alerting and preparing the population while emphasizing the courage, strength, and resilience of the Australian people; minimizing racial abuse and threats of such abuse when some populations may be seen as sources of potential terror; and ensuring that the preparedness aims at alertness, appropriate action, and positive expectations and does not lead to excessive anxiety, demoralization, and helplessness. Outreach now involves these themes both acutely and over time, as well as the capacity to handle uncertainty.

I have been involved in outreach with many other "disasters" small and large in the Australia context; these include slow disasters such as the current drought and toxic waste sites and their profound and ongoing impact (Dunne et al., 1990) as well as more emergent events, such as a fire in an amusement park. I have been involved in many and have intervened with and treated those affected. In addition, I have seen disaster victims many years after the event, as in the case of a peacetime naval collision (the *Voyager* incident), and I have seen the hidden and profound morbidity that remains. I have been privileged to learn much during this work with those that disaster has affected—both individuals and communities. Some key themes have emerged for me over the years of outreach.

Key Themes of Psychiatric Outreach in Disasters

1. *Complex environmental, social, and personal dynamics exist following disasters.* They need to be recognized, understood, and taken into account in determining mental health response. These dynamics are relevant to training, preparation, emergency response, and recovery (Raphael, 1986).

2. *Chaos and helplessness are frequent and often overwhelming elements of disasters.* In providing outreach, the importance of practiced, knowledgeable, and informed response with clear role delineation cannot be overemphasized. Mental health issues are vital throughout the response, and a structured, informed response from mental health providers will be of value. This should not override the humanitarian, compassionate response of one human being to another, however. Nor should the sense of helplessness lead to mental health providers' requiring structured interventions such as critical incident stress debriefing (CISD), perhaps primarily for their own reassurance, but rather they should respond to the individual need that is evolving and different for each person (see Raphael and Wilson, 2000).

3. *Identifying and responding to the different stressor experiences are of value,* both with individual assessment as well as in estimating and projecting population services needs.

There has been an intense focus on traumatic stress, the shocking encounter with death and psychiatric sequelae such as posttraumatic stress disorder (PTSD; Wilson and Raphael, 1993). This is clearly important and needs to be addressed.

Reactions to the stressors of loss and the grief that follows the death of a loved one in circumstances of disaster are different and are frequent and profound in their effects. The unexpected and untimely nature of the deaths, the violence and the mutilation, the absence of a body or an opportunity to see the body, the public nature of the deaths, the religious and personal needs of the bereaved, and many other factors make these complicated bereavements with significant psychiatric morbidity (Raphael and Martinek, 1997).

The dislocation from home in many disasters, particularly with natural or other catastrophes that destroy home, neighborhood, and community, creates significant vulnerability. This may have an impact over time, especially if family members have been separated, there are repeated moves and no secure home in which to settle, and those affected face the welcome, or lack of welcome, of new communities.

Then there is human malevolence—the violence and cruelty, the intent of "evil" and the cycles of fear, perpetrated injustice, and further violence that may result if this stressor is not dealt with. Of course there are many other stressors and often multiple stressors (Raphael, 1986; Raphael and Wooding, 2002), but those core themes must always be assessed, and outreach and response must be targeted to needs so generated.

4. *Should stories of disaster be told?* A constant theme is how much should be told about disaster; which narratives are significant; whether narratives should be encouraged; and when the telling of the story becomes a ritualized repetition, a fixation to the experience and the role of victim, rather than the process of moving on. These questions are important for intervention because there has been a belief that such stories must be told and discussed, but there is little evidence that this will make things right (Raphael, 1986; Raphael and Wilson, 2000; Ursano et al., 2000; Raphael and Ursano, 2002). Giving testimony to survival, to suffering, and to the past may be elements of many psychotherapeutic programs and may aid recovery, as may the sharing of the experience with teammates or loved ones. What is clear is that there are many individual ways of coping that should be respected: timing, person, place, and differential patterns may all be significant. There is no "right" thing to do that will ensure all will be well. Talking can externalize, and allow sharing and catharsis, but it does not take away, undo, or remove the reality of the experience.

5. *Disasters occur over everyday life.* The stress of a disaster experience may be worsened by the way in which it adds to the stress of complex underlying events and family life, adversity, or other crises. It may dominate experience and become the attributional focus for all problems, but it may also heighten awareness of life, death, and the value of loved ones. It may also trigger a link to past experience with factors such as war, other disasters, loss, and grief. These issues need to be taken into account when working with disaster-affected persons and in outreach. It may also be difficult for those who have experienced a disaster not to be defined by it as either a victim or a survivor and to relinquish it and return to everyday life. A balance between the excitement and feeling of doing something worthwhile, as well as the arousal and "adrenaline" of fear, versus the comfort of security and predictability may be difficult to achieve.

6. *Structural roles and response systems must be in place.* As emphasized earlier, it is vital for mental health and psychiatric outreach to be a formal, knowledgeable, and accepted part of disaster-operating systems with clear, recognized, and agreed-on roles. Psychiatrists should be comfortable with a leading role in such situations as doctors who can contribute to the system of health response. Mental health outreach should involve all relevant expertise focused on effective and evidence-based strategies, as well as

humanitarian, compassionate, and practical assistance. Psychological first aid is a good concept for the initial response, focusing on the expectancy of recovery and a targeted response to those in need, including specialized resources for children, adults, and older people. This response system will require training and preparedness as well as sustainability. Disasters are unpredictable, and no system can be eternally ready. Linkages to other emergency response systems such as emergency departments and responders to motor vehicle accidents can fine-tune the response and familiarize other emergency personnel with the value of psychiatric outreach.

7. *Disasters can cause wear and tear on workers.* The emotional demands of dealing with horror, death, and loss both directly and vicariously, of repeated demands, and of high levels of need may all exhaust workers and lead to burnout, overinvolvement, or "compassion fatigue" (Raphael, Singh, and Bradbury, 1980; Raphael and Wilson, 1994). Those providing psychiatric outreach should not become victims themselves (Raphael, 1983b, 1984b). They need to establish systems of structured and limited tours of duty and ensure that there are opportunities for review and operational debriefing, for respite with and care from loved ones, for professional training, and for educational opportunities. Being a disaster "expert" in mental health has additional demands related to public expectations from others and oneself, as well as ongoing demands of anticipating yet another catastrophe.

8. *Research and evaluation are difficult and inadequate in this field.* Ethics of intervention and research with acutely stressed populations make methodologic requirements almost impossible to meet. Nevertheless, it is vital that knowledge is expanded to support the development of effective mental health intervention with opportunities for prevention, early intervention, and effective treatment (Raphael et al., 1989; Raphael and Wilson, 1993). Psychiatric outreach should, whenever possible, contribute to the growth of knowledge in the field.

9. *Hope is vital.* One of the most rewarding and striking things about working with disaster-affected persons and populations is the great courage, resourcefulness, altruism, humanity, and resilience that most people show—even in terrible adversity. It is no surprise that a research study on mental health outcomes following the earthquake in Newcastle (Australia) showed that personal hopefulness was the single factor that best predicted who would do well in the aftermath (Lewin, Carr, and Webster, 1998).

My own experience has been one of great respect for and hope in the human condition. The darker side of human nature does show its face, but the courage, hope, and compassionate response to those affected is for me the dominating paradigm.

References

Caplan, G. (1964), *Principles of Preventive Psychiatry*. New York: Basic Books.

Carr, V. J., Lewin, T. J., Kenardy, J. A. & Webster, R. A. (1997a), Psychosocial sequelae of the 1989 Newcastle earthquake: III. Role of vulnerability factors in post-disaster morbidity. *Psychol. Med.*, 27:179–190.

_____ _____ Webster, R. A. & Hazell, P. L. (1995), Psychosocial sequelae of the 1989 Newcastle earthquake: I. Community disaster experiences and psychological morbidity 6 months post-disaster. *Psychol. Med.*, 25:539–555.

_____ _____ _____ & Kenardy, J. A. (1997b), Psychosocial sequelae of the 1989 Newcastle earthquake: II. Exposure and morbidity profiles during the first 2 years post-disaster. *Psychol. Med.*, 27:167–178.

Consensus Workshop on Mass Violence and Early Intervention (2001), *Mental Health and Mass Violence: Evidence-Based Early Psychological Intervention for Victims/Survivors of Mass Violence*. Warrenton, VA. Available at: http://www.nimh.nih.gov/research/massviolence.pdf.

Dunne, M. P., Burnett, P., Lawton, J. & Raphael, B. (1990), The health effects of chemical waste in an urban community. *Med. J. Aust.*, 152:592–597.

Kenardy, J. A. & Carr, V. (2000), Debriefing post disaster: Follow-up after a major earthquake. In: *Psychological Debriefing: Theory, Practice and Evidence*, ed. B. Raphael & J. P. Wilson. Cambridge, England: Cambridge University Press, pp. 174–181.

Kinston, W. & Rosser, R. (1974), Disaster: Effects on mental and physical state. *J. Psychosom. Res.*, 18:437–456.

Lewin, T. J., Carr, V. J. & Webster, R. A. (1998), Recovery from post-earthquake psychological morbidity: Who suffers and who recovers? *Aust. N. Z. J. Psychiat.*, 32:15–20.

McFarlane, A. C. & Raphael, B. (1984), Ash Wednesday: The effects of a fire. *Aust. N. Z. J. Psychiat.*, 18:341–351.

New South Wales Health Department (2000), *Disaster Mental Health Response Handbook*. Sydney, Australia: New South Wales Health Department and Centre for Mental Health.

Raphael, B. (1976), National disasters [monograph]. *Roy. Aust. N. Z. Coll. Psychiatr. J.*

_____ (1977a), Preventive intervention with the recently bereaved. *Arch. Gen. Psychiat.*, 34:1450–1454.

_____ (1977b), The Granville train disaster: Psychological needs and their management. *Med. J. Aust.*, 1:303–305.

_____ (1979–1980), A primary prevention action program: Psychiatric involvement following a major rail disaster. *Omega*, 10:211–226.

_____ (1981), Personal disaster. *Aust. N. Z. J. Psychiat.*, 15:183–198.

_____ (1983a), Psychiatry consultancy in major disaster. *Aust. N. Z. J. Psychiat.*, 18:303–306.

_____ (1983b), Disaster: The victims and the helpers. *Spotlight*, 4(4):14–20.

_____ (1984a), Psychosocial aspects of disaster: Some Australian studies, and the Ash Wednesday bushfires [editorial]. *Med. J. Aust.*, 141:268–270.

_____ (1984b), Rescue workers: Stress and their management. *Emerg. Response*, 1(10):27-30.

_____ (1986), *When Disaster Strikes*. New York: Basic Books.

_____ Lundin, T. & Weisaeth, L. (1989), A research method for the study of psychological and psychiatric aspects of disaster. *Acta Psych. Scand. Suppl.*, 80(353):1–75.

_____ & Martinek, N. (1997), Assessing traumatic bereavement and posttraumatic stress disorder. In: *Assessing Psychological Trauma and PTSD*, ed. J. P. Wilson & T. M. Keane. New York: Guilford Press, pp. 373–395.

_____ Singh, B. & Bradbury, L. (1980), Disaster: The helper's perspective. *Med. J. Aust.*, 2:445–447.

_____ _____ _____ & Lambert, F. (1983), Who helps the helpers? The effects of a disaster on the rescue workers. *Omega*, 14(1):9–20.

_____ & Ursano, R. (2002), Psychological debriefing. In: *Sharing the Front Line and the Back Hills*, ed. E. Danieli. New York: Baywood, pp. 343–352.

_____ & Wilson, J. P. (1993), Theoretical and intervention considerations in working with victims of disaster. In: *International Handbook of Traumatic Stress Syndromes*, ed. J. P. Wilson & B. Raphael. New York: Plenum Press, pp. 105–117.

_____ & _____ (1994), When disaster strikes: Managing emotional reactions in rescue workers. In: *Beyond Empathy: Countertransference in the Treatment of PTSD*, ed. J. P. Wilson & J. D. Lindy. New York: Guilford Press, pp. 333–350.

_____ & _____, eds. (2000), *Psychological Debriefing: Theory, Practice and Evidence*. Cambridge, England: Cambridge University Press.

_____ & Wooding, S. (2002), Violence and prevention. In: *Proceedings of the Second World Conference on the Promotion of Mental Health and Prevention of Mental and Behavioural Disorders*.

Singh, B. & Raphael, B. (1981), Post disaster morbidity of the bereaved: A possible role for preventive psychiatry. *J. Nerv. Ment. Dis.*, 169:203–212.

Ursano, R. J., Fullerton, C. S., Vance, K. & Wang, L. (2000), In: *Psychological Debriefing: Theory, Practice and Evidence*, ed. B. Raphael & J. P. Wilson. Cambridge, England: Cambridge University Press, pp. 32–42.

Wilson, J. P. & Raphael, B., eds. (1993), *International Handbook of Traumatic Stress Syndromes*. New York: Plenum Press.

9

Disaster Psychiatry Throughout the Americas

Raquel E. Cohen

For many people, a disaster is an event witnessed on the news. For others, the event can have an immediate and unforeseen catastrophic impact on their lives. Disasters are most often natural, like earthquakes, hurricanes, and tornadoes. Yet in our post–September 11 world, we have come to experience the devastation of man-made disasters that can be more destructive or frightening than anything nature has wrought. For millions of people, disasters are personal tragedies that create an unpredicted, immediate, and overwhelming loss. It may be the loss of a loved one, a home or personal possessions that make up a lifetime fabric of living. Today, as we face a time when we may often ask ourselves how we will be able to manage if or when we are the survivors of a disaster, it may be helpful to understand the reactions of survivors. Because through that knowledge, we can learn what to expect in the process, understand how our own emotional systems develop coping strategies, and recognize the importance of support systems that will strengthen our own mental health in crisis situations.

How do you cope when you are the survivor of a disaster? What happens emotionally when you are the survivor of a disaster? And how do you endure the overwhelming experience of loss and grief? These are the questions that I have sought answers to for more than 30 years as a psychiatrist in the field of mental health needs of disaster victims. When I began to work in this area, there was no "field" of disaster mental health. I had to develop a system based on my personal experiences in the field and my professional training in mental and public health. And, while over three decades we have been able to create a mental health system to respond to the needs of disaster survivors, each disaster is really a response to the hundreds and thousands of personal tragedies of each individual who is suffering tremendous change and loss.

I have often been asked how I became interested in the mental health of disaster survivors. As a native of Lima, Peru, I am sure my early experiences feeling the world tremble as an earthquake shook the foundations of our home gave me a predisposition to understand the fear of natural disasters. I left Peru to study medicine in Boston, first receiving my master's degree in public health from Harvard and then becoming part of the first class of women to graduate from Harvard Medical School. As a psychiatrist, my interest always focused on community mental health and public health issues. This public health orientation comes from a deep personal feeling that prevention is the best way to help people in need. I believe that these were the influences that motivated me to combine the mental health and emotional issues of individuals in crisis with the public health concerns of large populations of people in distress.

One of the first events that clearly provoked my interest in the mental health needs of survivors occurred in 1970 when I was visiting my family in Lima. A massive earthquake had recently killed more than 70,000 citizens in the Callejon de Huaylas, high up in the Andes Mountains. This catastrophic event left hundreds of young orphans stranded in the remote region. The minister of health, who was in charge of the rescue operations, asked me an important question: "What would be the best rescue plans for the children? Should we leave them in their hometown with their surviving relatives, who themselves were in dire need, or should we transport them to Lima and offer our urban resources?" The massive needs of the people and numbers of orphaned children left me speechless. I found little knowledge acquired during my training as a psychiatrist on which to base an intelligent answer. Intuitively, I suggested keeping the children in their town instead of removing them from their natural environment and adding to their losses.

I returned to my job in Boston, Massachusetts, challenged by this new awareness of mental health issues in disasters. I continued to ponder the questions raised in Peru and discuss them with colleagues such as Gerald Caplan, a pioneer in crisis intervention, and Eric Lindemann, a pioneer in community psychiatry. I had also contacted Bert Brown, then director of the National Institute of Mental Health (NIMH), to find out if we could send resources to assist the authorities in Peru. My petition was not successful. Although professionals in Washington, DC, were sympathetic, their lack of resources to respond to the situation was an obstacle to my efforts. Sadly, another disaster eventually created a new opportunity to respond to a catastrophe.

Two days before Christmas in 1972, a devastating earthquake struck the city of Managua, Nicaragua. More than 10,000 people were killed; the capital of Nicaragua was virtually destroyed. The United States and Nicaragua formalized an agreement to fund the efforts of bicultural and bilingual mental health volunteers. Professionals working in Washington who were linked with Nicaragua and NIMH representatives promoted the agreement. The agreement was reached through active negotiations between a Nicaraguan psychiatrist who traveled to Managua and established personal linkages with the Somoza government after the terror of the disaster. I was asked to be part of the volunteer team. After a brief training in Washington, we boarded a plane, organized into groups and planned our approach while flying to Central America. As the plane descended into Managua, I asked myself what I would find in the city and how I would be able to help. It is a question that still goes through my mind each time I face a new disaster situation.

At the airport, a representative of the minister of health received us. He briefed us on priorities for service and the arrangements for shelter and transportation. As we began to move through the city, the extent of the damage and overwhelming destruction was apparent at every turn. I remember the chilling sensation of seeing clocks on the buildings that were still standing all stopped at the same moment in time when the earthquake had struck. We set up in a kind of tent city established by the international rescue operations. As I began to develop a mental health outreach program, I was about to learn an important and lasting lesson about the emotional needs of rescue workers and caregivers in disasters.

I had been invited to make a presentation to a group of physicians. These professionals had been forced to leave their destroyed offices and hospitals and relocate to a nearby town. I prepared a science-based conference, thinking that these professionals would be best served by a technical presentation. Halfway through my presentation, as I was looking down on my notes, I heard a sob. I lifted my eyes and saw someone in the audience leave. As I looked around the audience, I could see the faces looking back at me were gloomy and sad. I then realized that they were experiencing the same pain and devastation that I had expected of their patients. I had defined them as health care professionals and expected that they would handle their emotions differently from the survivors that they were charged with treating. I then realized that they, and subsequently every caregiver affected by a disaster, were experiencing the same loss and emotional grief as any victim. I changed the tone of my presentation and suggested that if anyone wanted to see me individually I would be pleased to do so after the presentation. Many of them accepted my offer. This episode sensitized me to the effect of disasters on all persons and has continued to reinforce the individuality of needs of everyone who comes in contact with the tragedy of these events. I strongly support the research, development, and organization of mental health support programs to all the rescue and emergency personnel involved in disaster work.

New Federal Legislation Affects Disaster Relief Programs

Based on my experiences in Managua and work with other professionals in this emerging field, I was invited to a series of national meetings and planning activities designed to address U.S. programs for disaster relief. In 1974 the Disaster Relief Act (Public Law, Section 413) laid the foundation for systematic organized development of mental health activities that included the Crisis Counseling Assistance and Training Program. This program, which is jointly operated by the Federal Emergency Management Agency (FEMA) and the federal Center for Mental Health Services, funds short-term public education, outreach, crisis counseling services, and referral to other agencies for long-term treatment. The awareness of the psychological consequences of disasters emerged because of increased leadership in Washington, including the notoriety and publicity of a disaster that occurred in Buffalo Creek, West Virginia, in 1972 where the sludge accumulated from a coal mine caused a dam to collapse following a torrential rainstorm. Mass quantities of mud, rocks, and debris destroyed a number of small towns, killing adults and children. Class action litigation between the victims and the coal mine corporation resulted in the victims being compensated for the "psychic trauma" described by the lawyers.

This federal mandate for mental health assistance gave a strong impetus to train professionals to be prepared to assist in disaster situations. I was invited to be a member of the visiting faculty of the Staff College, a training arm of the NIMH. As I began to develop curriculum and train a number of professionals around the country, I adapted the research and literature on trauma, crisis, loss, bereavement, support systems, coping, and adaptation to the field of disaster mental health care. This collection of rather simple materials and articles has today grown to a worldwide rich, vast, and ever-growing body of disaster publications. To expand my own knowledge of the Emergency Response System, I invited representatives of every disaster-related system I could identify. Representatives from the Red Cross, FEMA, and civil defense agencies, as well as clergy and police, were asked to become the teachers in the presentations to the mental health professionals. Not only did I increase my knowledge from these experiences, but they also initiated a reciprocity by which many of these agencies began to invite mental health professionals to teach to their staff, something that had never happened before.

I still remember the puzzled looks of firefighters and police who were attending different training sessions in Emmitsburg, Virginia, the FEMA training facility. Their puzzlement also taught me an important lesson. One day, while I was eating in the staff cafeteria after presenting my work to a group of mental health professionals, one of the policemen asked why I was there. They wondered what a "shrink" could offer the emergency rescue efforts in disasters. It is a question that mental health workers have had to answer slowly, over time and through example. When people are addressing the immediate and painful needs of medical trauma, shelter, food and disease control, mental health may seem like a "soft" need. For many years, the public and survivors didn't and still don't see themselves as "mental health patients" in need of mental health assistance. That lesson was exemplified during the Great Storm of 1978 in Boston.

It started to snow one day that January, and then it seemed like it would never stop. When the storm ended, the city was buried in snow, communities were without power, and people were stranded. At that time, I was the superintendent of the Lindemann Mental Health Center, a comprehensive mental health, retardation, and drug abuse program. My responsibilities extended over part of Boston and several of the towns that bordered the Atlantic Ocean and were particularly devastated by the storm. This geographic area was part of the center's "catchment area," so I was able to mobilize a large number of resources to develop a mental health program focused on the event. Government leaders in Boston, who were interested and sensitive to the mental health needs of the survivors, assisted us in obtaining federal funding to organize several response teams. This opportunity to design, implement, and evaluate an intervention response taught me further how mental health programs need to be carefully integrated into the complex public and private agencies that assist victims.

I had advocated having a space in the FEMA center, where all the services were assembled in a large school gymnasium, called a One Stop Center. I assembled and organized a mental health team and we set ourselves up in the gym. Our table had a sign that said, "Mental Health." Because of the sensitivity of the content that the victims might want to reveal, I asked that the area should be curtained. We took our seats and waited. And waited. After several hours without any people stopping at our table, I decided to walk through the area where hundreds of individuals were forming long lines for Red Cross, housing, and loan assistance. As I walked through the large gym, watching anguished individuals negotiate their future, I realized that traumatized individuals do not see themselves as "patients" in need of mental health. They were traumatized individuals dealing with the immediate needs of survival. I recognized that survivors do not seek mental health assistance while they are struggling with survival needs.

In subsequent disasters, this awareness helped me learn to observe signs, expressions, thoughts, and behavior of survivors as normal expressions to cope with abnormal situations. I learned that their behavior in most of the cases were efforts to deal with the effects of the trauma events and were not expressions of psychopathology. This emerging awareness allowed me to conceptualize new ways of assisting them by focusing my interventions in supporting coping behavior and return of function. I also realized how the premise of community psychiatry, which recognizes the importance of coordination and collaboration with grassroots agencies, clergy, schools, and human service agencies, assisted in developing a well-designed emergency response program. During the activities in the Boston disaster I became aware of the well-organized programs of the Red Cross to assist survivors. I developed good relations with many of their leaders, who asked me to add my knowledge to their training content. This collaboration grew through the years and resulted in their inclusion of mental health into Red Cross disaster manuals.

Cross-Cultural Issues in Disaster Relief

As a Peruvian and a psychiatrist with a specialization in cross-cultural communication, my knowledge and experience of cross-cultural universal human response to the tragic impact of disasters has expanded through my work in Latin America.

In 1980, South Florida became part of history as it responded to the Mariel Boat lift. This exodus of people from Cuba brought thousands to the shores of Florida. At the invitation of the University of Miami Medical School, which had received a grant from the federal government, I was asked to participate in the program to assist more than 1,000 Cuban children who arrived on the boatlift without parents or adults. This program consisted of housing them in three federal national camps, where they would be diagnosed, referred, and placed in appropriate sites throughout the country.

Again, all the accumulated knowledge of disaster guidelines was useful in designing this yearlong program. Because of the nature of the youths' ethnic and cultural background, their differing psychosocial development, and, in many instances, traumatized childhoods, the concept of populations at multiple risks presented a challenge to our techniques. Our first priority was to house them and establish a sense of safety and fairness in dealing with all their needs. During the next year we studied each child individually and recommended their future planning, which consisted of a variety of placements: foster care, group housing, special schools, hospitals, or finding relatives with whom they could stay.

My subsequent decision to accept a tenured professorship from the University of Miami Medical School as the head of child psychiatry training paved the way for me to work more closely with Latin American countries.

One night in 1985, as thousands slept in their beds, a major volcano erupted in Colombia. A riverbed guided an avalanche of mud and stones toward Armero, covering the city with millions of cubic feet of boiling mud and stones, killing more than 20,000 citizens. The number of deaths was painfully high because there was very little warning of the impending disaster. Rescue operations were impeded by torrential rain and the difficulty of driving emergency vehicles on the deep mud surface. Terrorized survivors held onto treetops or tried to stay above the mud that reached up to their chins. Eventually a small fleet of helicopters rescued some survivors, one by one, flying and dispersing them to hospitals all over the country. Many had to have their legs amputated because of the infection developed during hours of waiting to be rescued. When I became aware that a catastrophic disaster had occurred in Colombia, I asked the dean of the medical school to contact the minister of health and offer our help. A few hours later we received a telegram inviting me to fly over and assist the emergency mental health program. I packed my bags for departure, and, as always, as we approached the disaster site, I asked myself what I would find there and how I would be able to help.

The Colombian Emergency Committee assigned me the responsibility of training all their deployed emergency and hospital personnel on mental health issues to assist the survivors, both wounded and well. For this to happen they organized a systematic schedule and attended to the logistics, transportation, lodging and attendance of the personnel that had to be trained at the site. This experience was one of the most tragic—and educational—of my career. This was the first time I worked in hospital trauma wards dealing with physically (amputations) and psychologically intense distress in large numbers of patients. Long hours of training and debriefing were spent with the nursing staff, who were also tired, grieving, and overwhelmed by the tragedy. Difficult situations also appeared out in the rural areas because of the constant reminder of the possibility that the events would be repeated; we received daily reports of the volcano's continued eruptions. The emotions of fear and anxiety were pervasive. I clearly remember its impact on my emotional state of mind during one incident. After a long day of consulting and training, I looked forward to bedding down at the inn where we were living. Tension among the participants was heightened that day because of several alerts warning that the volcano was erupting again. People were advised to seek shelter up in the hills. While resting on my bed, I wondered how real these alarms were and had a fantasy vision of the next day's headlines: "Disaster Expert Succumbs Under Volcanic Lava." As I tried to laugh about my fears, the electricity was cut off—no light, no radio, no alerts. I panicked, grabbed my flashlight and gathered two of my colleagues. We hiked, guided by our flashlights in the dark, and slept in a tent high in the hills. I became intimately aware how denial is a helpful defense when working in painful situations, but at the same time, intelligent self-care is a necessary response as well.

In Armero, I also learned another important lesson about the importance of bereavement processes when the body of the deceased cannot be mourned or buried. Because such a large number of dead remaining under the tons of mud were never recovered, the families had a very difficult bereavement. It ranged from the obsessive belief that the loved one was somewhere in a hospital to the slow, but painful realization that maybe they had not survived. I have seen similar types of reactions from families whose loved ones have died in airplane crashes where the bodies could not be recovered. The inability to have the emotional closure of a burial process and ritual can cause additional emotional consequences. Families from different cultures mourn their loved ones observing traditional ceremonies, but their need of visually seeing the bodies are similar. When this is missing, the expression of pain needs support and assistance so as not to rely on pathological defenses. Techniques to confront slowly and then bear the reality of the loss are helpful in these instances. The assistance of spiritual or religious guidelines and support are used throughout this process.

The next disaster experience in which I participated struck close to home. In 1992, the Category 4 Hurricane Andrew made landfall in South Florida, destroying hundreds of homes and becoming one of the most costly disasters in U.S. history. I had been active with the Red Cross program in Miami and accepted an invitation to be part of the team at its emergency center. After I left the center the day after the storm, I was still uncertain how I made it back to my apartment. The world had been turned upside down, with boats strewn across the roadway like litter; familiar roads, street signs, and landmarks had disappeared. Like many of my experiences in preceding disasters, there were new lessons to learn. Two of them remain in my memory. The first was the change in the subtle but powerful social environment that enveloped our daily lives. Whether at work or in recreational or social situations, all our concerns were linked to the effect on our lives of the destruction around us. The number of dead and wounded was small relative to other hurricanes, but the physical destruction of homes, roads, and neighborhood infrastructure was massive. The disappearance of familiar surroundings plus the loss of physical landmarks had a powerful effect on our emotions.

The second experience was the effect of the disaster on organizations and institutions that have bureaucratic structures and well-defined guidelines for daily working activities. These include schools, businesses, and government agencies. One such experience presented itself when my employer, state attorney general Janet Reno, asked if I could help her 600 employees by informing them of the emotional consequences of postdisaster responses. I was the director of the Children's Center, a unit of the State Attorney Office in Miami, the function of which was to interview children who allegedly had been abused. The state attorney asked all her staff to attend these sessions. After introducing the basic knowledge about normal emotional response to abnormal situations, I opened the session to discussion of how to solve some of the problems of personnel who had been traumatized and yet were still expected to produce documents or meet deadlines for cases in the judicial and criminal system. There were many examples that highlighted what happened when the working product relied on a human team who, for the moment, had lost its efficiency. Discussion on how much tolerance, anticipation, support, and time allowance to finish briefs or to research and investigate crimes, were some of the issues raised by lawyers and clerical staff.

In 1998, Hurricane Mitch devastated the Central America countries of Nicaragua, Honduras, El Salvador, and Guatemala. Human losses were counted at 6,500. Almost 12,000 people disappeared, and more than

1 million lost their homes and were placed in shelters. Worldwide assistance responded generously, and several international teams for psychological help traveled to the affected areas. I was invited by the Pan American Health Organization to participate in training and consultation with the members of the Coordinating Government Committee established to deal with the mental health of the survivors. During one of my consulting appointments, I was taken by helicopter to a faraway region because the roads were nonexistent. The experience of that bird's-eye view of hundreds of houses filled with hard, drying mud that reached the second or third floor was painful. A vivid memory that remains is of a worker's reaction as we walked through a cemetery, and she realized that the coffin of her grandparent had broken open and filled with mud. In that program, we worked with the director of mental health and the top representation of all the government ministries. Their dedication and interest in developing a good response enabled me to deliver and participate in an effective way. They organized each of the activities that consisted of daily training sessions, consultation to emergency teams, and information to government leaders. In addition they attended to logistic issues and gathered the members of the groups, which consisted of doctors, nurses, teachers, counselors, and students of all the disciplines. Their efforts reinforced my central belief that an effective disaster mental health program has to have the strong support and involvement of the top leadership in the devastated country.

Future Challenges

Over the past 30 years, I have been a participant and a witness to the evolution of the field of mental health in disasters. From the time when I landed in Peru and advised the minister of health about the earthquake, I have learned important lessons with each experience and from the exceptional collaboration of disaster workers. I have seen the body of research and published literature expand so that today there is a well-developed understanding of the mental health needs of disaster survivors. Today we face new challenges. These are not natural disasters but man-made tragedies. In the post–September 11 world and with the growing threat of international terrorism, the impending mental health needs that may be created through the devastating effects of nuclear attacks, poisonous gas, and germ or biochemical warfare have strengthened the awareness of the professionals in our field. The need to prepare and organize large numbers of trained mental health personnel was painfully clear in the response to the Oklahoma City bombing and the terrorist attacks in New York and Washington, DC. As professionals grapple with the best intervention strategies and the need for scientifically based research, it is evident that finding answers will be a challenge. Another large question in need of an answer is which methods and techniques developed over the last 30 years are most useful to assist survivors of terrorism. Individual resilience and support systems that reinforce coping and adaptation may be an important area for future research that will offer hope and guidance to the next generation of mental health workers. Public health models may be most useful to assist and help large populations of survivors. As I participate in adapting our knowledge to the new, evolving training efforts that will prepare us to help victims of terrorism, my thoughts often come back to the questions I have asked myself every time I land at a disaster site: "What will I find? How can I help?" I believe that we will continue to seek answers to these questions as we aim to assist those who are affected by disasters and who lose so much of what is most important in our lives—home, health, loved ones, and community.

10

All They Can Do Is Kill Me
Psychiatry in the Gaza Strip
John W. Raasoch

I never intended to end up in the Middle East. I traveled to the Congress on Social Psychiatry in Washington, DC, to establish contacts with Russian psychiatrists for my upcoming sabbatical in the Soviet Union. Having spent a three-month sabbatical in northern Italy in 1984, I had the "bug" for another overseas professional experience seven years later. There was a small workshop on trauma for Palestinian women and children. Should I go to the presentation? Was it safe? My association was to the Palestine Liberation Organization leader, Yasser Arafat, the only Palestinian I'd ever heard of. What would my Jewish friends think? I felt sorry for Dr. Eyad Sarraj, the presenter, as the professional audience verbally attacked him during the discussion. It was suggested that the Palestinian parents had a death wish for their children who they purposely sent into the streets!

I invited Dr. Sarraj to lunch, and he accepted only on the promise he could reciprocate with lunch in the Gaza Strip. By the end of lunch, I was convinced Gaza was to be my next sabbatical, as he was the only practicing psychiatrist for a million Palestinians; I was needed there much more than the Soviet Union and warmly welcomed. I have never regretted this life-changing decision.

My sabbatical was funded through Monadnock Family Services (a rural community mental health center) in Keene, New Hampshire, a long way from the Middle East. I had no previous ties to that part of the world—I grew up in Wisconsin, and my heritage is Scandinavian. Once Eyad sold me,

I struggled to learn very rudimentary Arabic from a colleague in New Hampshire.

Along with Arabic, I learned the geography of the Middle East. In 1992 Gaza was part of the Palestinian territories under Israeli occupation since the Six Day War of 1967. Gaza is a narrow strip of land, 25 miles long and up to five miles wide, bordering the Mediterranean on one side, Israel on the other, and connected at its tip to Egypt.

Major differences exist between acute and ongoing chronic traumas. A local school in New Hampshire experienced a hostage situation in which students were held at gunpoint, which was terrifying for the grade-school students. The community mental health center's intervention was to support and reassure the students that no matter how terrifying school was yesterday, today school is safe.

In Gaza, Israeli soldiers would drive by the school at closing time; students would be shot every day and frequently killed. Here, there was no reassurance that school could be safe on any day. Ongoing trauma needs a supportive home and, preferably, two comforting parents.

Coping with professional or vicarious posttraumatic stress disorder (PTSD) leaves a "wounded healer." Listening to intense stories can lead to suffering, despair, hopelessness, and nightmares. Reactions can vary from denial to overidentification.

Having a sense of social responsibility can help contain the horrors of trauma. Involvement in professional associations and political action are often coping mechanisms.

While some may question how this is related to disaster psychiatry, a visit to both Israel and Palestine would expose one to the chronic PTSD shared by the peoples of both. Israeli and Palestinian children are growing up in a war zone, exhibiting symptoms of flashbacks, intrusive thoughts and images, and hyperarousal. While I heard more detailed accounts of Palestinian trauma resulting from the occupation, merely asking Israelis for directions in Jerusalem was met with intense paranoia.

The Nightmare

1/12/92

I began a journey that would change my life. When I stepped off the plane at Ben Gurion Airport, I naively expected to catch a bus from Tel Aviv to the

Gaza Strip. Getting transportation to the occupied territories was akin to crossing over a front line in a war zone.

My first encounter of the hostilities and animosities between Jewish-Israelis and Palestinians occurred with airport security. I suffered a three-hour interrogation at the airport because I listed Marna House, Gaza, as my destination in Israel. While other passengers on my flight were given blue passes, mine was pink. This earned me special attention from an Israeli security agent. She immediately scurried me off to an interrogation room. I asked, "Why am I being singled out?"

The security agent assured me that it was purely routine. She then asked me repeatedly why I was going to Gaza, who I knew in Gaza, and how long I was going to stay. Did I have any contacts in Israel? Did I know any Israeli psychiatrists? Why didn't I know any Israeli psychiatrists? Why on earth would I want to go to Gaza? These questions, with slight twists and variations, were repeated over and over for the next several hours. This process was duplicated by a second security person. I wondered how, as a mere visitor, I could pose such an enormous threat to the state of Israel.

Finally, they let me go.

Through my exhaustion, I wondered how I would ever get to Gaza. When I asked people at the airport how to get to Gaza, I understood how complex a journey this would be. Resigned that it would take several hours to find connections to Ashkelon, which was only close to Gaza, discouragement set in. Finally, leaving this unfriendly and unhelpful airport, I exited near a large metal fence, under the watch of armed Israeli soldiers. I was surprised to see a Palestinian cab driver holding a placard with "Dr. Raasoch" on it. He seemed friendly enough but was somewhat unkempt and spoke virtually no English.

He gestured to his cab and said, "Dr. Sarraj." Sarraj was the director of the mental health program where I would be working and my only connection to this part of the world. I hoped that it was the same man. My journey might now be less complex, but hundreds of questions raced through my mind. I was helpless to communicate them to my Arabic-speaking driver.

I had been to Israel as a tourist in 1986. Although that week's visit had been intriguing, I knew that this experience would be a much greater adventure. My readings about Israel–Palestine and the intifada had prepared me for a conflict. My naivete had not even begun to appreciate the magnitude and intensity of the hatred that had torn apart these two cultures.

After an hour of silence and inner panic, we approached the armed border crossing at Erez. I realized that there was no turning back. The border,

the soldiers, and the machine guns all demonstrated the dramatic demar-
cation between a First World country and a Third World occupied territory. I felt propelled back at least 200 years in time by traveling only 50 meters. Litter was everywhere, and the primary means of transportation
became donkey-drawn carts.

A few kilometers down the road was the city of Gaza. The poverty was
overwhelming. Extensive litter covered every street corner. The rubble of
demolished houses looked as though the city had suffered a nuclear blast.
The driver first stopped in a neighborhood filled with deeply rutted and
potholed streets. Children played and rolled in its dust. Thinking that this
was my new home, Marna House, I wondered if I could survive the first
three months. I was relieved when the cab moved on.

Intense terror caught me off guard. I am still uncertain what triggered the
flooding of emotions that day. Was it the different culture, the poverty, the
language barrier? Was it the sense of isolation or my growing anxiety as I
pondered my decision to come to this place? I had usually felt confident and
relatively comfortable even in poor sections of American cities. To Gaza, I
had brought a stereotyped image of every Palestinian being a terrorist and
the sense that my life was at stake.

I arrived at Marna House, owned by Ayla Shawa, who rented a few rooms
to foreigners. It became clear that staying here meant abiding by her rules.
She really did not like Americans, except for a few special individuals over
the years.

After settling into a small room with few amenities, I confronted my fear
head on. I forced myself to go for a walk in the neighborhood. Everybody
seemed to be staring at me, and I must have seemed a strange sight. One
building or street seemed the same as the next one. In place of familiar neon
signs, there were only hand-painted Arabic signs that looked like fancy
swirls. I immediately got lost and disoriented. It seemed certain that every
stare, even from a child, came from a terrorist who was about to kill me. I
was sweating and began trembling.

I realized that I had to be home by the 8:00 p.m. curfew. If I was perceived
to be a Palestinian by the Israeli soldiers, I could be shot on sight. At best, I
could be perceived as a foreigner by the Israelis and would be most likely
stopped and harassed. As it was beginning to get dark, I could be mistaken
for a Jewish settler by the Palestinians and executed. Finally, an elderly Palestinian helped me find an English-speaking Palestinian who eventually
gave me directions back to Marna House.

Relief at being alive and back at Marna House did not last long. A distant, but motherly Alya sat me down in front of her TV, and put on a BBC

special about the intifada. It was about the Palestinians shaking off the Israeli occupation. *Do They Feel My Shadow* was a gruesome and powerful depiction of the intifada. The BBC crew had stayed at Marna House and made a good connection with Alya. This video was very moving and terrifying.

My first night in Gaza left me sobbing to myself. I was isolated in a distant and foreign land, wondering what was ahead. Feeling exhausted and emotionally drained, I climbed the rickety stairs to my tiny, second-floor room. It had essentially no heat and an antiquated electrical system that produced less light than a gas lantern. I wrote briefly in my journal and quickly dozed off. The many ideas and solutions that floated through my mind woke me up. I had many articles to read. I began writing lists of questions for Sarraj.

I had questions for Alya on how I could be direct with her without offending her. She was a major puzzlement, and I felt like an intruder in her home. I was aware that I had irritated and offended her many times on this first day. I finally drifted off to sleep, only to suddenly awaken to a huge riot.

I heard police, soldiers, voices, and a lot of noise. Faced with the dilemma of wanting to go and see what was going on, I feared for my safety and my life. I struggled over whether I should stay in the relatively safe confines of Marna House or not. After a few minutes of this dilemma, I realized that what I was really hearing was the crowing of a rooster at three in the morning. Obviously, the riot was only in my head and unconscious, a residue of the BBC commentary.

1/13/92

In the morning, Rula gave me a ride to the Gaza Community Mental Health Program, the GCMHP. I immediately rolled up my sleeves and immersed myself into my professional identity as a psychiatrist. My first patient was a 32-year-old Palestinian who had been married for 15 years and had seven children. I saw this man and his wife, with Ahmed, a Palestinian psychologist. The man had been unemployed for the last five years, had been abusing heroin for seven months, and, as of January 13, had been 17 days without heroin. In light of the previous day's experience, I was desperate to make a meaningful intervention with my first patient.

I precipitated the first crisis for the staff when I offered to hire this man as my Arabic tutor. Doctors Aziz, Ahmed, and Sarraj approved, but Rula, the clinic's training officer, vetoed the idea. Rula was responsible for foreign visitors to the program and shared a sense of protectiveness with Alya for my safety. Rula felt that it was too dangerous to have this patient as my Arabic tutor. The fundamentalist group, Hamas, would threaten his life because of his heroin addiction.

Hamas's usual routine with drug users would be first to threaten the addict. The second time they would break his arms or legs. Then, if the addict had not stopped, they would execute the person. Indeed, one of the addicts I interviewed was subsequently executed. I do not know the ultimate fate of this first patient.

The first day of the program, I not only heard patients' stories, but learned of the plight of the GCMHP staff. Eight weeks before I had arrived, two staff members had been arrested, as well as one of the physicians from the local hospital. I learned how easy it was to be arrested for "administrative detention." A Palestinian simply disappeared for 18 days. No one could obtain information on his whereabouts. Parents searched for lost children and wives for husbands.

After 18 days, the Israeli authorities would notify the Red Crescent (Red Cross), which then informed the family that the person was imprisoned. During detention the Palestinians were routinely tortured, the details of which became clearer to me over my stay. While imprisoned, only one family member was allowed to visit every one or two weeks. This administrative detention usually lasted six months to a year. Because of the military occupation, there was no need to give cause for arrest. The Palestinians did not have a right to legal representation.

Recurring Nightmare

1/14/92

Eyad described his refugee status. He went back with his father to the home his family had been forced to evacuate when he was four years old. Together they knocked on the door of their former home. Both cried when they talked to the new inhabitants, Jewish immigrants from Poland. The Jews were also victims who had been given the house by the State of Israel. Eyad and his father were not invited in. They were left crying on the doorstep. It was hard to find anyone within the boundaries of Israel who had not experienced severe victimization.

Eyad also had been arrested twice. The first time was 10 years earlier, for not paying taxes to the Israeli government to support the military occupation. The second arrest was within the last year, for reasons still unknown. Because of his international political contacts, he was able to avoid prison.

In my first days, I sat in on several therapy sessions. I saw children with night terrors and children with head injuries caused by beatings and gunshot wounds from Israeli soldiers. I saw women trying to keep their families together while their husbands were in prison. One case that especially affected me was a 32-year-old woman seen with her six-year-old son. She had four children and her husband had been in prison for two years. She had no money and really no clothes for her children. The family lived in two rooms with broken windows, and cold air swirled into the rooms. She cried throughout the interview and I cried with her.

That evening I set out to explore more of my surroundings. When I made eye contact with a video storeowner, he gestured for me to come over and offered me a chair. His English was clear and quickly a crowd of 30 Palestinians gathered as word spread that an American doctor was there. They were mostly kids and adolescents. Onion, Caleb, and Weasel made the greatest impact on me. First, they brought me a Coke and a falafel sandwich from the stand across the street. As I sat in the crowd, groups of three or four army trucks and jeeps raced by every five to 10 minutes.

"How can you live like this? Don't the soldiers and the trucks get to you?" I asked. I experienced my first urges to throw stones at these 40-mile-per-hour, gray army trucks with wire mesh over the windows. This increasing presence and show of force became a personal affront and seemed to invite or even to provoke a response. I realized that it would be very easy for me to get caught up in this dynamic. This street corner felt like a tinderbox, just waiting to be ignited. I did not want to support or initiate a riot that could have resulted in the death of one of my newfound friends.

I was invited to the rooftop of Onion's house to observe Gaza. He led me through a long, dark, treacherous path. We first went through a dark alley and then up four flights of pitch-dark stairs. I could see nothing. My heart began to pound as if it would come out of my chest, and I wondered whether I had been too trusting of these strangers. A door finally opened onto the roof to a beautiful view of the sunset over Gaza. My instincts had been correct.

1/15/92

I returned to the program in the morning where I met Fadel, who was in charge of research. Fadel was a real Palestinian success story, having completed a Ph.D. in psychology. He had five brothers. Two had been in prison, and one had been shot in the neck by Israeli soldiers. Fadel had himself experienced three night raids by the Israeli Defense Force, the IDF. A night raid consisted of the soldiers barging into your home between midnight and 3:00 a.m. to search your home and to humiliate you in front of your family. Often, Palestinians were taken outside and ordered to whitewash the walls across the street that had been spray-painted with political messages in Arabic. A fourth night raid was to take place a month later during my stay in Gaza.

According to Fadel, in December 1988, his family was awakened at midnight by the IDF. Fadel was dragged out of bed in his pajamas to clean the graffiti off of the walls of the house across the street. This humiliation occurred in front of his children. In June 1989, Fadel's 14-year-old brother was shot when he and other boys came running through the alley near his house. The door to his home opened and Fadel's wife was inside cleaning. The IDF entered his home and severely beat his wife, striking her on the face, arms and legs. She had to spend four days in bed. Fadel's 10-month-old son witnessed his mother being beaten. When Fadel came home, his wife was in bed and his baby was crying and unattended. Later, Fadel also noticed that some tape cassettes were missing.

Twenty-four hours later, the IDF returned to ask again about his 14-year-old brother. Fadel told the officer in charge about his wife being beaten and the missing cassettes. The IDF officer ignored the description of Fadel's wife, but offered to replace the missing cassettes. "The IDF is always honest," he said. Fadel's wife still suffered many symptoms of her trauma, including insomnia and difficulty walking. She had severe headaches, especially when she saw the IDF.

1/16/92

Four days in Gaza, and I had cried every day. Back in America, I probably averaged a good cry once every 10 years. This day was about to become one of my more memorable and emotional days. It began in the Gaza Strip and ended in Tel Aviv. I began the day with home visits to the El Nuserat Refugee Camp with a Palestinian social worker, Samir Zagguit. We made the trip in a broken-down, French-made car that had difficulty staying in motion. Four large men were squeezed in like sardines in a tin. That morning there appeared to be a problem with the steering and there was a clunking noise in the right front wheel. I figured if we survived the IDF checkpoints, we could still die horribly in a car accident. Samir promised to service the car before we proceeded.

To my amazement, the service station consisted of a small junkyard that was run by two not quite 12-year-old Palestinian boys. In place of a car hoist, a three-foot-deep hole allowed them to crawl under the car. They tried banging on the wheel and eventually welded something onto either the axle or the fender. We sat in the car and I wondered whether the welding torch would ignite an explosion. Finally, we gave the boys a few shekels and were about to be on our way. Suddenly the boys disappeared rapidly in an apparent panic.

Samir gestured for silence. I was terrified when an Israeli patrol banged on the metal corrugated gates. One soldier thrust a bayonet through a small hole. It was now obvious why the Palestinian boys disappeared with such dispatch. Fortunately, the patrol passed by and we quickly opened the gates and slunk away. We felt like criminals.

Driving a few blocks, we entered Nuserat Camp and asked directions to the family we were to visit. Suddenly, an Israeli foot patrol of 30 IDF soldiers surprised us. As they approached the GCMHP vehicle, one of the soldiers lowered his rifle and sited it on someone or something very close to our driver, Samir Fascia. The soldier was less than 10 meters away and as I looked down his gun barrel, I thought, "If he misses a small amount to the left, Samir is dead. If he misses far left, I am dead." I was sitting in the front seat next to Samir. Fortunately, he did not shoot and raised his rifle. He was probably just trying to intimidate someone in the street. He certainly succeeded in intimidating me!

We finally reached our destination, the home of Nasser, a 35-year-old former teacher who was in a wheelchair. We attempted to elicit his story, but he was physically shaking and somewhat incoherent. He eventually told us that he was having a hard time with the interview because his sons were at school. He had heard that the Israelis were patrolling the camp. Rumors were flying that shots had been fired and that there were many injuries. He cried as he told us that he did not know if his sons would come home alive that morning. The interview proceeded much more smoothly when his sons walked into the room and were okay.

Nasser had been caught in a clash/demonstration two years earlier while walking to school. A rubber bullet had lodged in his neck between two cervical vertebrae. Israeli surgeons told him that this was inoperable and the new paralysis was permanent. In general, he had been treated well by Israeli physicians. One Israeli physician, however, had spat on him and told him that his injury could not possibly be from the IDF.

During the videotaping of this interview, we met at least 10 of his children and his father-in-law. Nasser, his father-in-law, and several of his sons each described how they had first heard about the shooting. Each cried as they told their story. I vividly remember the interview and how cold and damp the room was. I have never spent a colder winter because, especially in the refugee camps, the inside temperature approximated the outside temperature. There was no central heating, only very small electric space heaters. January was also their rainy season, and most of the corrugated metal roofs in the camp houses leaked.

I had Nasser's five-year-old son sitting on my lap and his red jacket was thoroughly soaked. He was barefoot and mucous dripped from his nose. He was shivering and so was I, but the physical environment was more comforting than the psychological one. I was sobbing along with each family member as they described their collective experiences.

An "incidental" finding during this home visit was a 17-year-old cousin who had a story to tell. This young adolescent lifted up a pant leg to show us a scarred knee where he had been shot. He then showed us his old gunshot wounds on his elbow and abdomen. During a clash within the last year, he had been shot and fallen down. An Israeli soldier had walked up to him and pumped seven shots into his abdomen from point-blank range. The family asked the soldiers if they could gather up what they thought was a corpse, but they were refused. When the soldiers eventually left, the family was amazed to find him still holding onto life. They rushed him to a hospital and after many months of rehabilitation, he was able to walk again.

While our intervention felt helpful and healing to this family, I was very frustrated. The Israeli patrol that day probably created dozens more new cases of PTSD. Rumors ran rampant, and I will never know exactly what occurred that day. We heard that one child was shot in the head and died while we were with Nasser's family.

That afternoon, I decided to go to Tel Aviv because a strike was likely the next day and no taxis would run. The strikes were called by any number of Palestinian groups. I had made a contact with ABC television in Tel Aviv and needed to keep my appointment with Bill Seamans. During those first days in Gaza, I realized that I needed to do more than plug holes in the massive dike of trauma. I hoped that American TV exposure might at least help decrease traumatic events. I wanted to slow down the trauma so that the healing process could take hold.

During my overnight stay in a Tel Aviv hotel, I met an ex-IDF officer currently living in Switzerland and employed as a banker. He tried to convince me that the reason that the IDF patrolled the refugee camps was to prevent the Palestinians from killing each other. He also told me that the IDF would never beat or shoot a Palestinian child because the penalty was a two-year jail term. He said that the Israeli settlers were not appropriating land because it actually belonged to them.

"The IDF would only shoot if 500 children were attacking them and if their lives were threatened." These were his words. I had been in Gaza too long to believe any of this. We shouted at each other for more than an hour, and I got to him. When he left, he forgot his glasses and had to come back to retrieve them.

After he left I began to look around the lobby. I saw a great deal of wealth. Many of the patrons wore expensive fur coats and jewelry. I began sobbing when I thought of my experience only a few hours earlier. I pictured the utter poverty of the Nuserat Refugee Camp. I wanted to run up to these people, grab them, and shake them. I wanted to scream, "Don't you know what is happening 100 kilometers south of here?"

I Feel Like Throwing Stones

1/17/92

I had lunch with Bill Seamans, who was the director of ABC television in Tel Aviv. He was turning the reins over to Jacque Grenier. It was helpful to be introduced to the new bureau chief. I was optimistic that I had a tentative commitment from him to come to Gaza.

Returning to Gaza was yet another adventure. A strike was called so it was very difficult to get an Arab cab. The Israeli cab driver in Tel Aviv questioned my judgment in wanting to go to Jaffa to pick up a service taxi. He asked me if I was crazy, if I knew "what those people did to Terry Anderson. The Palestinians could be very friendly initially, but they could turn on you in a second," he warned. He tried every trick he knew to discourage me from returning to Gaza, especially by Palestinian cab.

Waiting for the Arab cab to fill with passengers, the admonishments went around in my head. It was the end of the work day and the Palestinian laborers would be returning to their families in the Gaza Strip. I wondered who would fill my cab. I looked around at the dust and sweat that covered the seats and compared it to the new, clean Israeli cab. One by one, men wearing *kayfeyahs* (checkered Arab scarves) and women in full-length camp dresses began to fill the cab, looking me over as they got in. My palms were clammy. I became uncomfortably aware of my foreignness and powerlessness to communicate in even the simplest conversation. Why hadn't I learned more Arabic before I came?

As the cab approached Erez, excitement and a furor broke out among several of the riders. They were trying to tell me something important. Arriving at the border, guns were pointed in our faces through the car windows as our identities were checked. Guilt crept over me as I handed the young Israeli soldier my American passport. My interrogation ended while the laborers struggled to respond to grunts with gun barrels in their faces. Palestinians constantly risked losing their identity cards, the source of their livelihoods.

The cab stopped again a few hundred meters past the checkpoint, and suddenly everyone jumped out. A hand reached out and dragged me out of the cab. I thought that we were on our way to Gaza City and that I would have a few minutes to regain my composure. I could not imagine what was happening. Before I had an answer, I was shepherded into another cab. Panic gripped me as this cab took a detour through an unfamiliar part of the strip. A huge rock suddenly crashed into the side of the cab. Thank God it hit below the window! A young boy of seven or eight stood triumphantly at the side of the road knowing that he had made a statement—no work and no driving on a strike day. Apparently our new cab driver was more of a risk taker than the first driver.

Around the next corner, we encountered 20 IDF soldiers in full battle gear. All wore helmets and black plastic face shields. They were patrolling Jabalya and engaging 10- to 12-year-old stone-throwing children. Our cab rapidly reversed direction to avoid getting caught in the crossfire of this clash.

Relief swept over me as the cab drove into the courtyard of Marna House. Just a few days before, Marna House had seemed so threatening. Now it was my safe haven. Suffering from emotional exhaustion, I plodded my way through dinner alone and felt uncomfortable with being catered to by a servant. What I wanted was friendship. I longed for someone with whom to share my mix of emotions. I felt a growing closeness with the Palestinians. Waves of humiliation and oppression washed over me and an inner anger began to boil. Intellectually, I knew that I had to contain these raw emotions to prevent them from turning into hatred and revenge.

My head was spinning as I made my way to my room up the dark and cold staircase. The room barely supported a single bed and a small dresser that was missing a few parts. Electricity was marginal. Fixtures resembled gaslight and put out about the same intensity. The electric heater in my room was barely functional and did not invite me to take off my clothes. The plumbing was antiquated, and drawing enough water to brush my teeth was a challenge. I did not even consider taking a shower. Sleep came as a relief.

1/18/92

This morning I needed a break from the mental health center, so I wandered across the potholed dirt street, through an abandoned building, and to the beach. I thought that this beach, being on the Mediterranean, would make a wonderful tourist destination. The only obstacles were the clutter of trash and the barbed wire enclosing the U.N. Beach Club. I walked along the beach and was invited to sit with an elderly Arab dressed in traditional robes. He insisted on teaching me Arabic, over my protests that I had to get back to the mental health center. Not caring about what I had to say or not understanding me, he picked up a piece of litter from the beach and began to write out the entire Arabic alphabet.

Back at the center, I was presented the case of a 28-year-old married woman with seven children. Her insomnia, tearfulness, and depression began several years ago, postpartum. She cried at the sight of other women breast-feeding their children. Her husband complained that her breasts were too small. He complained that she "looked like a man" and stated that he would take another wife. He stopped having sex with her. When she watched TV and saw other well-endowed women, she would burst into tears. The mental health team thought that she needed a medical workup and a gynecologic examination for her small breasts. Seeing this as a marital issue, I recommended family therapy instead.

Not all the distress in the Gaza Strip comes from the occupation. There are many culturally oppressive factors, especially for women. I was not well received when I coined the *second occupation* being the Palestinian men of the Palestinian women.

Another case was a 17-year-old boy from Gaza. This young man came from a family of five children and was brought in by his father. He complained of pain in his eyes, decreased vision, headaches, insomnia, and crying. He had seen numerous physicians who were unable to establish any physical reasons for his symptoms. After his father left the interview room, the truth emerged. He said that he was continuously compared negatively to his siblings and that his father would strike him in the head. When he cried in the middle of the night, his father made him tea and spent time being supportive to him. The team's recommendation was to prescribe multivitamins. My solution, family therapy, got us into a heated discussion about the negative cultural implications of not prescribing medications when the patients expect them.

What became apparent to me during these two discussions was how unaware and presumptuous I was with respect to Arab culture. A new

dilemma faced me: How could I effect some significant change without in-
sulting my hosts and their culture? I felt inept at juggling the sense of omnip-
otence placed on me and my own emerging feelings of humility.

My local colleagues were looking to me for some new insights, but were
struggling with traditions and having difficulty considering change.

Everything that I believed in regarding psychiatric treatment was being
challenged. Psychoses were treated pharmacologically as in the West, as
well as by faith healers in Gaza. After sitting in on several patient interviews,
I began to wonder about the accuracy of diagnoses and specific use of medications. My awareness grew of a strong rivalry between the disciplines of
psychiatry and psychology. How was I going to introduce my concerns without alienating my peers who were already fragmented among themselves?

Returning to Marna House that evening, I watched another BBC documentary on Gaza, which added images to my accumulation of words and
stories. House raids at night, interrogations, humiliations, beatings, and
gunshot wounds now had faces and jumped to life before me. Technical descriptions of the range of bullets used by the IDF, everything from plastic to
rubber, brought back my interview with Nasser. His 17-year-old cousin had
been left for dead in Nuserat Camp.

Alya had some other visitors staying at the house. One, Heather Grady
of Save the Children, watched this documentary with me. Turning to
Heather, I referred to the Gaza Community Mental Health Program as
"our" program. This signaled the beginning of my strong identification
with pain and suffering of the occupation and my own intifada. That night
I dreamed that I was actually one of the people I had seen oppressed. I
hated being controlled, losing my freedom, and having even the minutest
aspects of my life dictated by an outsider.

1/19/92

I sat in on a case presentation and met Samira, a six-year-old from Jabalya
Refugee Camp. She presented with severe fears, headaches, dizziness, and
crying night and day. Previously she had been successfully toilet trained,
but now she was bed-wetting and defecating in her clothes. Her father dis-
played bizarre behaviors, such as walking around the home naked and
talking rapidly whether anyone was listening or not. He had been beaten as
a child by his mother who was now 90 and living in the home. The father
hit Samira, often times in the head. Samira was also beaten by the IDF. She

had experienced and incorporated beatings as a source of power and would, in turn, beat her younger brother.

In a culture that had lived under occupation for more than 50 years, an undercurrent of hopelessness existed. A major source of personal power came through physical dominance. In Gaza, children were often victimized by two sources, their parents and the IDF. Parents often beat their children into silence while the Israeli soldiers were patrolling the refugee camps. If the IDF heard any noise from a household, they were more likely to enter. The occupants were more prone to be subjected to humiliation, severe beatings, and prolonged interrogation. Children during these periods were frequently kept in bed all day and were not allowed to leave the house.

While visiting Nuserat Camp, I met Basil, a 28-year-old married man who developed a seizure disorder after reportedly being beaten a year earlier by the IDF. His seizures resulted in loss of consciousness and occurred randomly, in public or in the privacy of his home. The staff considered these seizures to be hysterical, not having an organic basis, or as being stress related. Couldn't these seizures be related to the physical trauma he received?

It was confusing to me that my colleagues seemed to dismiss or not place any relevance on the trauma that they lived with daily. They appeared to be numb and accepted the condition of their lives, as though it were normal. An example of this was the daily curfew of 8:00 p.m. As a visitor to this environment, the curfew was painfully restrictive; yet my hosts would only complain about a 24-hour curfew imposed for several days in a row.

After visiting Basil's home, neighbors learned that an American doctor was in the area. They insisted that I come to the home of Rania, an emaciated, blind two-year-old girl with epilepsy. Cold, damp air rushed through the leaky roof of the cinder-block home. The corrugated metal roof was held on by rocks and tires. It was dark, there was no electricity, and I removed my shoes, as was the custom. I sat on the floor because there was no furniture. The thin sleeping mats that were used by the family were piled in the corner because the living room also served as the bedroom.

The child was wrapped in a tattered blanket and handed to me to examine because she had been crying night and day for several days. She was grabbing at her ear, and my first impression was that she might have an ear infection. I struggled to recall my antiquated knowledge of pediatrics. My experience consisted of a six-week rotation in the subspecialty of pediatric hematology. I had only reviewed the blood smears of children with leukemia. This brought back memories of feeling powerless when my own two-year-old son lay in a coma from meningitis.

My training as a doctor had not prepared me for this. I feared that Rania would die in my arms while I held her. The extended family and my colleagues looked on expectantly. I helplessly attempted to explain that I did not think that adjusting her phenobarbital for her epilepsy would resolve her crisis. My best educated guess was that Rania initially might have had an ear infection, easily treated by antibiotics. By this time, things had possibly progressed to meningitis, a much more serious infection involving inflammation of the lining of the brain. If not treated, it could be fatal or result in serious neurological impairments. I recommended immediate transport to the U.N. Hospital.

After dealing with Rania, 23-year-old Nabil, who had been in the same room, came forward with a history that was in my area of expertise. He had seven children and had been beaten by both the Egyptian soldiers and the IDF as he attempted to immigrate to Egypt. He described the Israeli soldiers as almost polite, compared with what he had experienced at the hands of the Egyptians. Nabil was having insomnia, nightmares, and depression, and he cried continuously. My intervention was listening and witnessing to his trauma, which by itself can be powerful and healing.

Exhausted, I took a walk to clear my head before returning to Marna House. Confusion and frustration soon gave way to clarity and assuredness. The streets were narrow, covered with dust and littered with refuse. As I turned a corner near Shifa Hospital, I dared to make eye contact with a shop owner seated in front of his business.

Eye contact was all it took to elicit an invitation to share a cup of *kawa*, Arabic coffee, or some *shay*, which is tea. After drinking in silence for several minutes, the owner eventually recruited a translator so we could have a discussion. Hassem, an attractive young Palestinian laborer, was just one of the 20 or so people who gathered over the next hour.

Palestinian hospitality was something that I had not experienced before, and the insistence of my new acquaintances was not to be refused. Darkness and curfew were approaching rapidly, and I was afraid of offending Alya again. Hassem would not end the discussion until I agreed to visit his home and meet his family.

Finding myself again in a long, dark alley where I could not see my hand in front of my face, I thought to myself, "Here I go again, naively following a stranger." Words of my friends back in New Hampshire suddenly flooded my memory: "Have you thought this through, John? Have you done your homework? Are you sure you understand the culture you're going to be living in?" I had dismissed these questions as unnecessary cautions, diluting the spontaneity and sense of adventure.

Relieved to be finally in the living room of Hassem's home, we were joined by his brothers and sons. We watched television in Arabic for what seemed like hours, and I almost missed curfew. We sat on the floor drinking kawa and eating food prepared by female relatives who remained in another room. It was the custom for the females to have no contact with any males other than the closest of family friends.

3/23/92

Eyad Sarraj hosted a farewell dinner at the program. The mood was festive. I was implored to share my favorite stories that I had frequently recited in broken Arabic. I was never sure if it was the content—the chicken in the stove and the mouse trapped and killed in Basil's house—or my delivery, which totally butchered Arabic. The outcome was always bedlam and hysteria.

In spite of my own immense pleasure with these stories, however, I declined. This night and my experience in Gaza, I did not want lost in humor. I shared how Gaza had been the most meaningful experience of my life. I had been honored to share their pain and oppression and to be accepted into their homes and their lives. They had become family, and I loved them. I felt great guilt in leaving them and returning to America. I would never forget them and would work extremely hard to tell their stories and to try to end their ongoing oppression.

My speech had been planned for days. I spoke directly to several people about what their gifts were and how much they meant to me. The occasion passed too quickly. I could not give as much as I wanted, nor could I take away their pain. I could not find the words to express my torrent of intense feelings. At least I kept the humor to a minimum, and I hoped my tears conveyed a deep and profound caring.

3/25/92

Leaving Gaza at 3:00 a.m. was perplexing. Outside of the cab, windows were dark. There were dilapidated buildings and desolated parts of the city for which no one in their right mind could have any possible affinity. Yet my tears could not stop, my guts were twisted and knotted, and my mind was at sea struggling to make sense of it. I had never experienced such a painful termination.

I learned firsthand the immense value of witnessing the stories of trauma. For victims, knowing they are not alone and that other people care, can be healing. In addition, there is also a validation of what was previously a unique personal reality. The context of trauma is also critical in determining the trajectory of its impact. Random deaths in inner cities, by drive-bys, have much less meaning and more impact than when there is a cause—for example, Palestinian statehood.

The cycle of abuse can pertain to nations and groups of people as well as individual physical and sexual abuse. The Holocaust plays a role in the Israeli–Palestinian cycle of violence.

Dealing with my own personal PTSD—by becoming involved in the media, research, and activism—allowed me to cope. Facing my own immortality and coming to the conclusion that "all they can do is kill me" freed and inspired me.

If the Palestinians can remain optimistic in the face of their plight, I think the rest of us should certainly offer our support. We need to break the cycle of abuse. More beatings, killings, torture, and martyrs are not the answer.

There are no good guys and no bad guys in the Middle East; it's the violence that is wrong on both sides. Terrorism, occupation, and oppression must end.

We will have peace in the Middle East when we love our children more than we hate each other.

11

The Acute Aftermath of an Earthquake in El Salvador

Lynn E. DeLisi

On January 13, 2001, an earthquake of the magnitude of 7.8 on the Richter scale hit El Salvador. As an immediate consequence, a hilltop water tower toppled and caused the massive movement of mud to pour down the hill, covering a whole community within the Las Colinas section of San Salvador. Anything and anyone in its path was buried within seconds. In the subsequent 24 hours, as people slept outdoors in tents, the slow cleanup revealed an official count of 850 dead from the landslide alone and countless others unaccounted for. In addition, villages throughout the country were diminished to rubble and scores of others were buried beneath. A quite peaceful and sunny Saturday morning turned into pandemonium. In the United States, news accounts of this earthquake were scarce in the midst of reports covering President Clinton and his last-minute executive orders and of a predicted snowstorm that would cause havoc along the entire Northeast coast. I was in the midst of dealing with the never-ending frustrations as a psychiatric academician and the usual tensions created by the need to meet grant submission deadlines and obtaining fundable scores on those already submitted so that research could progress.

Thus, in the midst of the usual daily crises in my own office, which focuses on schizophrenia research, I received a short message from a colleague in Manhattan requesting psychiatrists who could donate a couple of weeks of time to help the people of El Salvador in the aftermath of the trauma that had just taken place throughout many regions of their country. Already the

International Red Cross, Doctors Without Borders, and many religious groups were assembling to determine how best to help this country.

The priorities of a continual research program with its ups and downs seemed mundane in comparison to the life-and-death struggles of such a disadvantaged population of people. On an impulse, I replied that I would go, using my accumulated vacation time. I would remove myself from my research with all its frustrations for a period of two weeks, something I had not done for several years, and for once try to help in my own small way a quite remote country and its people. We were given updates on necessary precautions for tetanus, yellow fever, hepatitis, polio, and malaria and told to bring toilet paper, sleeping bags, food, water, and lots of medications. It took a while to dawn on me that we were really going. It was only when I had my plane ticket in hand that I began wondering what I as a psychiatrist could offer these people. Although we had meetings about it and proposed things to do and to take, I was wary that our help was not what these people needed and questioned whether psychiatrists really had a role in the face of an acute disaster.

I arrived at La Guardia Airport on February 3, 2001, with more baggage than I ever had before in all my travels, and American Airlines tickets, which I ridiculously upgraded for a last bit of luxury on route to San Salvador. I, and the others on this mission, still did not have a clue as to what we would do or how we would help. We brought Spanish-language research surveys to gauge posttraumatic stress disorder (PTSD), but we didn't have the vaguest notion of how we would implement them and how we would use what we know to help people from a culture very different from our own who were in acute distress. We stuffed our large suitcases with sample tranquilizers and sedatives given to us free by various drug companies and had the promise of more to be shipped to us in San Salvador once we arrived.

El Salvador is the smallest but most densely populated country of Central America, sandwiched between Guatemala to the northwest, Honduras to the northeast, Nicaragua to the south, and the Pacific Ocean to the west. Despite its size, there are several volcanoes within El Salvador's borders that are said to be active at times. The country was ravaged by civil war in the 1980s, the opposition reaching a peaceful settlement with the government only in 1992. It is hard to find a woman who hasn't lost sons or a husband through war. Many people and their families have been displaced from their original land as a result of the war.

Although farming is the main occupation of most, it is rare to see lush greenery and vegetation from irrigated fields. Alongside barefoot children at play are large, dirty pigs; a thin breed of cattle; and roosters roaming the dirt roads of each town. The land is vastly dry and brown. Men carry loads of materials by balancing them on their shoulders, while often stringing a large metallic machete at their waist or holding a rifle in one hand for protection. Women balance the family water supply in jugs on their heads as they walk. One resident told us that since the war, there is so much distrust that weapons are a necessity for self-defense. Food store chains have counters selling a variety of large guns.

Transportation is by pickup truck. Twenty or more people can be seen standing in a tight squeeze, as in a New York subway during rush hour, except they are riding in the back of a pickup. We were warned not to travel at night on the roads because people, particularly foreigners, have been kidnapped. Although we didn't heed this advice, we nevertheless felt the anxiety of it all. These were the baseline conditions that existed at the time we responded to the acute damages caused by an earthquake.

In our first week in El Salvador, we felt it was important to see the consequence of the trauma instilled on the people we spoke with. Rosita, a nurse who lived on the outskirts of Las Colinas and lost her husband and friends in the landslide, tearfully gave us a tour of what remained and told the story of Las Colinas, a middle-class neighborhood with neatly gated, colored two- and three-story houses placed along the side of a mountain for good views of the city. This was considered a desirable neighborhood, with new houses being completed even higher up the hill. A church, a seafood restaurant (which her husband had owned), a variety of markets, and streets packed with fashionable cars existed until that Saturday morning when a 20-second tremor caused a water tower to break on the top of the mountain and mud to pour down in such force that houses, cars and all human life within were crushed and pushed down a mile to a tightly compressed standstill.

Although the official toll was 850 dead and 1,500 missing, no one knew how many people had died instantly, because they were many whole families with no one left to search. One Red Cross rescue worker we later saw in a group debriefing session tearfully described the bulldozer picking up multiple body parts—all that remained of the human beings who lived and worked in this area. When we had the opportunity to see Las Colinas, all that remained was a side pile of mangled cars, shattered bordering houses, and a large leveled-off field of dirt sprinkled with a powdery antiseptic.

Rosita's two children survived, but their friends did not. As we toured the region, she pointed to the plot where her husband's restaurant stood only a short while earlier. Another location she indicated was that of the church; nearby was the house of a man she knew and recalled was so happy to have recently gained custody of his young son, who had just moved in with him, both of whom died. We walked to her home, still standing but uninhabit-able toward the boundary of Las Colinas. One block away, nothing stood. She reached her hand through the iron gate and delicately removed a lone red rose seemingly out of place in the rubble. She tearfully handed it to one of us as a gift, but we could not take it. The rose was hers and a symbol of her anguish and what remained of her former life. We asked her if she needed someone to talk to or some medication to sleep, but she refused and was clearly not ready to resolve the grief she felt. We gave her our e-mail addresses, and she promised to write after we returned to the United States, but she never did. We knew she felt embarrassed that she was talking to psychiatrists.

During our stay in a small neighborhood hotel that was a gathering point for many foreign aid groups, a minister from the United Kingdom re-counted one story about the remarkable recovery of the two lone survivors (a mother and daughter) who were pulled out of the path of the landslide despite being buried several feet down. Both suffered multiple fractures, and he urged us to visit them. When we arrived at their temporary shelter provided by a friend, the mother, only 42, described how grateful she was to God that she, not her beautiful 18-year-old daughter, was the one who lost her leg. This family received a great deal of publicity while we were there, including visitors from newspapers and TV, but they were suffering emotionally. We recommended antidepressants for the mother, and she gratefully took them. Despite many follow-up phone calls, however, we were unable to relocate this family and to determine whether our visit had been helpful.

Santa Tecla, by far the biggest tented community, had been established by the government for all those inhabitants of San Salvador who had lost their homes. Santa Tecla was an awesome sight. It could be approached from high above with a view of 1,000 pointed, white tents neatly lined up in the distance. It appeared quiet and peaceful. There were fast-food stands on top of the hill outside the gate. A guard with a rifle prevented visitors from entering, except when told, such as in our case, that we were *medicos*. The camp headquarters on the hill above was operated by the mayor's office, which oversaw the operations of the camp. Food (rice, beans, cornmeal) was delivered in large quantities daily and handed out in food lines. There appeared to be volunteer organizations set up everywhere. Rosita worked in one of the makeshift clinics, which was where we met her. A pharmacy tent enabled patients to get prescriptions filled as ordered by doctors in the clinics. Boxes of donations of a variety of medicines were strewn over the floor and pencil marks indicated whether they were for diarrhea, pain, or infection. The individual containers were dirty from the ground dust, and it was unclear how the tablets were actually distributed.

On our first visit to the pharmacy, one of the volunteers admitted that the need for medications for anxiety and depression was great—they have none, except "benzos"—benzodiazepines—which a member of the Red Cross told us were "given out like candy." I promised to call my drug representatives back home to get medications shipped as soon as possible and took note of what they had or didn't have, although I later saw how the government confiscated these shipments. Just to the left of the pharmacy stood a complex of two tents labeled *Doctores Sin Frontieres*. We were told that they were administering a mental health program for the camp, but had no idea about the extent of psychiatric symptoms among the residents. To our amazement, the ministry of health tents were a few feet away in another complex, but we found that in practice there was no real coordination for the provision of health care between them. In fact, both groups almost seemed in competition, and one could sense the tensions between both sets of staff.

At the ministry of health complex, we were told that the first helpful step might be for us to obtain a survey of all inhabitants of the camp to determine the extent of psychiatric problems among them and to detect those who needed treatment. We all suspected that people were not asking for help with sleep or anxiety but suffering silently in their tents. They had to be drawn out somehow. We were enthusiastic about this task because it was one thing we could do well, and had come equipped to do so with questionnaires to measure just about everything. So after a meeting with the local tent division leaders that evening in which we were given support to implement our project, we found ourselves having a role in this unique community.

The next day we gathered some local psychology students and began to visit each tent in the most systematic way possible, interviewing people in Spanish with a one-page set of questions aimed at detecting any type of stress and its severity. Language was, of course, a problem for us, although we had a bilingual psychiatrist-in-training among us. We set out in pairs, one of us providing Spanish-to-English translation and the other interpreting the presence or absence of psychiatric symptoms. The danger was that often we were not confident in our knowledge of the language and would hear things that appeared with entirely different content once translated. But the messages in general were clear.

We selected the Davidson Trauma Scale, a questionnaire that consists of questions to determine all items necessary for a psychiatric diagnosis of

PTSD. With this scale, we conducted 276 interviews—70 with men, average age 38, and 206 with women, average age 39—using a Spanish translation of the form that one of us was able to complete. This was a random sample of approximately 10 percent of the inhabitants of the camp that week. Those individuals who were perceived as having at least one severe symptom or a few moderately felt symptoms were considered at risk for a psychiatric disorder and potentially in need of treatment.

Only 2.5 percent of all subjects were considered not to have any symptoms, whereas 97.5 percent had at least one severe symptom of post-traumatic stress or generalized anxiety. Many of them had considerable difficulty sleeping or disturbing thoughts about the earthquake that prevented them from thinking about their present and future needs; others simply felt numb and wanted to avoid talking about what had happened to them or seeing anything that reminded them of the event. We also noted that women reported significantly more distress than men, but we felt this could have been due to the need of many of the men to appear strong. The men would often tell us that they were okay, but we should visit the wife who spent much of the day crying.

Shortly after beginning our project, we sat compiling initial data on a table in an empty tent, when a psychologist and French volunteer from Doctores Sin Frontieres approached us for a meeting. Happy to be useful to her organization, we invited her in to discuss how we could work together and go directly to the tents of those whom we had identified as being in need of help. Her agenda, however, was different. "I don't like your questionnaire," she said in a thick French accent. "It is making people sick . . . because of your questioning. . . . People are in need of treatment. They are becoming anxious and crying. One lady was dangerously left alone in her tent [she claimed by one of our interviewers] and had to be given medication."

The psychologist continued, "We have already gone to each tent to find out whether people are in need of treatment. Why are you doing this, and don't you know that you are making things worse?" When she calmed down, we could see what the problem was. We had somehow moved into her territory. We felt we had done some good. That if after talking to us, people were seeking help, then we had accomplished our purpose. So once we assured her that we would give her our entire list of people who were detected as in need of treatment, she softened. Of course, on leaving we gave the same list to the ministry of health and only hoped that both worked together eventually in the end to help each individual. We even managed to see a few patients ourselves in a small corner of the ministry of health tent clinic examining cubicles. One woman was medicated with Zyprexa for an acute psychotic reaction, and one man whose job and dignity were lost obtained the antidepressant Prozac from us to help gain some energy to rebuild his life.

After spending our first 24 hours in the country sleeping in a rural warehouse with no running water, toilets, or food, we set up base in a small city hotel known as Casa Grande. By any imagination this was not a grand house, but it did have character and was run by an El Salvadorian extended family with a couple of hired cooks. The bathrooms had cold-water showers hooked to water heaters that the owners claimed worked, but we never could understand how. Breakfast was rice and beans with some plantains and eggs, but one had to be able to request these in Spanish; otherwise nothing would come with the weak grainy special coffee. Dinner also could be had with the family. In the center courtyard were round tables where we would sit and meet with the other guests, many of whom were relief workers with other organizations whom we amazingly would encounter on our travels throughout the country. It was there in the courtyard that one such worker spread a map out for us and pointed to specific towns with the most severe devastation that were in need of our help. We worried about the safety of this "grand" old house should an earthquake strike again. Where would we take cover? The owners appeared not to have any contingency plans, except that we would all congregate in a small courtyard, but privately we worried if we would be hit by the surrounding walls caving in on top of us. The other problem was the double set of iron doors that were closed and locked from 11:00 p.m. until 7:00 a.m. Should another earthquake strike, there would be no way out without the key. We eventually left Casa Grande for the luxurious comfort of a new Comfort Inn, a solid structure with hot water, a business center with a computer, and American-style rooms. We settled with this in the middle of our second week following a second major earthquake.

The anxiety about our personal safety was real; from the moment we stepped off of the airplane, we were confronted with continual daily ground tremors and the realization that although we came there to help people, we were not free from danger. Our high level of anxiety continued to underlie all of our interactions with each other and extended to those we tried to help.

We were told not to miss seeing the U.S. Embassy on this trip because it is said to be the second largest in the world. The embassy was indeed a large fortress, with lines of people outside waiting for visas. We tried to get a visitor's visa for our local driver, but did not succeed. It would require a minimum of two months wait, and he would only be able to come back home with us if there was a funeral or terminally ill person awaiting him at the other end. We wanted to give him that free trip as a bonus for ruining his car on all the rough roads for two weeks. He thought of surprising his two sisters living in New Jersey whom he hadn't seen in 20 years. We left him the last night promising to write and with a standing invitation to a group reunion sometime in the future. But in the time since, this has not happened.

Why would our country choose El Salvador for such embassy headquarters? A young man actively pursuing civil rights issues for his "people" reminded us that not so long ago, his country was at war. In 1978, he recounted, an election was held and "the people's candidate" won, but the government in power refused to let the elected officials take over. When opposition and demonstrations ensued, those whose opinions were deemed dangerous were arrested and disappeared. We were told that they were tortured in several ways. Some were thrown in swimming pools with electricity pumped in. Others were slaughtered and thrown into the Pacific en masse. Many young university students and professors, whose worst crime was believing in the rights of the people, disappeared, never to be found. The protesters were labeled "communists" and later became proudly known as the guerillas. We met some former guerillas on this trip. Despite U.S. support of the corrupt previous El Salvadorian government (as our informer referred to it), he said not to worry; they did not hold a grudge against the American people, just our government. They were very sensitive to the separation between people and government. What we learned from this, however, as psychiatrists, was that this country was suffering from a considerably more chronic set of trauma than the acute trauma we thought we had traveled to help the people overcome. The psychology that existed was certainly more complicated than we were initially led to believe.

On February 13, 2001, at 8:21 a.m., our continual fears were realized. A tremor shook our car as we were driving out of the city to an appointment we had to visit the National Psychiatric Hospital. It had taken a week and a letter from the dean of the university medical school to get this appointment. No earthquake would prevent us from seeing what psychiatric care was like in El Salvador. But the streets in the few seconds of tremor turned into chaos. People were running fast in every direction, grabbing sides of buses and pickup trucks and scurrying to pick up children at school. Schools were emptying, and people were running from something they couldn't see or control. We recalled in jest the expression "standing on firm ground," because this was meaningless. There was no such thing. Fears and rumors were circulating with no scientific understanding of the events that were taking place. We continued on. Within the hour, a Spanish news station was broadcasting that a school had collapsed and a town had been destroyed at the epicenter of this new quake—just at the one-month anniversary of the first one that had killed so many people. The name San Vicente repeatedly played on the radio. We asked our driver to take us there. We would provide aid—whatever we could do. We later regretted how we had left many basic medications, stethoscopes, and blood pressure cuffs in storage back in Casa Grande.

The hospital was a small structure that seemed to survive, although because of the earthquake, it had more of an outside than in. Tents were set up within the walled-in upper courtyard, and one became a triage center. Doctors and students from the medical school had already arrived and were examining the injured, who were stretched out on old mattresses or tarps on the ground. Most had multiple fractures and serious wounds. A portable x-ray machine had lost power. We bravely announced that we were medical doctors specializing in psychiatry from New York, although I'm not sure anyone heard the word *psychiatry*. No one asked for our credentials. We were told to just begin with any patients we saw and suture their wounds as needed. A lower level with some tents but lots of open area in the hot sun had perhaps 100 wounded lying on the ground. Many were groaning and dehydrated. Some had IVs with saline started; others had nothing. We watched a young doctor remove some badly placed stitches and try again with no antiseptics. Limited analgesics and antibiotics were available. No tetanus vaccines were available. We thought of how these people were injured, buried in the dirt and stones before they were rescued. We had some miscellaneous medications in our car, mainly a bag filled with antibiotics for distribution to an upcoming mobile pediatric clinic. We had a few bottles of our drinking water as well. All of this we emptied and began distributing. How could it be that we were the ones to bring the hospital supplies and even water?

We looked for paper cups or any type of receptacle that could hold water and distributed the water to as many people as we could. Little plastic bags or even the inside of latex plastic gloves that sufficed were used and these were handed to many grateful of the wounded and their distraught relatives. Rule number one, we remembered from the disaster training we had, was to look for what was needed most and do it, regardless of whether it fit with the role of a doctor or psychiatrist. We took pictures to record the event as it was happening. One man, particularly in pain and severely injured, was waiting for transfer by helicopter to El Salvador. His hand was held up by a nun offering prayer. As we worked feverishly in the hot sun, the ground kept shaking with aftershocks, but there was no time to worry about something far worse. Most locals felt the ground would completely swallow it all. We learned very quickly about the significance of numbers on the Richter scale, which obviously we concluded advanced exponentially. But was it infinite? How high does the Richter scale go, one could ask, before a whole country or all of Central America is destroyed?

The town of San Vicente looked war-torn. Walking through the small city, we felt we were part of a World War II movie. Military units with guns discouraged our passage, but we moved on, taking care not to walk too close to sides of buildings that could tumble down with the next tremor. In the town square, a clock tower still stood, with its arms displaying 8:21, the moment the earthquake had hit. The municipal building had fallen down, as had a historic old church at the park entrance. We spread out and talked to families huddled together on chairs, benches, and the ground, not knowing what to do next. There they would stay the night as the mayor's command post was being set up nearby. Any food we had in our car was given to these people one by one. Occasionally we gave them some anti-anxiety medications we carried with us, but was there anything more we could do for them?

The next day, we were on to San Miguel, another hard-hit community. Again, there were wounded being cared for out in the open courtyard, and we talked to families one by one about their plans and how they would cope. Most people were in shock without any thoughts of the future. They would wait and hope that aid would come.

This community had a special problem. It was high on the side of a mountain that made up one wall of a volcano. Down below was the crater containing a beautiful, misty lake. The mist, our driver told us, was steam. The water was bubbling, a warning of impending trouble or implosion of an active volcano cooking below. The rumors were also flying fast that the earthquakes had destabilized at least this, if not more, volcanoes. An eruption of this one would wipe out San Miguel completely. We were told on the radio that Japanese volcanologists had been flown in to analyze the situation. Back in our hotel, we saw them at breakfast and approached one, asking the ultimate question: Would it occur? Unfortunately, the experts understood no English.

We eventually went back to all the towns to which we had traveled and to the people we had met to see how they were surviving. Our best efforts were spent walking from tent to tent asking people if they knew how to get food and other supplies, if they knew what was happening, and whether we could help them consider how to rebuild their lives. Overall, a certain apathy had set in among the people, the rescue workers, and national and local officials. It reminded us of some of the theories about learned helplessness. What you can't control gets you down, leading to a kind of helpless feeling. There was little planning for the future, and the people without homes sat and waited for the government to come and get them out. Would this happen? We were doubtful. Whether the people to whom we talked and gave medicines became active to get some control of their lives remains unknown to us.

On February 17, 2001, we boarded planes back to New York, back to our university positions, and back to the comfortable stresses of everyday American upper-middle-class life. We showed pictures of our experiences and recounted tales to colleagues. They listened silently with some interest, but, in the end, they said they were glad we were back, because there was a lot of work to be done. No one commented on the sadness of the pictures of barefoot little girls and the injured lying on stretchers. They were all too busy with their own thoughts of getting the research grant deadlines met and making progress in the laboratory. Although we were psychiatrists who had gone to help victims of a disaster, we too felt traumatized and needed to process all that we saw and experienced.

Did we help people during those two weeks? In reflection, I see a lot that we accomplished. Our survey of some very traumatized victims caused individuals to receive help for depression and sleeplessness that they otherwise would not have sought out. We conducted some education sessions for medical workers in affected villages to mobilize there awareness of the symptoms subsequent to trauma that many of their inhabitants could be feeling, and we spent some time aiding many individuals, not only with food and medicine, but with words of encouragement. Although we remember each face very distinctly, we have no follow-up information as to whether we were effective.

In the least, this experience taught us about the nature of disasters, and how people respond in a region of the world where medical care is primitive compared with that of the United States. We learned that as psychiatrists and physicians we need to step in and provide whatever is needed for the moment, even if that is simply a container of water. Finally, we learned about the politics of disaster response and how many groups can, in a tenuously coordinated and competitive fashion, step in to aid victims. We needed to make sure that the primary goal of helping those who were suffering was maintained above all, and we recognized that along with physical trauma comes psychological sequelae to both the direct victims of the disaster and to those who treat them.

Acknowledgments

This mission was sponsored by the American Jewish World Service and Disaster Psychiatry Outreach. It was organized by Craig L. Katz, M.D., who was one of the participants, along with a pediatrician, internist, psychiatric social worker, and bilingual psychiatric resident. I thank Dr. Katz for providing suggestions and edits of the final manuscript based on his firsthand experiences on this mission.

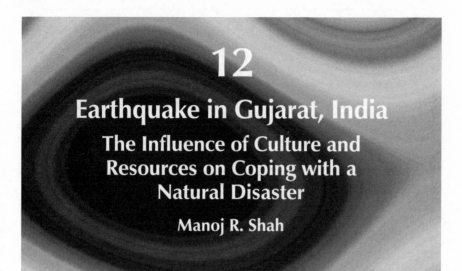

12

Earthquake in Gujarat, India
The Influence of Culture and Resources on Coping with a Natural Disaster

Manoj R. Shah

On January 26, 2001, about 8:42 a.m., my mother was making tea in the kitchen and my father and a cousin were chatting, waiting for the morning tea. Suddenly, the building started shaking violently, the tea kettle fell to the floor, and it dawned on my parents that they were experiencing an earthquake. They told my cousin to run out of the apartment building, while they sat down on the floor and began to pray. Because of their age and difficulty with walking, they were unable to rush down the stairs. Fortunately for them, they escaped unhurt, though the apartment building was severely damaged. Another lady in the neighborhood was not so lucky; while rushing down the stairs, the stairway collapsed, and she did not survive. There are numerous stories of miraculous escapes, rescue after several days of being buried under the debris and unfortunate deaths.

The earthquake hit on the 50th Republic Day of India, a national holiday. The schools and offices were closed, and there were flag-raising ceremonies being held outdoors. Except for a few who had decided to sleep late for the holiday, most of the folks were up and able to get out of their apartments and houses when the earthquake hit. Thus, many were able to escape injury and death.

The intensity of the earthquake has been placed at 6.9 to 7.9 on the Richter scale. The epicenter was the small village of Bachau (the word in Gujarati means "saved or survived") in Kutch, a region in the western state of Gujarat, India; it borders Pakistan. Many villages in Kutch were entirely destroyed and needed to be rebuilt from scratch. Bhuj, the capital of Kutch, suffered severe damage, destruction, and death. Ahmedabad, the commercial capital of Gujarat, located about 150 miles east from the epicenter, was another major city to suffer severe damage and casualties. Figure 12–1 shows major earthquake areas in India, and Figure 12–2 shows the location of the epicenter and the areas affected by the earthquake in Gujarat.

I arrived in Ahmedabad exactly 48 hours after the earthquake, and my plane landed two minutes after a major aftershock. The trip had been planned before the earthquake, and I decided to go ahead with it despite instructions from my parents and pleas from my children not to go. I was born and raised in Ahmedabad and had completed my medical education there before immigrating to the United States. New York and Ahmedabad are the only two homes I have known; the disasters of TWA and Egypt Air were fresh in my mind, which made me determined to undertake the journey. The work that awaited me as a psychiatrist and the small contribution I was able to make were immensely gratifying.

The people of Ahmedabad were understandably in a state of shock. The population of about two million appeared scared and insecure. Many were not sleeping indoors even though their homes were intact and had not suffered any damage. Those who slept in the homes avoided their bedrooms if they were not on the first floor and slept close to the main door to escape in case there was another earthquake. One family had a water bucket hanging from the ceiling, which would tilt and spray water to wake them in case the earth moved. Any minor aftershock made everyone scurry out of the homes. Even if there was no aftershock, someone would feel a slight movement and yell to make everyone rush out the front door. The astrologers had a field day predicting when and where the next earthquake would hit. Everyone was praying, making offerings to gods and performing *yagnas* (specific forms of religious cleansing and offerings to gods) to prevent further devastation. The businesses had come to a standstill, schools were closed, normal activities of life had ceased, and everyone was obsessed with when and if there would be another quake when they might not be so lucky. Yet water and electricity were freely flowing, milk and vegetables were available, as were other daily necessities, and roads were open.

Bhuj and Kutch were a different story. There was no water, electricity, or communication. The daily necessities were not available, the devastation was severe, the death toll was high, and relief efforts would not reach these areas for several weeks—a fact documented in newspapers and reports from various government and international relief agencies. As I did not visit these areas, I limit my report to what went on in Ahmedabad.

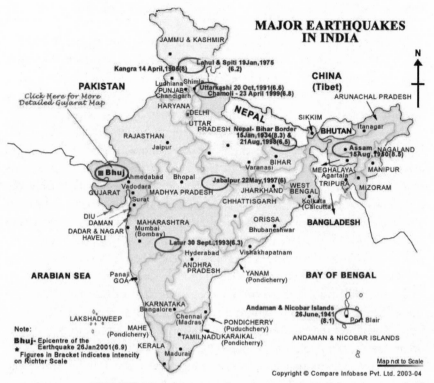

FIGURE 12–1. Major earthquake areas in India.

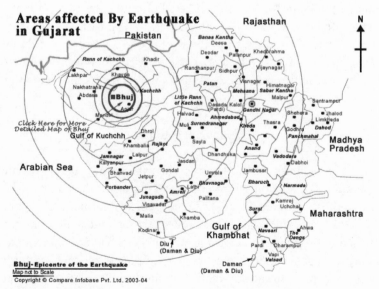

FIGURE 12–2. Epicenter and areas affected by the earthquake in the state of Gujarat, India.

Driving through the streets of Ahmedabad did not give the impression of an area that was devastated. Most of the buildings were intact, then suddenly one came across a building reduced to ruble or another building tilting dangerously. There was a newly married couple trapped under the debris of a building who were pulled out uninjured after three days. There was a family that lived on the fourth floor of an apartment building, and when it collapsed, the family walked out the window, which was now at the ground level, while the families living on the floors below them perished. One of my relatives, whose apartment building was severely damaged with the bottom two floors buried in the ground beneath, had no damage to her china. A family planning to take a ride in a new car was waiting for the last person to come down from the apartment when the earthquake hit; the family perished. Surviving relatives and neighbors of these victims were seen in the counseling center that was established to help them.

The federal and state governments began to organize efforts to deal with the disaster. The national guard and the military were mobilized. Many nongovernmental organizations (NGOs), industrial corporations, religious organizations, and political parties joined in these efforts, but there was little coordination among them. Medical personnel and volunteers also came from the other states of India. International relief agencies contributed material and human volunteers. The United Nations, Red Cross, World Health Organization, and individual nations sent in food, clothes, medical supplies, equipment for housing and shelter, and expert personnel. They brought much needed expertise and a plan to deal with the disaster from their experience in other parts of the world. The government and international agencies as well as NGOs all came up with blueprints of how to deal with a disaster of this magnitude, and in many respects they were similar.

Rescue and Relief

The first order of business was to assess the damage and plan rescue and relief operation. The people who were buried under the debris had to be rescued, and those who were injured needed medical treatment. Camps had to be set up to house the homeless, food distribution and sanitation arrangements had to be made, and clothing and blankets had to be provided. Appropriate arrangements had to be made to dispose of remains, both human and animal, to prevent the outbreak of communicable diseases. Transportation links had to be reopened, and debris had to be cleared. Communication had to be reestablished. The relief work, undertaken by various government and international organizations and NGOs, had to be coordinated. These steps had to be taken urgently and had to be completed successfully before moving on to the recovery efforts.

Rehabilitation

The rebuilding of the devastated area includes repairing the damage to all aspects of life that a human being cares about and works for. This is a long and arduous process that takes years. At a concrete level, houses, schools, libraries, temples, playgrounds, roads, bridges, airports, and railway stations have to be rebuilt. Those who lost their livelihood have to be assisted to restart their work or business. Cash has to be provided in the form of charity or loan to help them tide over the immediate hardship. Children have to start going back to school. Providing medical care for those who were injured and rehabilitation therapy for those who had lost body parts and preventing the outbreak of communicable diseases required careful planning and allocation of resources. Providing safe drinking water and sanitation remained a major challenge as long as people remained in the camp.

The plans provided by all the agencies did mention psychological rehabilitation, but they were mentioned only in passing under medical help and not laid out in any detail, as were plans for vaccination, transportation, rebuilding bridges, and providing acute medical care.

Psychological and Psychiatric Rehabilitation

At the human level, families have to be reunited, those who have lost loved ones have to be helped to deal with their grief and loss, those who have been injured have to be rehabilitated. At the psychological level, the loss of loved ones, of one's livelihood, of one's confidence, and of all that is familiar is more difficult to come to terms with. That this was a natural disaster in which people had almost no control, and that it could happen again without any warning, left people with an intense sense of vulnerability. The fear that gripped the city of Ahmedabad in the immediate days after the earthquake was palpable.

The initial rumors were that more than 100,000 people had perished. The final official figure was 20,005 for all of Gujarat and 751 for Ahmedabad. The figure for the injured was 166,000 of whom 20,717 were injured seriously, again for all of Gujarat. Many of the injured from all over Gujarat had to be brought to Ahmedabad or flown to Mumbai for treatment.

One of the roles that the media played was to provide facts and educate the public about the fundamentals of earthquakes. The scientists countered the rumors about the wrath of gods and when the next earthquake would strike (according to astrologers) by providing on TV graphic representation of the tectonic plates and how earthquakes occur, and how to protect oneself when earthquakes strike. The myth that the earth gave way because there was too much sin in the world, and that Armageddon was imminent, needed to be dispelled. One of the humorous results of all these belief systems was the exodus of daily wage earners, maids, household help, and cooks to their native villages. The middle class and rich of Ahmedabad were reduced to doing housework and cooking on their own, and one of my first jobs after landing in Ahmedabad was to go look for household help! All the five families (including my parents and myself) that were huddled at my in-laws' house had to share household chores.

TV was also helpful in reuniting families or sending messages to relatives by broadcasting a brief message from an individual describing his or her whereabouts and health. These messages were broadcast at various fixed times of the day. Psychiatrists also appeared on TV and wrote articles in newspapers to educate and reassure people who were deeply fearful and scared. The major task was to normalize the fear they were experiencing— giving simple, concrete directions about how to handle it and how to reassure and take care of children and to encouraging people to resume normal, daily activities.

The psychiatrists were busy in their practice taking care of their patients who were experiencing anxiety-related symptoms or having a relapse of a preexisting disorder. New patients with acute symptoms of severe anxiety, panic, or nightmares were placed on minor tranquilizers. Mental health workers had little time to provide therapy; the major task was to provide services to as many people as possible in dealing with the pervasive fear and to prevent the emergence of disorders such as posttraumatic stress disorder.

Status of Psychiatric Care and Mental Health in Ahmedabad

Ahmedabad, with a population of about two million, has two medical schools with a residency program in psychiatry. They have between them about 30 acute inpatient beds and an active outpatient service. There are about 60 psychiatrists in private practice, a few with their own five- to 10-bed inpatient facilities. These are all open units. There is also a state mental health hospital, which is a locked inpatient facility for chronic, long-term patients. There are a few, small, low-fee outpatient clinics, supported by religious or charitable organizations. Almost all the psychiatrists are members of the Gujarat Psychiatric Society, a district branch of the Indian Psychiatric Society. Psychologists and social workers have doctorates and master's-level degrees granted under the auspices of Gujarat University. These mental health professionals work at the medical schools; few have private practices.

Mental health and psychiatry are increasingly accepted by Indian society and recognized as part of mainstream medicine. The Mental Health Education and Research Trust has run several programs, educating the general population and medical practitioners (through the Ahmedabad Medical Association) on various mental disorders. I have participated in these programs during my annual visits to Ahmedabad, particularly on issues of child mental health.

The practice of psychiatry in India, however, is primarily limited to psychopharmacology and electroconvulsive therapy. Individual or group therapy may be practiced by a rare mental health practitioner and is referred to as "sittings" or counseling. Psychologists or social workers, either at medical schools or in private psychiatry offices, generally provide these services. The sheer number of patients at these clinics or in private practices leaves little time for therapy. In other words, the field of psychiatry post–managed care in the United States is where psychiatry has always been in Ahmedabad, India.

Being aware of the state of mental health in Ahmedabad, as a psychiatrist with exposure to the TWA and Egypt Air disasters off the coast of Long Island and Nantucket, I decided to go to India to provide assistance. There was a personal aspect—namely, to provide support and comfort to my parents who had gone through a severe trauma and were uprooted from their home. And Ahmedabad, my hometown, had an emotional pull; I wanted to give back to the community that had raised me and was instrumental in my education and accomplishments. I had maintained my ties to the community through my annual visits and my involvement in education in the area of mental health.

Mental Health Education and Research Trust

I have been an advisor to the Mental Health Education and Research Trust, a philanthropic organization, for the past several years. A meeting of various mental health professionals was held to assess the psychological trauma suffered by the population, to discuss ways to help alleviate the fear and anxiety that gripped the people, and to prepare the community to get back on its feet.

A meeting with the trustees was arranged under the chairmanship of Dr. Anil Shah.[1] The sheer enormity of the task was daunting. The total number of people who may need psychiatric services and the limited number of resources were a focus of intense discussion. The trustees readily agreed to have the resources of the trust available to provide free counseling service to anyone who needed it. It was up to we mental health professionals to come up with modalities of intervention that a few professionals can provide to reach a large number of people. Based on the concept of bereavement groups, I suggested that a group-counseling center be established. A therapist can see a group of about 8 to 16 for three or four sessions, which facilitates serving a maximum number of patients who need immediate assistance. We did not want to develop a waiting list because these patients were considered to be in a crisis situation and the goal was to provide relief of emotional distress on demand. Group therapy has been found to be helpful in various conditions, including bereavement, trauma, phobic and panic disorders, and substance abuse, to name a few.

A building near public transportation was secured courtesy of the Ahmedabad Municipal Corporation (City Hall). The Mental Health Education and Research Trust provided funds for administrative expenses. Residents in psychiatry training programs at local medical schools, as well as psychology and social work interns and students, agreed to volunteer their time. Senior psychiatrists agreed to provide supervision and even run some groups. The groups were formed according to members' experiences:

1. Those who had lost a loved one.
2. Those who had lost their belongings or business.
3. Those who had suffered no material loss but felt traumatized from the experience.
4. Those who had suffered from, or were actively suffering from, emotional disorders independent of the traumatic event.

---

[1] Dr. Anil Shah is a past president of the Indian Psychiatric Society and a former advisor on mental health to the government of Gujarat. He was professor of psychiatry at B. J. Medical College, where I received my medical education.

The Indian culture fosters interdependency and is sociocentric rather than egocentric (Desai and Coelho, 1980). Individuality and privacy are not encouraged, and family identity, sharing, and lack of boundaries are valued (Viswanathan, Shah, and Ahad, 1997). These characteristics lend themselves to group therapy. At the center, group members were encouraged to talk about their feelings and fears, the losses they had suffered, and their worries about the future. Venting frustration (directed at contractors for building structures that were substandard, for example) and sharing fears and worries were common activities in these groups. Group members were taught relaxation and breathing techniques such as *pranayanam* and *savasan* (yogic exercises). Meditation and yoga are indigenous to Indian culture (Chopra, 1987; Ornish, 1990). Deep breathing, chanting a mantra (both individually and in groups), and concentrating on a mantra (which can be deeply relaxing) are generally part of the daily routine as part of the morning prayers. These were incorporated as therapeutic interventions to reduce anxiety and panic, and the patients could use these techniques on their own (Mehta and Ochaney, 1987).

The patients who had histories of emotional disorders were referred to their own psychiatrists after the group sessions for ongoing treatment. A few patients who required medication for acute panic or ongoing nightmares were given a prescription and then referred to psychiatrists in their community for monitoring of their medication. There still remained a vast number who could not come to the center, including people in camps, nearby villages, and the community at large. Mental health professionals made some strategic decisions involving establishment of mobile crisis teams, training highly educated non–mental health professionals, and conducting meditation and yogic exercise in parks.

Mobile crisis teams were established to provide outreach services to the camps and nearby villages. Group therapy and supportive therapy teaching relaxation techniques were the main tools employed during these on-site visits, and in severe cases of anxiety, medications were prescribed and referral to a local psychiatrist was made. The mobile teams did not do psychiatric assessments. In the refugee camp, we came across a middle-aged woman who had lost all her belongings when her apartment crumbled. The only article that survived was a picture of her late mother (the frame and the glass were intact), which she was clutching to her heart and sobbing uncontrollably. She was consoled, encouraged to talk about her mother and later about her own fear of near death experience. She was then seen in group therapy.

A middle-aged man was upset and angry at the illegal construction (a swimming pool on the roof of his apartment complex) that resulted in the collapse of his building. His life savings had been lost, and he was distraught. After the initial venting of his anger, he was able to talk about how he had struggled and eventually prospered, how he was looking forward to a comfortable life, and how the earthquake had shattered his dream. He was seen in a group with other refugees with similar experiences.

The educated among the community, such as judges, lawyers, priests, and housewives with master's-level educations, were trained in meditation and yoga so that more volunteers were available to provide services in the community. They did not conduct psychiatric assessment of the people they saw, but only served as a means for people to vent their emotions and frustrations; they also taught meditation and yogic techniques to promote relaxation when panic or anxiety set in.

Many in the community go to the parks every morning for walks. This allowed us to gather large groups to conduct exercises in meditation and yoga (already part of the culture), thus reaching a large number of people who may otherwise have been reluctant or unable to come to the center (Singh, 1986). There was no psychiatric assessment of this group. One of the unintended benefits was the ability of those gathered to form small, impromptu groups to discuss and validate their feelings.

The counseling center functioned for about a year, and about 400 clients were served. Afterward, about 16 percent of the clients met the criteria for posttraumatic stress disorder. Acute panic and phobic disorders were the other most common diagnostic categories, and these subsided in the course of a few weeks. A few patients experienced a relapse or worsening of past disorders such as schizophrenia and affective disorders.

Personal Reflections

In 1956, a severe earthquake devastated Kutch. Tremors were felt in Ahmedabad, but there was no damage. As a junior high school student, I remember collecting money and used clothes from the neighborhood to send to the victims in Kutch.

The 2001 earthquake had caused considerable damage to Ahmedabad, a city in which I grew up, and the vivid pictures on CNN brought back those painful memories. I felt an inner drive to see the destruction and to help. An urgent call came from my parents, who instructed me not to come because it was unsafe. I was concerned about leaving my wife and children in the

United States and exposing myself to possible danger, but I decided to go. It was an extremely emotional experience.

Fear gripped the city initially, but the community pooled its resources and came together, the rich and the poor, the Hindus and the Muslims, the educated and the illiterate, the businessperson and the union worker. Young people worked night and day to dig out those buried under the debris and to rush the injured to the hospitals. Neighbors and relatives opened their homes to those who had lost theirs. Community kitchens sprang up in neighborhoods to feed those who had lost everything. The religious organizations and political parties pitched in with tremendous outreach at the grassroots level. The federal government, all the states of the Indian Republic, other countries of the world (including Pakistan, with which India has strained relations), and international organizations contributed to the relief and rescue efforts. Money, food, clothes, blankets, supplies, medicine, and personnel poured in. The natural disaster had brought the world together.

As these facts were registering in my psyche, filling me with positive emotions about the essential goodness of human beings, I was also aware that there was no systematic effort to help heal the psychological trauma that people suffered. The Mental Health Education and Research Trust provided a vehicle through which we were able to bring together mental health professionals, local government officials, and the business community. Resources were scarce, and the challenge was to use them efficiently. Incorporating the indigenous cultural value system and the alleviation of panic, anxiety, and fear through extremely powerful but inexpensive tools such as meditation and yoga was a creative breakthrough arrived at through deliberation with many gifted, caring, and giving professionals. Because the modalities of treatment were indigenous to Indian culture, we were able to reach a significant number of people, even with our very limited resources. Because this was a natural disaster, a strong fatalistic belief among the population was helpful in accepting what had happened (Viswanathan et al., 1997).

At a personal level, this was one of the most emotional and gratifying experiences of my career—emotional because it happened in the city in which I grew up and because my parents could have perished, and gratifying because I was able to give back to the community that had given so much to me. Finally, it taught me that the most important resources are not material, but human; when human beings join together, they can work wonders, and they can conquer any adversity. Cooperation and interdependency should be fostered worldwide as cultural values.

Summary

The earthquake that hit Gujarat on January 26, 2001, was one of the worst natural disasters in the history of the state. It claimed more than 20,000 lives, devastated the lives of millions, and left most of the population of 130 million people frightened. The relief efforts appear elaborate on paper but were marred by lack of coordination and communication between different organizations.

Psychological effects of disaster and interventions were a low priority for the major relief agencies. Group therapy, with emphasis on relaxation techniques and yogic exercises, was found to be helpful and could be taught by people outside the mental health professions. Expanding delivery to schools, colleges, parks, and gardens allowed a small group of mental health professionals to reach the population at large. Using indigenous techniques was also extremely cost-effective, and this is particularly important in a developing country with fewer resources.

On the basis of our experience, we have made the following recommendations to the state and federal governments:

1. Psychological rehabilitation should be an integral part of response to any disaster.
2. A mental health professional should be part of every medical team that responds to a disaster.
3. A manual should be prepared describing psychological interventions that include indigenous modalities, integral to the community, as demonstrated in our project.

References

Chopra, D. (1987), *Creating Health: Beyond Prevention, Towards Perfection*. Boston: Houghton Mifflin.

Desai, P. & Coelho, G. (1980), Indian immigrants in America: Some cultural aspects of psychological adaptation. In: *The New Ethnics: Asian Indians in the United States*, ed. P. Saran & E. Eames. New York: Praeger, pp. 369–386.

Mehta, M. & Ochaney, M. (1987), Assessing the efficacy of home practice relaxation procedure. *J. Pers. Clin. Stud.*, 3:145–147.

Ornish, D. (1990), *Dr. Dean Ornish's Program for Reversing Heart Disease*. New York: Ballantine Books.

Singh, R. H. (1986), Evaluation of some Indian traditional methods of promoting mental health. *Activitas Nervosa Superior,* 28:67–69.

Viswanathan, R., Shah, M. & Ahad, A. (1997), Asian-Indian Americans. In: *Cultural Issues in the Treatment of Anxiety,* ed. S. Friedman. New York: Guilford Press, pp. 175–195.

13

Occupational Psychiatry, Community Psychiatry, and Cultural Considerations in an Aviation Disaster

Mark L. Dembert

On September 2, 1998, Swissair Flight 111, bound from New York's JFK International Airport to Geneva, Switzerland, crashed at about 10:30 p.m. six miles off the coast of Nova Scotia, Canada, approximately 30 miles southeast of its capital city, Halifax. All 229 passengers and crew members aboard this McDonnell-Douglas MD-11 jumbo jet perished immediately. Subsequently, the Canadian government requested a large U.S. Navy diving and salvage ship with excellent lift capacity and many divers to assist Canadian Navy divers in recovering passenger remains and plane debris. Although U.S. Navy divers are used to working in hazardous diving environmental conditions and have recovered victims from military aircraft disasters, they have much less experience in recovering a relatively large amount of human remains, including those of children. This is where I came in.

On July 16, 1996, TWA Flight 800, bound from JFK to Paris, crashed off the Long Island coast after exploding in midair, killing all 220 passengers and crew members. Navy divers provided the major effort to recover human remains and debris. Mental health support was established for the divers by the navy's Special Psychiatric Rapid Intervention (SPRINT) Team 2 based at Naval Medical Center, Portsmouth, Virginia. Members of this team were sent in case divers or the ship's crew members had significant psychological distress in dealing with the human remains that had to be retrieved and then transferred to a temporary morgue. The diving conditions were murky, and the currents were strong. Diving operations took place around the clock, so divers were separated from their families for weeks. Few of the divers had any experience in recovering a large quantity of human remains.

I was involved on site as a member of the SPRINT team during the latter part of the operation. Subsequently, Lieutenant (LT) Chris Leffler, M.D., a navy physician assigned as diver support, and I conducted a cross-sectional survey of many of the divers to investigate the possibility of posttraumatic stress disorder (PTSD) or other anxiety disorders stemming from the operation (Leffler and Dembert, 1998). We found that the TWA 800 navy divers reported the recovery of adults' and children's remains and personal effects in an isolated diving environment, far from home support, to be more stressful than the hazardous nature of the diving. There was no evidence of cases of PTSD among the divers, compared with a set of navy divers unexposed to TWA 800. Last, the best coping factors were the rigorous navy diving training, phone contact with families, a sense of mission purpose and duty, and humor (especially gallows humor).

When the Swissair 111 disaster occurred, I was quickly requested to participate on site in a preventive occupational psychiatry role. Aside from being an experienced military psychiatrist with many years experience on SPRINT teams, I had additional preventive medicine residency, public health, and epidemiology training and practice. Perhaps most important for this mission, I had been a navy diver and diving medical officer for many years at the beginning of my career, and I had continued to work professionally with navy divers in various clinical and research policy positions until the Swissair disaster. The divers saw me as "one of them"—I had maximum credibility and entry into their tightly knit group.

I made detailed preparations for a trip of uncertain duration, weather extremes, and both physical and psychological demands. Aside from military uniforms and leisure clothes, I packed outerwear for the cold, blustery, late-autumn Canadian Atlantic maritime weather and athletic gear for exercise. Regular toiletries were augmented with a one-month supply of prescription and nonprescription items that could treat a spectrum of potentially impairing health problems. I also included a well-equipped Swiss Army knife, a glasses repair kit and an extra pair of glasses, an assortment of bandages, a finger cot in case of a small fingertip cut (especially problematic for typing and for pushing the camera shutter release, if on the dominant index finger), and a moleskin patch to cut and place on any foot blisters. I packed my toiletry kit keeping in mind that disaster response efforts would not wait while I took time, personnel, and a vehicle to search out a pharmacy in a far-off town to replace forgotten items.

I wore around my waist a flat, waterproof, under-the-shirt security pouch that contained my checkbook, my passport, my credit card, cash, and traveler's checks to cover any money requirements. I pared my wallet down to a minimum of photo identification cards. I wore dog tags around my neck that had basic information (civilians could have something similar made) for ease of identification if I were injured, for example, in a jogging accident or killed in a plane crash or other accident en route or on site. I also made sure my will was current and readily available to my wife. I never viewed myself as immune from a disaster befalling me when I traveled to a separate disaster affecting others.

I then completed the other arm of preparation, which was local briefings (with disaster mental health colleagues, flight surgeons with forensic aviation accident investigation experience, and navy diving and salvage authorities) and long-distance telephone briefings with navy staff on the diving and salvage ship USS *Grapple* at the crash site. I was most concerned about the divers regarding the environment (weather, ocean, living, and eating conditions), their mission readiness, their morale and camaraderie, the emotional climate on the ship in preparation for a psychologically unsettling task, and the current working relationships between the senior and junior divers.

My previous research on TWA 800 divers was put to good use in this operation, because a process of staged desensitization was used by the senior divers for the junior divers' advantage. In this, there was a gradual exposure, in the days before departure and after their arrival in Canada, to increasing amounts of information—technical diving, logistics, travel, and, most important, grisly aspects of remains recovery and hazardous diving conditions. A final step in this preparation involved showing underwater video footage, taken by a unmanned underwater drone, of the crash scene at the ocean floor, including whole and fragmented bodies either in the wreckage or floating eerily free in the currents.

The often turbulent, five-hour journey by small twin-engine military turboprop aircraft from Norfolk, Virginia, to the Halifax military airport on September 12 was an anxious one. I was queasy from the roller-coaster ride. I also frequently wondered if this was the type of ride and the anxiety the passengers and crew on the doomed Swissair jet experienced before it became clear the plane was doomed. I was happy to land safely at the Halifax airport, despite a driving late-afternoon rainstorm. The next morning I took a long walk through fog-enshrouded suburban Halifax streets. In practicing a previously helpful pattern of acclimation, I got a feel for the weather, the

terrain, the tempo of daily life, the traffic, the commercial aspects, the history, the recreation resources, the media, the language, the cultural nu-
ances, and the people through these initial walks. I stopped at a convenience store for needed currency exchange and a newspaper and talked
with the clerk about how the disaster was seen locally.

Later that morning, at the large naval installation in Halifax, I met up
with the rest of the U.S. Navy contingent in time for a comprehensive brief-
ing by the Canadian admiral in charge of the entire operation. Assembled in
the windowless command center were Canadian military personnel, Royal
Canadian Mounted Police (RCMP), Canadian and U.S. transportation
board investigators, Canadian government and ambassador representatives, and U.S. consular representatives. The RCMP were the overriding
authority on the handling of all wreckage, remains, and personal effects, because these were considered evidentiary in light of the undetermined and
thus suspicious cause of the crash.

The tempo and procedure of the daily briefings for the admiral were set:
the answers to his probing questions were to be brief, informative, and
without speculation; no one spoke unless first asked a question by the admiral. When I impulsively offered a spontaneous comment on the challenge of recovering human remains, I was met with uniformly disapprov-
ing glances from the admiral and his staff. I had learned this protocol
lesson the hard way.

I had first requested quarters on the *Grapple* but was informed that there
was no extra room. Thus, by midafternoon I was settled at the Century
House, a homey bed-and-breakfast inn along the tiny shoreline of the
wind-whipped village of Blandford, some 40 miles by car from Halifax. I
asked for the room whose window faced the direction of the crash site over
the near horizon. Looking out of the window provided a sobering emotional
link to the mission on days I didn't visit the *Grapple*.

Daily support runs by boat of personnel and supplies to the crash site left
from Blandford; the local fishing industry made available its factory and
docks in full support of boat transportation (including their own boats at
times) and storage of supplies and diving gas. This was also the staging point
for transporting VIPs to the site.

About 15 driving miles back up the coast was the 55-inhabitant village
of Peggy's Cove, apparently the land point closest to the crash site, six
miles away. Peggy's Cove had been a tourist attraction primarily because
its scenic location, its massive shoreline granite rock formations, and its
whitewashed lighthouse above the crashing waves had become a photo

opportunity and a post office rather than the crucial navigation beacon it had been for generations of fishermen. In response to the Swissair disaster, the international media congregated in Peggy's Cove because one could see diving and support ships on the horizon directly from this village, and the historic stone promontory and lighthouse became a backdrop for all of the media-generated human interest stories as well as for updates on diving operations.

By evening that first day at Blandford, I had formulated a comprehensive plan of goals and roles for me, not limited to mental health support for the divers.

My disaster psychiatry work over the years had been informed by two philosophies. First was a caveat I conceived: *When you see an individual, think of a group; when you see a group, think of an individual.* Simply explained, every person I come in contact with during a response effort brings with him or her the family of origin, family mythologies and traumas, personal successes and failures, personal traumas, relationships to the community, as well as past and present work relationships and attachments to the organization and the formal building(s) where work is done. All of these shape the current physical and mental state of that individual. When I work with a group, I look at preexisting and expected within-group interactions and dynamics and the group's relatedness in the context of the larger community of families and businesses. But I also keep in mind how each individual within the group shapes group context and response. Both aspects of that caveat are mutually dependent and interlocking and represent the essence of the challenge of disaster mental health efforts.

My second philosophy has always been that I could be the most effective consultant and counselor when I knew as much as possible about the lives of the dead and the survivors, as well as the jobs that first responders and those who recovered wreckage and human remains had to do. I had to put myself in others' shoes no matter how physically or emotionally challenging the experience. I knew that there was a risk of becoming so involved in some aspects such as mortuary work that it could be psychologically traumatizing for me, but I countered that with good judgment, controlled exposure, and informal talks with workers such as pathologists and mortuary technicians during coffee breaks. I also knew that taking photographs of every situation and every community provided me with a sustaining visual connection to the land, the people, and the culture, both for my time there and for after I returned to Virginia. Finally, I also knew that by traveling around to local communities and through the city of Halifax—walking, talking, sitting, seeing—or even to places where I could sojourn and simply absorb the weather, the coastline, and the geography, I would further immerse myself in the culture and local perspectives of recent events.

To be the most effective consultant and resource in disaster mental health work requires taking on many roles, many of which I have assumed in clinical psychiatry work. I have routinely served as a parent, a family authority figure, a religious figure, an anthropologist or sociologist, a journalist, a historian, a teacher, and so forth—sometimes for a single patient, at other times for a group. Following are among the roles I foresaw as most challenging and most fruitful in this operation, pending approval (later granted) from my seniors:

1. To serve as a consultant to my boss, the commodore, on any mental health matter, even if not applicable to the divers.
2. To provide routine or emergent psychiatric evaluations for any military personnel at the site or billeted nearby on shore.
3. To set up a surveillance system for mission-impairing psychopathology among ship's crew and divers, both during the operation and on return to Virginia.
4. To work closely as a disaster mental health expert with assigned Canadian military physicians.
5. To be available as a mental health consultant on the psychological hazards to military mortuary personnel and RCMP staff handling human remains and personal effects of adults and children.
6. To serve as a consultant resource for Canadian military or civilian mental health care providers in conducting short-term or crisis intervention groups, as well as setting up long-term support groups in Halifax and coastal communities around the disaster site.
7. To travel to local coastal communities around the crash site and informally assess the impact of the crash on each community's daily life, its citizens, and its economy.
8. To immerse myself in the history of maritime and other disasters in Nova Scotia.
9. To set up an effective reunion-and-homecoming adjustment program for the divers and the *Grapple* crew on their return to Virginia.

My mission began in earnest the morning of September 14 and finished on September 28 with my flight back to Virginia. I established a daily routine: a long walk for stress management, regular meals and good sleep as much as possible, review of notes and writing while observations were fresh in my mind, planning for the next day, review of newspapers and magazines for coverage of the disaster and all of the international commercial and legal manifestations, laundry, and venturing out in the nearby towns and villages. I was on call 24/7 by cell phone for meetings, briefings, advice, emergencies, consultation, telephone calls from the SPRINT team leader in Virginia, and changes in departed boat runs from Blandford to the *Grapple*.

When I first arrived in Blandford, I met with the navy diving medical officer LT Fred Lindsay and the *Grapple*'s master diver about the work schedules and the rotations to allow each diver a 24-hour period on shore to "recharge batteries" mentally and physically. The ocean water was very cold, and the currents, both at the surface and 190 feet below, were strong. The operations would involve precise timing of divers entering the water, reaching depth, leaving the bottom, going through partial required decompression stops on the way up, and then being quickly brought up for rapid removal of diving suits and gear and immediate recompression in the shipboard hyperbaric chamber (down to the equivalent pressure of the outside last depth stop in the water) with a final controlled decompression to the "surface." This was truly hazardous diving all around. The risk of injury from sharp debris, air embolism from unplanned sudden ascent, decompression sickness from too long at depth, or emotional shock from human remains suddenly popping up into the beam of an underwater light—essentially right in the diver's face—were omnipresent.

I phoned the *Grapple* for updates on days when I was not scheduled to visit it. When LT Lindsay and the master diver were on shore for brief R&R, I could catch up on how things really were, over a cup of coffee or a beer. It was important that I worked behind the scenes. The divers knew I was around, several of them knew of my past work as a navy diver and diving medical officer, but the last thing needed on a small ship was a psychiatrist watching everyone. It would be distracting for routine, the ship's crew would use a lot of energy to keep away from me for fear of being evaluated, and divers would worry that something must be going wrong for me to be there so often.

In the military, the psychiatrist is challenged every day with fitness-for-duty and workplace evaluations. There are many personnel who welcome the chance of an evaluation and hope to convince the psychiatrist of the need to recommend discharge from the service. For those with special training and positions such as divers or pilots, however, a psychiatric evaluation for whatever reason, even if for brief counseling or stress management for nonmilitary issues, is generally feared as a black mark in the health record and a likely recommendation for removal from special duties. This is unfortunately based on stigmatization of mental health problems, the frequent use of mental health evaluations to remove a "bad apple" from a command without any chances for rehabilitation, and lore among specialty groups that to see a psychiatrist means one is "crazy." From a system perspective, in my experiences, military psychiatrists are traditionally viewed as tools used to find out what is wrong in a situation, an organization, or a person, not what is right or adaptive. For me to accomplish the latter on the *Grapple*, I needed to be involved, aware, and vigilant, yet only peripherally visible. I had to be an observer of group dynamics and varying stress levels. So I maximized my time by getting around unobtrusively: talking to crew at cigarette breaks, going inside to watch underwater video surveillance of the operations, visiting the communications "shack," hanging out with the cooks in the galley, perusing maps and weather charts, and using my binoculars to watch what all the other ships out there were doing.

I walked out to the fantail area at the stern of the *Grapple* when there was a break in diving operations. I looked out over the water, and then looked down at the water surrounding the ship. We were moored directly over the crash site. Water does not soften the impact of an airplane crash. It is like hitting concrete at high speed. I thought of people on board at that time, realizing imminent death as the crippled and smoke-filled plane lost flight ability and turned downward, perhaps rolled, and then dove several thousand feet straight down. I thought of the words of Nova Scotia's chief medical examiner, Dr. John Butt, in his makeshift office at the airfield hangar morgue. He privately told me the impact was so great that the sudden acceleration forces caused some bodies literally to pop out of their skin. He described how the huge tail engine compressed the rest of the fuselage in front of it at impact, shattering the plane into possibly millions of fragments. This was supported by the divers' recovery efforts to date, which found, aside from intact landing gear, few pieces as big as a small car and most less than 10 feet in any diameter.

I shuddered when I looked at the water around the ship and thought of the terrible destruction below. Previously seeing it on the basically two-dimensional ship's video monitor did not elicit a comparable emotional reaction. I hoped that the flight surgeon present with Dr. Butt and me was right when she said that passengers and crew may have lost consciousness before impact due to the tremendous G-forces of the plane's final dive. The likely voices and screams of passengers during that initial dive were hard to keep out of my mind. I looked around the fantail at the fenced-off piles of wreckage. I looked at some of the body bags, filled at the bottom with remains and zippered shut so that no one would have to see them here at the surface. They were taken by small boat transfer to the Canadian command ship and then flown by helicopter directly to the large morgue set up back at the Halifax military air base.

In my previous disaster response work, I had made sure that I got to know the expectations and ground rules quickly, not only from the highest in charge but also from the person who was responsible for overall site operations and safety. In the present situation, my commodore was completely responsible for my well-being and my performance at all times, and I knew what he expected from me. But I also met with the commanding officer (CO) of the *Grapple*, Lieutenant Commander (LCDR) Dave Davis. A ship's CO has ultimate authority and responsibility for the welfare of everyone on his or her ship as well as for who can be on the ship and who cannot. The CO is like the old-fashioned boss mayor of a small city. The captain's eagle on my collar and the diving and submarine insignias and the ribbons above my uniform shirt pocket all gave me initial visual credibility with him and his officers. How I conducted myself, however, first as a naval officer— knowing when and how both to speak and act in a military manner and then in other situations with familiarity—and how I presented my professional role in supporting his ship and divers earned his respect. I told him he could reach me for assistance in any matter, psychiatric or not. He knew I would stay out of his way on the ship and generally not talk with him unless, again, he spoke first. When diving operations were at a lull, chatter and banter did appear, however.

Although all of this traditional protocol was commonplace in the military, it applied equally well in civilian operations, including the earning of respect, because of the increasing use of an incident commander and the hierarchy of command, control, and emergency operations center systems.

LCDR Davis was also ultimately responsible for the safe conduct of everything diving and nondiving that went on aboard the *Grapple*. He and the diving operations were under constant scrutiny from the media, U.S. and Canadian admirals, consular officials, RCMP, Swissair representatives, and the Canadian and U.S. transportation safety board senior investigators. In my opinion, it seemed that these and other stakeholders who were not ship's crew or involved in diving operations wanted to be on *Grapple*, even for a very brief visit. I sensed a hint of entitlement or insistence that many times lurked behind altruism. It was enough to be on the ship, but meeting the CO appeared to confer almost reverential status on the visitor. There were bona fide reasons related to the mission to visit, but other reasons could have had deeper psychological explanations.

Bottom line, this was a disaster in which a large number of people from all walks of life and ages had lost their lives suddenly, in a situation beyond their control, and yet they were undoubtedly aware of facing death and had time to reflect on it for several minutes. It happened at night, and thus there was no visual orientation, no ability to see land or to gauge distances to a hoped-for safe landing. Most did not have their full families present for comfort. Although death happened instantaneously on impact, it is up for speculation whether passengers and crew were awake and aware of impending death during the agonal dive. This method of dying, in contemplation, is for the average person the "worst nightmare." Perhaps in a sense of unconsciously confronting one's worst fear of dying, visiting a crash site and especially people in charge, may confer a magical sense of "This can't happen to me, now, because it happened to so many other people, right here."

By visiting the site and seeing the operations and talking with people in charge, it may additionally confer a sense of undoing or absolution: "I am having these grisly and morbid thoughts, but these people here must have these also. Therefore, it is okay for me to have them, and I won't be punished for them or die like the people here did." Perhaps there is a healthy element to this: "If I visit this site where this happened to so many people, I can conquer my fear [of an interpersonal conflict, extreme emotion, or impairing behavior] and go about my life in a renewed and more satisfying way."

I based these explanations on what came into my own awareness as I monitored my feelings and thoughts during my visits to the crash site and to the morgue; I assumed they could apply to others. I emphasize another caveat: This "I was there" phenomenon should be considered by cognizant mental health consultants before undertaking any response effort to a disaster in which many perished in circumstances of possible awareness of impending death. The individual human need for connection on the basis of the previous hypotheses can interfere with the ability of those in charge to remain focused on the safe and effective conduct of rescue or recovery operation, as well as place visitors who do not really need to be there in harm's way.

A very necessary goal was to develop a good working relationship with LCDR Heather Mackinnon, M.D., who was the Canadian Navy's fleet support medical officer assigned to the operation. She was a flight surgeon and diving medical officer in her own right. She had been a military physician at sea and in foreign countries for many years, and she was highly regarded for her organizational and consensus-building abilities. We met at the Century House late afternoon my first day there. She was in the chain of command of more senior operational medical officers and ultimately with the Canadian admiral and thus handled many "hot potato" issues, from all over the world, daily. I helped her by doing "reccys," her term for community and military reconnaissance and information gathering. In other words, I became her direct eyes and ears for the progress of the diving operations on both the U.S. and Canadian diving ships. I also visited, with her introduction, the Canadian Navy command ship HMCS *Preserver* and offered any assistance to the CO.

LCDR Mackinnon invited me to consult with the military social worker at the Halifax military hospital who headed up all Critical Incident Stress Management (CISM) efforts for this operation. CISM is a system of brief, focused mental health interventions initially developed in the United States to provide support for first responders (EMT, fire, police) who can be overwhelmed psychologically or emotionally by small or large disasters with a significant magnitude or spectrum of loss of life (Mitchell and Everly, 1996). This system, now international in use, includes the standard Critical Incident Stress Debriefing (CISD) model and has expanded in application to incidents where there is psychological or physical trauma but no loss of life. It has also been used for survivors of an incident and their families, classmates, and coworkers, as well as for human remains handlers. In this disaster, the social worker recommended it be made mandatory for all those involved to go through, even if they did not have any psychological symptoms, did not see a need for it, and were functioning well in their eyes and the eyes of superiors.

I took a somewhat different view and expressed my opinion that it should not be made mandatory but be reserved for those persons who requested help or whose bosses were in a position to request such help. Otherwise, I had found that similar to the TWA 800 disaster, camaraderie and mission purpose were very strong group and individual coping skills for any expected situational psychological symptoms. Even when some type of intervention was needed in other disasters, I described how a tailored approach with elements of CISD admixed with group dynamics or follow-up support group venues were highly effective for specific workers or survivors. My opinions were respectfully considered, but, in the end, CISM was used extensively.

LCDR Mackinnon and I agreed we were sailing uncharted waters in this disaster recovery effort. This type of disaster was unique in Canada, where maritime populations are sadly accustomed to losses of fishermen at sea. Canadians were not used to airplanes "falling out of the sky." This one, although it did crash at sea off the coast, had circled around settled coastal areas while it was in distress, and many of the local citizens heard it that night. Many smelled the aviation fuel dumped on land before its hoped-for emergency landing at Halifax, and many heard the actual explosion at impact. Local fisherman spontaneously went to sea to investigate and found adult and children remains, personal effects, and wreckage surrounding their boats. Others living along the coast found body parts or personal effects or wreckage washing up on shore, even near homes. For the first time, the Canadian citizens—some in Halifax, but many along the shore—felt vulnerable with the realization of jumbo jets that routinely traced paths over their areas on nightly transatlantic flights from U.S. international airports to Europe. Besides, fishing boat losses claimed adult lives, and except for isolated deaths of children due to trauma or diseases, Canadian citizens were not used to having children die in a large numbers in such a horrific way, all at once, near their shores.

On board the *Grapple,* there were no diving-related injuries or cases of decompression sickness, the divers' physical output was huge, and morale and camaraderie were outstanding. Many of the junior divers reported that they were better prepared by the staged desensitization for the grisly task ahead of them. They felt supported by the senior and master divers. The scheduled 24-hour off-duty rotations on shore helped immensely, as did phone calls to home. LCDR Davis took time to hold an awards ceremony one afternoon to reinforce crew and diver morale. The senior divers absorbed much of the anxiety and day-to-day worry, but it helped greatly when they vented among themselves or to LT Lindsay or me. There was one case of decompression sickness in a Canadian diver, but his treatment was straightforward and successful.

There were no reports of possible stress disorder symptoms from LT Lindsay or the master diver over the 15 days. Aside from these verbal reports, however, I set up an informal surveillance system at the building where the divers ate and slept off duty. I took the navy cooks assigned there aside on my second day, complimented them about their food after eating a meal with them (they appreciated that from a senior officer!) and talked to them about the stress of being deployed, the uniqueness of this mission, and some of the stresses to be expected on the divers. The cooks knew that the divers were a macho group overall (men and women divers alike here) and that they tended to keep fear and anxiety well compartmentalized and usually well hidden. I told the cooks they could really assist me by being my eyes and ears, watching for any signs of divers in the chow line or at tables acting out of character, sullen, excessively reactive or withdrawn, or even anxiety stricken, smoking if never before or now in larger amounts. When I told them I would check with them daily, and I met with them and their supervisory chief petty officer (giving the cooks compliments in front of the chief cemented the deal), they were "on board." They did a good job and eagerly reported what they saw. I also hung out at meal times when possible, but not too much to raise suspicions, and ate with the divers or ship's crew and engaged in banter, all to take the emotional pulse as a whole. We saw no early indications of stress disorders.

With introductions arranged by my Century House hosts David and Mieke Martin, I was able to meet with hosts of other local inns where senior navy divers spent off hours. I set up an informal surveillance system whereby the hosts could contact my hosts, who would then tell me if there were any indications of problems brewing as discussed by the senior divers.

At LCDR Mackinnon's request, I visited the billeting and operations sites of the Canadian divers on shore. I also walked along the shoreline accompanying Canadian soldiers on wreckage and remains reconnaissance. I felt a sense of excitement at finding some small pieces of cabin insulation. I also experienced the sinking feeling in my gut and the visceral apprehension when I spotted pieces of colorful fabric and as I approached each one of them, wondered if there would be a head or torso or hand or a foot or a chunk of flesh attached to it. (I remembered quite well in the first *Jaws* movie when the torso of the woman swimmer was confirmed with the emetic accompaniment of the police deputy!) I never did discover remains along the shoreline.

I confronted this issue head on when I first learned about the huge temporary morgue set up at the military air base. Dr. John Butt was thrust into the international spotlight from the first day of the disaster, and it remained along with intense governmental and media pressure for weeks and weeks. He described how families of victims called him at all hours from around the world, wanting to know if a loved one's remains had been identified, how that person(s) had died, and when the remains could be released for burial. He did not have many answers at all for the first many days, and callers were angry. He described a rapid and intense burnout that required him to step away from the case for small periods of time. He was feeling better when I met with him, but he lectured me on the need for any psychiatrist involved in mass disaster work not to overlook the emotional states of the medical examiners and quietly and collegially take them aside before burnout starts.

Dr. Butt took me back to the actual morgue area. I looked at all of the equipment for remains identification. I picked up and handled clear specimen bags filled with pieces and parts of torsos or extremities or organs or flesh and muscle, tagged but waiting to be identified.

I went into autopsy rooms and stood with forensic pathologists or dentists over torsos, almost all headless and cut up. I looked at family-supplied dental x-rays posted on view boxes beside x-rays of mandible or maxilla fragments, used in hopes of finding a match with the actual specimens on tables in front of us. Finally, I met with the courageous young soldiers who handled and tagged remains and assisted in autopsy rooms. They had volunteered for this job; several of the women and men said they were mothers or fathers and they felt very deeply for mothers and fathers who lost children or adult parents in this disaster. They said it was the least they could do to help the operation, to work in a job that most did not want to do. They coped in many ways—smoke breaks, gallows humor, being able to take breaks when they wanted, being able to call home freely to other parts of Canada, and having a supervisor who in this situation was not as keen on uniform appearance as he was on working as a team.

Not to be forgotten, and no less of a stress, were the personal effects. I handled small sealed clear bags of personal effects in the presence of the RCMP investigator who was assigned on the Canadian ship to husband them until their helicopter transport to the base. With an increasing sadness I sifted through luggage pieces, dolls, clothing items, jewelry, reading glasses, books, papers, pens, cards, business items, diaries, and gifts. Most disturbing to me, as I held one in my hand, were passports. I looked at one of a very attractive, blonde, 30ish-looking woman in apparent business suit, smiling at the camera. I read her name. I was so upset by this, seeing the face and knowing she no longer existed, that smile full of hope and travel. I turned the passport over immediately, noticed that it was a non-U.S. passport, and handed it back to the RCMP man. When I took a photograph of him with the pile of bagged personal effects, for future lecture purposes, I made sure any passports were turned cover side out. He said he coped knowing it was part of his duties, but the sadness etched on his face silently asked me to talk no more about this work.

I drove to Peggy's Cove along scratchy dirt roads alternating with paved narrow roads that wound and catapulted and dove along the variegated coastline of conifers on one side and homes and lobster traps along the other. On this little spit of land I finally found a parking spot, hidden from view behind a gift store with all of the media trucks and RVs and their gardens of antennas and satellite dishes. In a biting cold headwind, blinded by a

dazzling sunshine reflecting as millions of diamond needles from the spar-
kling blue water, I walked up the road to the light house, sitting precariously
on the rocky promontory pounded by large waves. I bought postcards at the
cozy post office, read history posters describing the origin of Peggy's Cove,
and listened to the veritable polyglot of languages spoken by curious tourists
from monster buses and frazzled media technicians decked out in the latest
Army–Navy store cold-weather clothing. I scanned the horizon with my
binoculars and recognized the *Grapple* and other support vessels six miles
away, little antlike silhouettes on the ocean surface. I imagined what it
might have been like to be sitting in a small boat out there on the night of
September 2, watching this large jet come speeding down from the sky and
crash into the surface. I couldn't think about it any more and walked back to
the gift shop, bought a stained glass window hanging of a traditional
three-masted clipper ship, and talked with the cashier about year-round life
in Peggy's Cove.

On an emotional dare to myself, I walked back up to the wall near the
base of the lighthouse. Mourners, tourists, and family members had left
large beribboned flower bouquets, stuffed animals, photos, poems, cards,
signs, and even clothing at this very poignant monument. I read the cards
and signs and slowly looked over all the objects. I spent a remaining few
minutes reading and rereading a beautiful card with a very personal and lyrical poem written underneath a photo of a couple obviously in love, with
heads touching at the temples, smiling, late 50s–looking, enjoying that moment. I took some photos of the cove area, the lighthouse, the horizon, and
the monument—from afar. Then I went up and took a close-up photo of the
couple and the card and poem. It was the reminder I needed, the photographic linchpin of any disaster psychiatry lecture in the future, on the
frailty and preciousness of human life.

Within about a 15-mile radius from Blandford, I went to several
small villages and dawdled over lunches in the typical convenience
store/post office/diner/bait-and-tackle shop/toy store/supermarket/currency
exchange/meeting place, all rolled into one. I usually wore my U.S. Navy
khaki uniform, which invited local civilians and military types to approach me and ask me how I happened into their village. I told them I
was a doctor on the staff of the U.S. Navy team assisting the Canadian
government and military in the Swissair recovery effort. That was an
excellent lead for me to ask them about their lives, their views of the
crash, and how it affected their village—for instance, human remains
washing up, the presence of aviation gas, the fears of local children, and
local history.

I perused bookstores and bought books while I talked with the managers. I only volunteered that I was a psychiatrist when someone asked me about my medical specialty. I had already talked with my bed-and-breakfast hosts, LCDR Mackinnon, and some of the mental health staff at the military hospital who lived and practiced part-time in this area. They had warned me that psychiatrists and counselors were looked on with a great deal of skepticism and wariness among the maritime communities culture. Mental illness was not something people talked about; admitting to mental or emotional symptoms was seen as tantamount to being weak-willed, and bearing sadness and despair privately in the context of personal or economic hardship was necessary so that the image and success of the traditional self-sufficient maritime family were maintained at all costs. The frequent response to my revealing that I was a psychiatrist was much nervous laughter with a comment to the effect that I may find a lot of mentally ill people in the area. It seemed to be their way of ending the conversation gracefully.

I visited groups of fishermen and talked with them on their boat runs out to the *Grapple*. Many had taken their boats into fuel slicks and had bumped against remains and personal effects and small debris that night after the crash or during the next couple of days. They didn't like talking about these experiences. What prompted talk was the economic impact of the government closing the rich fishing and lobstering grounds of the crash site while recovery operations went on; the closure extended for miles because of the current's effects on the wreckage field. This was an important time of year, before the winter arrived, for fishing and lobstering. There was talk of financial subsidies and reparations to the fishermen, but many uncertainties swirled around who would pay this money, whether it would be enough, and whether it would come in time. I looked beyond their extremely vocal discussion on this topic and saw underneath psychological hurt and confusion over the enormity of the disaster and the exposure to remains and personal effects. I saw these were fairly well masked to maintain the age-old bravura needed for this way of life. A few said they would consider counseling or even CISD, but they were not enthusiastic about it.

To round out my appraisal of the magnitude of the disaster, I spent a day of appointments at the Halifax military hospital, meeting with other fleet medical officers like LCDR Mackinnon and talking to them about my experiences with many disasters at sea or in hospitals. I also met individually with members of the mental health department, predominantly social workers and psychologists, some retired military. They provided me with their observations of Halifax, the province of Nova Scotia, the military, the civilian sides of disasters, and the coping strengths and weaknesses they have seen in their civilian practices and military patients. The culture accepts violent deaths of fishermen at sea and loss of their boats from storms or accidents as a necessary risk of growing up and working and providing for a family here. People did not seek mental health care for such losses, and traditionally church and community banded together to help the bereaved. Violence in the form of fights, even alcohol related, was accepted as tradition. While death from an accident at shore was accepted, however, murder in general and violent deaths of children were exceedingly uncommon and thus hard for communities to resolve. Many times the first true appearance of problems from these was noted in comments or questions by schoolchildren to teachers and parents. Mental health care was sought if the counselor or therapist was a local-born person who came back to practice. A mental health care provider not from the local community would not be trusted and would be used only reluctantly. The Swissair crash was completely out of the expected, and already some of the mental health care providers were hearing patients nervously talk about, "What does it mean for this area?" and "Why did it happen here?"

I drove to Halifax on other daylong occasions. Aside from military briefings, I walked the downtown areas to get an urban feel for Nova Scotia nationality and culture and commerce. I went to historical museums. I was introduced to a very gracious and engaging retired couple, Allan and Margaret Green, who welcomed me into their home, gave me tours of Halifax, and invited me to Rosh Hashanah services for the Jewish New Year. Notwithstanding my spiritual needs being taken care of, I was very moved by the services, the congregation, and the formal recognition and prayers for those passengers on Swissair 111 who were identified as Jewish.

Halifax was not without its visible history of maritime disasters and personal losses. One cemetery I visited, a peaceful, grassy, hillside enclave set beside a busy thoroughfare, contained graves of more than 150 *Titanic* dead. I looked out over the harbor where the huge 1917 explosion of a French munitions vessel in Halifax harbor killed more than 2,000 people and destroyed half the city. Many Nova Scotia young men who joined the military as duty never returned from world wars.

As the recovery effort yielded debris to generate hypotheses and remains to identify most of the 229 victims, and with winter weather approaching that would make it absolutely untenable for diving operations, the U.S. Navy effort began to wind down.

I had completed two psychiatric evaluations on request from LCDR Davis and the master diver. One, a fairly experienced diver, had earlier requested permission to stop diving and go home. There was a tremendous amount of family stress over preparing for a move to another duty station across the country, which would happen soon, and he was having trouble focusing on his work. After I reassured the master diver there was no stress disorder or other cause, he was given permission to leave. The second evaluation was for an older but lower ranking sailor on the ship whose eccentricities and interpersonal friction had so isolated him, he talked of suicidal or homicidal thoughts. I made a diagnosis of likely personality disorder that was a detriment to morale now and likely for continued service. LCDR Davis agreed to send him back to the squadron office in Virginia to be off the ship and for further mental health evaluation. The sailor was in a calmer frame of mind as he flew out the next day.

Right before I left Nova Scotia, I wrote up a two-page reunion-and-homecoming advice memorandum for all the navy members of the mission to read before their return to Norfolk. I described how this particular mission had been a psychological challenge to diver and nondiver alike. I described some of the expected stresses they might feel on returning home to family and friends who had no idea what it had been like up here; I discussed the frustrations of trying to explain what they did as well as needing time to decompress and not talk about the mission. I ended it with a list of helpful and practical daily strategies for reunion.

LT Lindsay and I conceived of a practical way for him and the master diver to keep an informal surveillance system going on return to Virginia, aided by the eyes and ears of the senior divers and the diving medical technicians. They would be on the lookout for symptoms of stress disorders or uncharacteristic individual patterns of poor work performance or attitude, drinking more than before, marital conflict, family violence, and dire financial straits. I would provide any urgent evaluations thought necessary. As it turned out, none were ever needed.

I checked out with my new Canadian friends and associates, getting their promises to send me future newspaper clippings, magazine stories, or books describing the investigation. I also arranged to keep in periodic contact with two therapists for updates on noteworthy community reactions to the disaster and the investigation.

As I prepared to leave, I reflected on my recognition that this operation was the milestone of my military disaster mental health career. It combined so many (cultural, occupational, community, preventive, organizational, individual, emergency, disaster, environmental) psychiatry roles, it required immersion in the lives and work of so many people, and it forced me to confront my own deepest fears of (loss of control over) death and dying in ways I never had foreseen. I had been in a situation in which I was most effective by remaining on the periphery with preventive plans set in place; had something bad happened, I would be under international scrutiny with the diving operations temporarily in the balance while I acted. As I boarded the airplane, I looked back with a measure of satisfaction that all did go well.

I flew back to Virginia on September 28 on the very same aircraft as my September 12 flight. This one was a smooth flight.

References

Leffler, C. & Dembert, M. (1998), Posttraumatic stress symptoms among U.S. Navy divers recovering TWA Flight 800. *J. Nerv. Ment. Dis.*, 186:574–577.

Mitchell, J. & Everly, G. (1996), *Critical Incident Stress Debriefing: An Operations Manual for the Prevention of Traumatic Stress Among Emergency Services and Disaster Personnel*, 2nd ed. Ellicott City, MD: Chevron.

14

Becoming a Disaster Psychiatrist in Turkey

Pamela J. Edwards

Long before I went to medical school, I wanted to work as a medical mission-ary, but once I decided to become a psychiatrist I concluded that wish would never be realized. Then one day, on the evening news in 1999, I saw footage of an American psychologist working with Kosovar refugee children in Al-bania under the auspices of Northwest Medical Teams International (a nongovernmental organization that provides medical care and supplies in disaster situations around the world). I thought that if they sent psycholo-gists, they would surely send psychiatrists. I felt called to this work, and be-fore the newscast ended I phoned Northwest Medical Teams and began a process that ultimately resulted in my being scheduled to go to Albania in August 1999. At the time, it appeared that the refugees would be in Albania for many months, far into the fall and winter. At this point, I did not person-ally know any psychiatrist colleagues who had disaster experience. Some colleagues admired my plan, and others asked, "Are you crazy?" Then in July 1999, far sooner than anticipated, the refugees returned to Kosovo, and the clinics where I would have worked in Albania were quickly closed. Thus, op-portunity to help in this disaster evaporated instantaneously. Despite my de-sire to go, I had a sense of relief because of the potential dangers involved. Other physician colleagues of mine who had returned from Albania before I was to leave told of experiences in which their lives were jeopardized due to open gunfire. Although I missed out on what would have been my first disas-ter, I was given pause to prepare myself psychologically for future disaster work, at least to the degree that this is possible without prior experience. With no end to disasters in this world, I knew another opportunity would avail itself, but of course I had no idea what, when, or where, and that uncertainty is one feature of disaster work that appeals to me—you never know what, when, or where, nor does anyone.

The second call to a disaster came from Northwest Medical Teams International several months later when I was asked to go to Turkey after the earthquakes and work in a clinic in an earthquake relief camp. By this time, the acute phase of the disaster had passed, the clinic was established, and most of the patients were being seen for typical outpatient maladies. I understood that I would function as a psychiatrist, incorporating some basic general medicine as needed. I and an internist from Seattle comprised the team and away we went, with surprisingly little orientation, which left me uneasy. We flew all night from the West Coast through Chicago, and on to Istanbul. We were picked up at the airport, hot, jet-lagged, and grimy, by an American physician who worked for World Relief and oversaw the medical clinics in several camps along the earthquake zone, which extended over a hundred miles. It was a 90-minute, high-speed ride (through air pollution so thick you could cut it with a knife) to Derince, a small town where the relief camp was located. The camp was situated on the outskirts of town, on a gently sloping hillside where shepherds with sheep meandered the hillsides. Verdant hills and beautiful vegetation surrounded the camp, and a winding river was visible in the distance. On arrival, there were 32 patients waiting to see the two of us. Never mind that we had been in transit around the globe for more than 24 hours, and hadn't even had time to wash up or take a rest. We looked at the patients, and they looked at us, and from the looks in their eyes we knew there was no alternative but to begin our work. I quickly became aware that none of the patients came to the clinic specifically for a psychiatric complaint; however, even across cultural boundaries, it was easy to detect a psychiatric problem. I made a rather instantaneous transition to a general physician and was surprised how much general medical knowledge was available to me from my own memory. A seasoned nurse from Oklahoma, who ran the clinic and had 14 years experience in the Middle East, told us it was not unusual for medical personnel to arrive, scope out the situation, and immediately return home, because they "just couldn't take it." This did not apply to me, but I could appreciate her point, as well as the sentiments of those who did turn around and go home. The human devastation and loss, the lack of amenities, and the cultural "blast" can be overwhelming, especially when you don't go home at the end of the day. At day's end, exhausted, we ate dinner in the mess tent, set up as a cafeteria by

German relief workers within 48 hours of the first quake. Afterward, we went to our quarters, which were freight containers with bunk beds, a lightbulb, and, specifically, no toilet, sink, tub, or kitchen amenities whatsoever. I hiked across camp to use the bathroom and cannot recall if I took a shower or not. Falling asleep in my container "home," I heard the Muslim call to prayer broadcast from the mosques every four hours, which became a familiar sound in the ensuing weeks.

Fortunately, I have found that in disaster and humanitarian work, nearly everyone has shared values of compassion, dedication, and teamwork, and what would initially seem impossible becomes doable and enjoyable because of the motivating esprit de corps. This is, in my view, the factor that makes nearly everything possible. Therefore, arriving in the exhausted and jet-lagged state that we did, with 32 patients waiting, we were able to begin our work. The family physician who was finishing his stint gave us an overview of the camp, the organization of the clinic, the common medical problems treated, and the medical supplies available. There were medications from many countries in a supply room attached to the clinic, the whole of which was constructed from two freight containers arranged in a T shape. The medications were organized by organ system in a workable fashion; only two selective serotonin reuptake inhibitors and one generic benzodiazepine comprised the psychotropic formulary. There were also supplies for minor surgical procedures and for making casts. We had no laboratory capabilities, except for urine dipsticks and pregnancy tests. Everyone who needed labs, x-rays, or more was referred to a local hospital. The earthquake victims, that is, camp residents, had great expectations in seeing American doctors, yet we were probably less equipped than the average physician in Turkey! The clinic nurse and her assistant were invaluable in their organizational skills and their knowledge of the culture, language, and the individual patients. Our work would have been next to impossible, however, if it hadn't been for our interpreters. We had three, who hailed from Romania, Lebanon, and Turkey. They each spoke at least three languages. Their sense of humor was a godsend, and they performed any and all tasks necessary in addition to interpreting. I cannot overemphasize the absolute necessity of such flexibility in disaster work. Being multitalented helps, and humor is essential. Our Lebanese interpreter specialized in singing Elvis Presley songs that he had learned at the American University in Beirut and performed for us ceaselessly and joyfully.

Although focus on the work at hand is essential, when you arrive in a devastated foreign land, finding drinking water and toilet facilities are high on the priority list. In fact, it is difficult to proceed without addressing this matter. We learned we must drink bottled or boiled water and fortunately this was available in adequate supply. We were introduced to the "Western potty" in the clinic, accompanied by a small sink with running water, which were the "luxury facilities." Otherwise, one had to trek across camp to a small aluminum shed, which contained a single "squatty potty" and a single shower, and which was for camp staff and volunteers, where there was often a waiting line. Camp residents used the primitive squatty potties and showers in a small building on the opposite side of camp. They obtained water from one common source on the campsite. All camp residents and staff lived in dwellings constructed from freight containers, which were small rectangular boxes with two windows and a doorway cut into one side. There were two lightbulbs in each container. Most residents had devised makeshift kitchens by finding a way to plug in a small burner and a small refrigerator. Camp staff and volunteers were fed three meals a day in the MASH-type tent, where meals were prepared by an ex-engineer and his wife who served as camp cooks. It was always enjoyable to visit with other camp workers over meals. Volunteers from seven countries were there with us and we all learned much from each other. The camp residents were friendly and respectful; in the evenings they often sang and danced and sat outside visiting with each other. I was told by camp staff that many of them would be living in the camp for five to 10 years! Although the camp may have had more amenities in its primitive state than many disaster workers encounter in other disasters, it was an adjustment for me, because this was my first disaster trip. I found every aspect of the experience novel and requiring adjustment. Fortunately, it agreed with me very well.

I was surprised at how easily I shifted into the general practitioner mode and how much knowledge from medical school and internship I still had. I did have to review the treatment of worms, as well as update myself on antibiotics for various common infections. The clinic nurse designated me as the physician for women and children, and my colleague saw many of the men and geriatric patients. We saw about six patients per hour, with a lunch break at midday. Looking in a child's ears with an otoscope or adjusting the dose of an antihypertensive, for example, was a far simpler matter and considerably less intriguing than evaluating a suicidal or psychotic patient in my office in the United States. I told my colleague I was reminded why I did not go into primary care—"too much earwax, plain and simple!" Obviously, it's not that simple, but it's hard to match the intriguing and compelling nature of our work as psychiatrists in any other speciality.

Another enlightening observation was that even though all work was done with the assistance of an interpreter, I found I could tell within a minute whether the main problem was psychiatric or purely physical. Facial expression, tone of voice, and posture told the story before I knew the words. I could easily see how primary care physicians are able to detect psychiatric issues so quickly. The healing impact of listening, empathy, and interest in the patient's subjective experience was powerful and needed no interpretation, and I experienced this repeatedly in its purest form. This was the most gratifying aspect of the work. I found the patients to be very amenable to taking psychotropic medication and to talking about their emotional problems, so I was able to practice some very helpful psychiatry. In addition, the patients were grateful and had no sense of entitlement. Between the immensely gratifying nature of the work and the absence of the "hassle factors" we contend with the United States, I knew by the second week that I wanted to incorporate disaster and humanitarian work into my professional life for the remainder of my career. This I knew in my bones. I happily went about my work and felt simultaneously energized, exhausted, and gratified until it was time to head home.

One of my most memorable experiences was being asked to see a woman in the camp who by all counts sounded actively psychotic. We had no antipsychotics in camp and decided to take her to the psychiatry clinic at a nearby university hospital to initiate treatment. On the morning of our agreed meeting time, the woman was nowhere to be found. Some said she went to town. The camp staff did not worry much about this because the vicinity was safe, the woman was not thought to be dangerous, and apparently this was not unusual for her. So the clinic nurse, the interpreter, and I drove to the hospital in the camp ambulance to seek treatment for this woman. We met with several hospital directors, drank strong tea with them (which is customary), and explained our dilemma. In several hours' time, we were escorted to a psychiatry clinic, where we encountered psychiatry residents and a psychiatry residency training director. They were very gracious and willing to help. We told them about this woman and asked for antipsychotic medication, which yielded a supply of olanzapine for our patient and a promise of ongoing care for her if we could get her to their facility. Notably, I learned that the challenges the psychiatrists face in Turkey are much the same as those we face in the United States.

When I returned home, I told the director of Northwest Medical Teams that I loved the experience in Turkey but would like to go as a psychiatrist on my next venture. As it turned out, I was told I was the first psychiatrist to do disaster work with Northwest Medical Teams, only at that point I had not yet functioned as a psychiatrist. Who could have known that the next disaster I was called to would be Ground Zero, to be a team leader for the first multidisciplinary mental health team ever sent to a disaster by Northwest Medical Teams? I must have passed muster in Turkey.

On September 13, 2001, I was called by Northwest Medical Teams to go to Ground Zero. A team of five mental health professionals was quickly assembled, a brief orientation was held, and we arrived in New York City on September 18, 2001. The request for our help came from Nyack College, a Christian college with two campuses, one of them five blocks from Ground Zero. We were to help the students, faculty, and staff in the aftermath of the terrorist attacks. Many of the students had jobs in the World Trade Center. Many watched the planes crash into the buildings and saw people jumping to their deaths and other traumatic sights. This situation was entirely different from that in Turkey. We arrived soon after the disaster, when chaos was the operative term and the terrorist aspect of the disaster had permeated everyone's psyche. In this context we had to become a functioning team, having met each other only two days before leaving.

Because this was the first full mental health team sent by Northwest Medical Teams, with no previously established team structure or roles, the team went through the typical stages of group development in an accelerated and challenging fashion. My leadership and group therapy skills were useful in this process. We ultimately set up two arms of operation. One could be best described as an emergency student mental health service for the Manhattan campus of Nyack College, where we conducted classroom education in stress response and coping strategies as well as individual and group sessions. We also formally met with faculty and the deans and gave recommendations we thought would be constructive for students and faculty as they weathered the impact of the disaster. We felt that we helped every individual with whom we had contact; however, many were reluctant to seek us out, so despite arranging structured services, much of our work was done informally in the hallways, bathrooms, and elevators. The fact that nonstructured services are often better utilized than structured services is common in mental health disaster work.

The second arm of our services was spending time at "the Pit," the steam-spewing center of Ground Zero, where we provided moral support and advice and helped other agencies such as the Salvation Army. On our first trip to the Pit, which occurred on the morning of our arrival, we were accompanied by the pastor of the church affiliated with the college. Without him, we may not have gained access to Ground Zero and made it into the Pit. I admit I felt reluctance making my way into the core of the destruction, but afterward I felt it was useful for us to have done so. Later, we found many New Yorkers were afraid to get near the destruction because of the emotional impact.

Remarkably, firefighters, police, National Guard, FBI agents, and even the mayor approached the pastor, who was easily identifiable by his pastoral collar, and asked to be prayed for—right in the middle of their work, right in the middle of the rubble and chaos. We, the mental health professionals dressed in our Northwest Medical Teams shirts and identification badges, were effectively bypassed! We often had to approach others to talk to them, and when we did, they appreciated it. Most of them wanted to know what to tell their children. One man, not realizing I was a psychiatrist, announced he had been constipated for eight days and wanted fast help. Obviously in disasters, the basics of human physiology are most important and cannot be ignored. Beyond basic bodily functions, it was clear that in life-threatening situations, people turn more to their faith than to psychiatrists and mental health professionals when it comes to coping with the emotional impact. There were signs advertising free crisis counseling dotting the vicinity, but it appeared there were few takers. This was humbling and enlightening and has given me pause to consider the role of psychiatrists and other mental health professionals in the acute phases of disaster. I also witnessed the tensions and conflicts between and within agencies on the scene—the Red Cross, the Salvation Army, police, firefighters, National Guard, and the FBI. Chaos and power struggles were part of the landscape, and situations changed daily.

Some of the difficulties we encountered included not being familiar with the local mental health system and resources, which we learned about promptly. Telephone service was spotty, and transportation systems were down in many areas, which presented logistical challenges. Not being able to prescribe medication was a disadvantage but eliminated the need to arrange specific psychiatric follow-up, which was limited. It was also difficult to appreciate one's impact, given the massive devastation and human loss, not to mention the impact of the disaster on myself. Handling the media demands could be a whole chapter in itself. An unexpected experience on return was that, compared with the life-and-death aspect of the 9/11 disaster, many usual concerns and duties seemed trivial, especially those of an administrative and bureaucratic nature, and it was difficult for others to understand what it was like to experience such a situation. It has also been challenging to help some colleagues realize that the scope of disaster psychiatry is far more broad than only preventing and treating posttraumatic stress disorder.

Ultimately, the disaster experiences I have had thus far have impacted my professional life significantly. I have become much more interested in trauma, stress, and cross-cultural work, as well as in disaster response systems in general. I have begun working with refugee groups in our Intercultural Psychiatry Program at Oregon Health and Science University (OHSU), the medical school where I am a faculty member. I have also become a member of the Oregon Medical Association committee responsible for overseeing the organization's response to the threat of bioterrorism, in coordination with other state and county entities. I am currently working on the Oregon Psychiatric Association's disaster response plan. I am also developing a disaster psychiatry program at OHSU, which would provide direct and consultative services domestically and abroad and provide training opportunities for students, residents, and fellows. Outside the military, disaster psychiatry is in its infancy, with much to be learned and refined. The role of psychiatrists in disasters is still being defined. In my view, the disaster psychiatrist has a limited, but important, twofold role, separate from and in addition to providing direct patient care. The first aspect of this role is to be on site and available to other disaster responders to assist when the need arises, which requires cooperative relationships with other individuals and entities and, ideally, inpatient and outpatient facilities for admissions and referrals. The second aspect is in mental health disaster response planning, which includes educating ourselves and others, including the public and the media, and synthesizing the knowledge and expertise of our field with the disciplines of psychology, social work, and myriad volunteer organizations. It is imperative that we become knowledgeable about all the agencies and entities involved in disaster response in our country and respect the long history that many of our colleagues in psychology and social work have had in the disaster arena so that we can all be effective in a cooperative way.

The most important result of my experiences thus far is that a far greater portion of my professional work is now in alignment with my personal values, which is deeply meaningful to me. In addition, I have clearly moved "out of the box" in regard to my shift toward compelling, action-oriented work. At this point, there is no turning back!

IV

Child and Adolescent
Disaster Psychiatry

The three essays in this section address a population that is often the focal
point of attention after disasters. Indeed, the effects of disaster on children
have been of great interest to researchers and the general public alike. The
well-being of children may well serve as a convenient object onto which society displaces any number of "adult" anxieties.

As these essays demonstrate, the impact of disasters on children and
adolescents can be enormous. Yet, developmental factors make it difficult to apply "adult" interventions, especially with young children. It
thus behooves all disaster psychiatrists to become familiar with certain
core principles involved in therapeutic work with children and adolescents. On the other hand, Carol Kessler's contribution raises the provocative idea of applying a child intervention, play therapy, to work with
adults. In point of fact, creativity and play are prominent therapeutic
factors in all three of these essays. Desmond Heath also illuminates the
value of environmental interventions in the aftermath of disasters. His
creation of the "Kids' Corner" at the Family Assistance Center is a telling example of how psychiatrists can powerfully intervene by addressing
the milieu in which disaster response occurs. Indeed, such systemic
interventions are an integral part of disaster psychiatry. Margaret
Tompsett's essay introduces another modality intrinsic to disaster psychiatry: work with groups. Since disasters are collective experiences,
groups—whether groups that have formed for single-session debriefings

or open-ended, long-term groups—are an inevitable vehicle for assessing and working through the effects of disasters. Children, for their part, are accustomed to being led in group activities in school. This familiarity may be an asset or a liability in the types of group work that follow disaster: Children may feel comfortable in the group or have difficulty differentiating the rules of a therapeutic group from those of their educational setting.

All three essays offer valuable insights into disaster psychiatrists, who in various settings may find themselves working directly with children, addressing the post disaster concerns of adults about children, or adapting the techniques customarily employed in work with children to traumatized adult populations.

15

Awakening Creativity in the Wake of Disaster

A Psychiatrist's Journey with the People of El Salvador

Carol Luise Kessler

As a child and adolescent psychiatrist who has spent the past 15 years making yearly visits to El Salvador, the events of September 11 brought home to New York City terrors that I'd grown accustomed to experiencing on foreign soil. For although *El Salvador* means "The Savior," the small Central American country that bears this name bears scars of events that wreak chaos—12 years of civil war; earthquakes, hurricanes, and dengue epidemics—events of mass destruction that might lead one to think that the country ought to be renamed *El Desastre*, "The Disaster." Yet journeying with Salvadorans over the past decade leads me to believe that "Savior" is a fitting name for their disaster-ridden land. For as a psychiatrist, one who cares for the psyche, in the wake of disaster, I have witnessed the birth of saving grace, as solidarity and compassion are sparked, in survivors' efforts to weave meaning and to keep hope alive.

The yearning for hope and meaning in the wake of disaster is not new. My theology background reminds me of a Biblical tradition in which from the beginning of time, humanity has wrestled with questions of how to go on when innocence is lost or when the floods of chaos threaten. It was in the wake of the "disaster" of exile that the people of Israel remembered the story of creation—a story wherein each day heralds new life and all is declared to be good. It was in the wake of the "disaster" of exile that the story of Job was woven—a journey into the mysterious question of why disastrous events befall the innocent. These sacred texts serve to remind me that the fragility of life is not new. Creation emerges out of chaos time and time again, and

189

when chaos strikes, we, like Job and his friends, are riddled with tormenting questions: Why has this happened? Am I being punished? How can I go on?

Such questions of the soul and psyche may find their way to the psychiatrist's office. In the wake of disaster, however, I as a psychiatrist have found that much as it was Job's friends who journeyed to find him covered with boils, seated in ashes, it is I who must journey to the ashes where the survivor sits. And, much like Job's friends, on encountering the horrific impact of disasters, I might be struck with silence, or tempted to reassure with lofty rationalizations. Yet, ultimately, I may discover that what I can best offer is my presence as a witness to a survivor's cries to the void or to her Creator—a companion in the survivor's search for meaning and hope.

The morning of September 11 started with my routine drive from the outskirts of the city into Manhattan, and ended with a frustrated yearning to go to the ashes, to take on my familiar role as companion to the survivors. Radio news spoke of an accident—a plane striking the Twin Towers. Reporters initially labeled it a bizarre mishap. A second plane struck, and the quest to label the unfathomable began. Was it an accident, a terrorist attack, or an act of war? I drove along and moments later learned that the Pentagon had been struck. Bridges to Manhattan would be closed. Security measures I'd grown accustomed to on Central American turf hit home. My yearning to serve as psychiatrist at the site was frustrated. Yet my years in El Salvador reassured me that my skills would not go unutilized. For the impact of trauma would ripple across survivors' psyches for years, if not generations.

September 12 dawned, and I was granted access through a police checkpoint to Manhattan island, where with colleagues I journeyed to a site where people gathered in search of missing loved ones. I sat with friends and families of the disappeared as they filed missing-person forms and shared photos and x-ray films with detectives. Most remained convinced of their loved ones' survival and saw no need for psychiatric support. Others suspected the worst and welcomed my presence as they struggled to find words to convey the unspeakable. One woman yearned to be with her beloved spouse in the heap of ashes. Another struggled to find words to tell her child that daddy, who worked in the mighty towers, at Windows on the World, wouldn't be coming home again. My fluency in Spanish was welcome, since it was the immigrant women who were the most isolated, and who sought a listening ear and a supportive presence. Police officers heard plea after plea to find a missing loved one, and later confessed to me, "I was there. There aren't even corpses. Only body parts." Yet who could shatter the hope for a loved one's return?

And who could shatter mental health professionals' desire to ease psychic pain in the wake of disasters? Indeed, volunteers flocked to offer assistance, and mental health clinics prepared for the arrival of patients, as solidarity was sparked in the wake of disasters. Yet most found that patients didn't arrive. As a psychiatrist, I journeyed with countless colleagues to the Family Assistance Center staffed with volunteers through Disaster Psychiatry Outreach. It was only in my role as consultant to the clergy and pastoral counselors of Lutheran Counseling Center that survivors flocked to me, searching for meaning, for answers from their Creator to questions that plagued the soul. Seeking the comfort of ritual and of sanctuary.

Indeed, a ritual I'd grown familiar with in Central America and the Southern Cone, and even in the South Bronx became enfleshed in a new way in the wake of 9/11. For Mothers of the Disappeared have marched with photos of missing loved ones for decades in Buenos Aires's Plaza de Mayo, and friends and family of those lost to Bronx violence continually transform walls into colorful graffiti memorials. A similar tapestry of hope emerged, as loved ones posted the faces of the disappeared of 9/11 on lampposts and city walls.

A few weeks after the collapse of the Towers, I boarded a plane to El Salvador, where my role as psychiatrist and companion to survivors has evolved over the past 15 years. Although I hadn't linked the word *disaster* with El Salvador before, events that threaten mass destruction of life and property have been woven into El Salvador's reality for years. Concepts such as posttraumatic stress disorder lose their meaning as events that would prove overwhelming to almost anybody become normative in the context of long-term civil war, repeated earthquakes and hurricanes, and constant threats of endemic infectious disease. Traumatic events are not, as the *Diagnostic and Statistical Manual of Mental Disorders* indicated up to its 1987 edition (*DSM-III-R*; American Psychiatric Association, p. 250), "outside the range of usual human experience," in this small country where, for years, the terror of political violence threatened all.

And so, as I journeyed to El Salvador in October 2001, in the aftermath of September 11, the plane was filled to capacity. Plane-induced terrorism had led many to temporarily abandon air travel, yet for Salvadorans terror wasn't a novelty. It was a familiar event. Many fellow passengers would say, "I left El Salvador fleeing war, and now I'm returning fleeing war." Acts of political violence sparked familiar terror and search for safe haven. In El Salvador, my friends mourned that others were now suffering terrors that they have long endured. The deep psychological sequelae of terror lead me to return to El Salvador each year to weave meaning with colleagues as I offer consultations in mental health to teachers, psychologists, and community workers.

My first journey to El Salvador was during its protracted civil war. As a medical student and volunteer with Aesculapius International Medicine and the Archdiocese of El Salvador, I lived and worked in a rural zone of conflict, tending to patients and training *campesinos* to serve as health promoters. Although I had initially worried that my newly acquired medical skills wouldn't meet the needs of war-torn El Salvador, I became struck by the numbers of people who'd walk hours to the clinic to disclose their sleepless nights, their deep affliction, their nervous state. In El Salvador, utterances depicting the horrors of daily reality were grounds for persecution; any story outside the bounds of the "official story" was considered subversive. It seemed that psychic pain became manifest in physical symptoms. We'd offer a compassionate presence, and perhaps some Tylenol. Hoping to connect more meaningfully to the emotional distress, I offered interviews to uncover signs of anxiety and depression. Many welcomed these interviews as a place to give voice to emotional burdens—burdens they'd attribute to the *situation*, a generic term, much like 9/11, that for those affected carries a terrorizing charge. Some felt safe enough to share the details of their particular *situation*—a murdered brother, son, or husband; bombings leading to displacement; witnessing of mass slayings; threats of forced military recruitment; earthquakes. Terrors that evoked hopelessness, desperation, aches, pains, sleepless nights.

Some sought safe haven, crossing borders to the United States. On my return to New York City, I entered psychiatric training, and connected to a Salvadoran center in Long Island, Centro Salvadoreno, where I volunteered mental health services to the growing refugee community. In a center created by Salvadorans to advocate for their "illegal" or undocumented community's rights, I encountered many who carried deep sequelae of the "disasters" they'd endured.

I remember a five-year-old girl, Maria, who graced the center's office in November 1989. She and her mother were seeking refuge from disaster. They had lived in Soyapango, an urban town to which they'd fled from a war-ridden countryside years before. One November night, a guerilla offensive on San Salvador sparked military counterattack, and Soyapango became the heart of armed conflict. Trenches were dug in the streets. Doors were kept open to witness the crossfire. Stores were looted. Maria's mother was enlisted to care for the wounded, leaving Maria with a teen cousin. For days, Maria huddled in the only room that had survived massive aerial bombardment. She pleaded to Papa God to make the bullets disappear in midair. Yet her teen caretaker was hit with shrapnel.

Maria's mother eventually returned, escaping crossfire and teargas, to find Maria behaving like a girl who'd gone back to find a time that was safe. She'd regressed to a time when she could trust that her mother wouldn't be taken away, and that her home would remain standing. She would only drink from a bottle; she wet the bed. Yet with mother, she fled, journeying through Guatemala and Mexico, to Texas, where she was confined in an INS (Immigration and Naturalization Service) Detention Center, before release and reunion with her father in New York. Her father had left years before and was now a stranger to Maria.

When I met Maria, I saw her five young years struggling to provide her with enough strength and wisdom to take care of all that was dear to her. She wouldn't let her mother out of her sight—day or night, waking or sleeping. During their last separation, she'd nearly lost her mother to the war. The nights she was able to find rest, Maria's depths would stir and rouse her with images of soldiers pointing their guns at her. In her dream, she'd play dead, and I wondered how a five-year-old knew to play dead in order to survive.

It was hard for Maria to trust that we could just be together. She'd run to the windows looking for planes. A baby's cry in the next room signaled danger; Maria feared that the baby would be killed.

Yet Maria and I met, and as I offered sessions of play therapy, she was able to use the safe space that I provided to convey what she'd endured. Over time, Maria moved from hypervigilance and regression toward active expression and creation. Toys became her words, and play became her language. I offered a bag of toys, and Maria found farm animals to build her grandparents' farm. She created a peaceful, pastoral scene. Yet it didn't stay safe. Maria sensed danger and urgently instructed the animals to seek shelter inside a box. "Shhhh," she whispered with urgency, as the toy car she'd initially labeled as the *Red Cross* transformed into the frightening police. She tried to barricade the car between blocks. Yet it still wasn't safe.

Maria sat a little doll girl within a brightly colored house, when all of a sudden crayon "rockets" banged fiercely on the rooftop, and Maria rhythmically, repeatedly asked me, "Will the little girl be okay?" or "The little girl will be okay, right?" *Which little girl?* I wondered, for it seemed that Maria was filled with anxiety for herself, for her mother, and for her wounded cousin, who though remaining in El Salvador, appeared in all of Maria's drawings, drawings in which big eyes dominated hypervigilant faces.

The little girl, Maria, would become okay, as she played over time. As a psychiatrist, I offered both a safe, predictable space and words that assured Maria that the disaster she'd endured was in the past. As Maria felt safe and connected to me, she was able to stage her horrifying memories in what has been called "posttraumatic play" (Terr, 1985). This play consisted of driven, compulsive reenactments of the disaster she'd endured. Yet Maria was now the active player. Rather than merely receive the assault of bombs and bullets, silently huddled beneath a bed, Maria could direct farm animals toward safety, and voice the hopes and fears of a little girl. In her play, Maria recapitulated events of the war she'd left behind, whose echoes waned over time, as her play became richer and more spontaneous. English words became interspersed with Spanish, as Maria wove her story on U.S. soil.

My role extended to that of family therapist, as I confronted the family's bewilderment that mother and child remained distressed despite their arrival in father's safe U.S. home. All were reassured that they weren't crazy, as I informed them of the psyche's reactions to traumatic events. I offered space for Maria's parents to move gradually from reliving an overwhelming past toward connecting with each other in the present and dreaming a collective future.

As a child psychiatrist, I'd learned to hear children's stories in their play, and during my years as a volunteer at Centro Salvadoreno, I witnessed disasters wrought by political violence etched in children's drawings, enacted in play. I witnessed the quiet, withdrawn faces of children who dared not play with their world. I sat with children, frozen in isolation and speechless terror. In sessions of play therapy, I witnessed children, emerging out of the depths of disaster to engage their world and to forge new paths.

In Long Island's Centro Salvadoreno, brave refugees indeed forged new paths. Although branded *undocumented,* they stood with concentration camp survivor Elie Wiesel to declare that "no human being is illegal." They strove for rights to housing, health, and indeed mental health care for Salvadorans in New York City, as they advocated for peace in their homeland. In 1992, peace would dawn, heralding a new space for healing of the sequelae of a 12-year war that had killed 75,000, left 9,000 missing, displaced one million, and scarred all.

The wounds were deep and far-reaching, and so, too, was a desire for healing and connection. Political violence had scarred neighboring Latin American countries in the 1970s, and solidarity was sparked, calling neighbors from the Southern Cone to share what they had learned along their healing journey. In 1991, I was invited to Argentina, a country whose years of dictatorship left it no stranger to disappearance, torture, and terror.

There, I met with the Solidarity Movement for Mental Health to learn of their journey with survivors (Solidarity Movement for Mental Health, 1987). Argentine colleagues shared that in the wake of long-term political violence, many of those affected would repetitively tell past traumatic events, others remained frozen in speechless terror, while others acted out in aggression or rage. To forge a new path, psychologists teamed up with actors, artists, and teachers and together fashioned tools that might enable survivors to play together. In therapeutic groups, survivors might gather together in the space before words, and emerge out of speechless terror, to create collectively new images, sounds, and stories. Years of political violence had shattered trust in shared space, and the Solidarity Movement for Mental Health worked to forge space where trust and relationship could grow through the language of play.

I had encountered the power of play in such private, one-on-one consultations as that of Maria, and so I eagerly entered the collective playspace of Argentine peers. In Buenos Aires, I learned tools that would enable me to fashion such space of creativity and play among Salvadorans. These creative tools work along three paths. First, there are games that involve movement, wherein one explores the innumerable ways to connect with self, one another, and the surroundings. There are games of sound and dramatizations, where memories are enacted and transformed in the group experience. The second path of creativity involves words. Games are fashioned that reclaim the creative power of words. In the third path, one plays with objects—newspaper, clay, cloth, balls. Collective drawings and collages can be fashioned.

Peace accords had recently been signed when, in collaboration with an Argentine actor, Luciano Suardi, I was invited to share these creative tools with the psychologists of El Salvador's Universidad Centroamericana. There, only three years earlier, the dean of psychology, Ignacio Martin-Baro, five other priest-professors, their cook, and her daughter had been slain by the military. It seemed appropriate to be offering workshops of creativity in this setting, for Martin-Baro had theorized that prolonged war changes the social fabric into one characterized by social polarization, violence, and lies, for war is a construct founded on the premise that might makes right. Social polarization ensues as battle lines are drawn—"You're either with us or against us." Efforts to weave meaning are challenged by propaganda and contradictory news reports from either side of the conflict (Martin-Baro, 1990).

The challenge to promote mental health in postwar El Salvador was therefore not solely a challenge to diagnose and treat symptoms of posttraumatic stress disorder. It was a challenge to heal a social fabric threatened by a framework of violence, social polarization, and lies. It was a challenge to create safe spaces, or in the words of British analyst and pediatrician Winnicott, "transitional spaces"—spaces of trust wherein survivors might meet one another and together create new symbols, new stories, new ways of being in relation (Winnicott, 1971). In El Salvador, Luciano Suardi and I offered tools to build such spaces.

During our stay, a psychologist requested that we share our playspace with a group of demobilized FMLN (Farabundo Marti National Liberation Front) guerilla combatants, who were preparing to enter a newly forming civilian police force that would replace a police force linked to death squads. We accepted the challenge and gathered in a classroom at the Universidad Centroamericana, with a group of 25 men and five women.

Luciano and I began with movement, inviting the men and women to put chairs aside and to walk as they wished. They accepted with enthusiasm and filled the room with liberated energy. To facilitate connection, we formed a circle, inviting each person to share his or her name as they threw a ball. The group created a game of movement from guerilla to civilian, as they shed their clandestine names and revealed their birth names.

To facilitate play with language and symbols, Luciano and I scattered newspaper on the floor and invited all to search and to tear out those words and images to which they felt drawn. The walls became transformed as group members covered them with words (*Peace Accords, VIOLATED, THESE ARE THE INNOCENT VICTIMS OF THE FMLN*) and with images (naked women, a detained student labeled *FMLN Sympathizer*, Richard Nixon). Group members gazed at the walls to discover how words had been torn from printed sentences and placed side by side, creating new meaning.

Shreds of newspaper covered the classroom floor, and Luciano and I invited the group to play with this object in a more dramatic manner. "Tear it up if you wish," I called out. There was a burst of embodied energy, as everyone created a whirlwind of newspaper. I entered into "battle" with one participant. We threw paper at one another, until I surrendered, and fell to the ground. I threw paper from below, and found myself becoming the target of an ever-growing crowd. Buried in newspaper, I heard a resounding chant, "Let's bury the dictator!" *Yanqui invasor, fuera de El Salvador. Yanqui invasor, El Salvador sera su tumba.* "Yankee, go home. Yankee, you'll find your grave in El Salvador." Words painted on the walls of the U.S. Embassy had arisen from the group. In play, I became the enemy, and the group enacted my assassination.

I reentered the group, as I felt my legs being pulled. Group members pulled me from beneath the mountain of paper, and glided me across the floor. I was invited out of the grave.

With torn paper scattered about, Luciano and I invited all to move from destruction to creation, by fashioning costumes from shreds of paper. Each person envisioned who they might become, and characters were gradually born. To encourage interaction and dramatization, I invited all to pretend that we were walking through a marketplace, where we could meet and greet one another. I saw the face of a young man who'd constructed a long nose. He sniffed the air, and walked timidly. I asked his name, and he responded, "Dumbito." I asked what Dumbito was doing in the market. "Looking for my mother," he responded. I took his hand and walked through the "market," searching for Dumbito's mother. We walked together, examining each face: man, woman, animal.

We searched and searched. We couldn't find her. Almost—"But she's taller, thinner," Dumbito would say. Until the search ended. We let go of one another's hands, and entered separate paths. Dumbito, without his mother, learning to walk alone.

Time passed, and I invited all to remove their newspaper disguise and to enter a moment of reflection. I wrote phrases on a blackboard that each member could transform into the first line of a poem. After writing, we formed a circle, and members shared poems that evoked memories of pain and fear, grief for lost childhood, and hope for justice and peace. I invited the group to call out words that came to mind. *Fear, hope,* and *love of life* were named.

Luciano invited groups to gather and to enact scenes conveying the words they had named. To represent *fear,* people walked with averted gazes and rigid bodies. *Hope* was portrayed as group members danced along a paper trail toward a sun etched on a chalkboard.

I then invited group members to create scenes as each participant felt moved. One man invited others to gather in a circle to share a meal. The meal gradually grew until all were seated together, and one woman invited all to join in song. The group then spiraled back to the game that had opened their play, as they threw an imaginary ball.

We closed by inviting all to reflect on their time together. There was surprise at the trust they'd developed, the creativity they'd manifested, and the joy they'd felt.

My playtime journey with Dumbito searching for his mother took on deeper meaning, when years later I returned to El Salvador as mental health consultant to the psychological team of Pro-busqueda ("Pro-search").

Pro-busqueda is a nongovernmental organization that emerged in the wake of peace accords. The wound that Pro-busqueda seeks to address is that of "disappeared" children.

In 12 years of war, hundreds of children were separated from their families. Some truly became orphaned by military operations that slaughtered mother, father, sister, and brother. Many were seized and falsely labeled *orphaned*. These children were adopted under false pretenses both within El Salvador and abroad, in the United States and in Europe. Pro-busqueda emerged under the leadership of Jesuit priest and professor Jon Cortino, as families began searching for their disappeared children. Father Cortino narrowly escaped death by coincidentally being elsewhere on the night his six colleagues were assassinated by military bullets at their residence at the Universidad Centroamericana. Over the years, the organization he helped found has grown into a team of lawyers, investigators, and psychologists that has succeeded in celebrating reunions of "orphans" with their families of origin. Disappeared children, now grown, are granted the right to reestablish lost ties and to learn of their history and identity. Parents and grandparents whose little ones are found are blessed with peace of mind and the possibility of renewed relationship.

Yet Pro-busqueda's work wears on the psyche and soul. Many young people and many parents search and search for years, yet find no trace of their kin. Others search and find that their disappeared child has died. Even when discovered alive, reunions are not always celebratory. Some adoptive families, threatened by the prospect of renewed biological ties, have thwarted reunions. Years of separation, often across cultural, class, and political lines, challenge efforts to communicate. Workers' efforts to investigate circumstances of disappearances lead them to challenge the past actions of the military and thus to fear their own security. Confrontation with a military granted amnesty for unimaginable acts of political violence leads to deep feelings of rage, frustration, powerlessness, and sorrow. The search for justice can be a lonely one amid cries to forget the past. Workers' interviews with family members lead them to hear continually tales of horror, as the circumstances of the disappearances are recounted.

Disappeared children are not new to Latin America. In Argentina, I met with Grandmothers of the Plaza de Mayo, whose children had given birth while in captivity. Their children were then murdered, while their grandchildren were fraudulently adopted, often into military families. The grandmothers organized to search for their grandchildren and to seek justice. Their courage serves as an inspiration to Pro-busqueda. It seemed fitting that tools of healing that had emerged in the wake of Argentina's "dirty war" might prove helpful in El Salvador. Pro-busqueda's staff therefore invited me to facilitate workshops of creativity—workshops that might benefit the staff as it equipped them with tools to use later with their searching clients.

We gathered for a day of movement, play, drawing, and dramatization. I invited all to utter words that came to their minds when they thought of disappeared children. I served as scribe for the words that emerged:

Pain	Joy	Tears	Confusion
Anguish	Road	Cry	Remember
Sadness	Anger	Military operation	Impunity
Gray	Rage	Pro-search	Adoption
Impotence	Courage	Dream	Massacre
Found	War	Worry	Identity
Hope	Harm	Reunion	Separation
Search	Fatigue	Isolation	Memory
Sickness	Reparation	Disintegration	Frustration
Action	Uncertainty	Loneliness	
Trauma	Indignation	Orphan	

I formed small groups and invited each to choose three or four words that they would collectively depict in a drawing. Three powerful images were created. The first group depicted *road, fatigue, joy,* and *hope.* They drew two people walking on a road through colorful mountains rich with trees, birds, and flowing water. They stated that they'd drawn Pro-busqueda members walking wearily toward hope, creating moments of happiness as they searched by appreciating the birds and the waters that surrounded them.

The second group depicted a fist shattering glass to represent *pain, anguish, frustration,* and *disintegration.* The fist donned a swastika and the words *Death to the Communists* as well as the symbol of the "elite, American-trained Atlactl Battalion"—soldiers who have been implicated in the massacres of hundreds of Salvadoran civilians. In the periphery of the fist was a cemetery. Saddened parents and children stood separated by fist and shattered glass. This sketch sparked much emotion as group members bemoaned the artists' negativity. One member shared that she was preparing for a reunion of a child with his family of origin and didn't want her hope to be shattered by such disturbing images. Others acknowledged a desire to cover up the harshness of what they'd endured in the past, yet voiced a need to accept that their world had been shattered, so that they might move forward in hope for reparations. "A boot crushed our reality," said one. "War tore apart the family," cried another. "This group dared depict what we all feel deep within," said another.

A third group chose the words *tears, hope, memory,* and *reparation.* They depicted a woman standing beside a shadow of the woman, in front of a building shaded by a flourishing tree. The group explained that the woman was the mother of a disappeared child. She now lived as two people with two hearts. One life was that of her daily routines, yet there was a parallel shadow life, filled with memories of the war and the consequent absence of her son. Her heart was filled with hope as she stood before Pro-busqueda's office. The tree of life, too, stood as a sign of hope for reunion, and for her child's reunion.

On the close of the day of creativity, Pro-busqueda's staff reflected that they, too, carried the shadow of war. This shadow came to the fore as they played, cried, and laughed together. The staff felt hopeful that these moments of creativity had served to deepen their ties, and they looked forward to sharing tools they'd learned with their clients. They hoped to be as midwives, enabling others to journey from paralyzing fear of the past, toward new symbols and stories. They wished to forge paths of hope and to break through isolation toward new connections.

These paths toward hope were forged as Pro-busqueda staff shed their professional masks. Early in the day, one individual shared that the staff themselves hadn't been affected by disappearances. Their role was to bring hope to the affected ones. Yet as the day unfolded and the group created images and dramatizations, deep responses were evoked. A subgroup enacted a story often heard by Pro-busqueda staff. In the scene, a woman prepared tortillas for her children and greeted their father when he returned from the cornfields. Suddenly, a soldier appeared, separating the children from their parents. He threw the parents face down to the ground, and shot them. He then departed with the children. This scene dramatized the drawing described earlier of a fist shattering glass. The "audience," those who didn't serve as actors, reacted with laughter. They then explained that their laughter disguised fear. They had been deeply affected by a brief scene that demonstrated how abruptly families had been shattered by disappearances.

Members of a second subgroup shared a scene they'd created, and laughter could no longer contain the deep emotions. In this scene, which dramatized the drawing of the road described earlier, a woman walked casually along, playing with her daughter. Suddenly, a fighter jet descends and a soldier appears. Mother and daughter flee, seeking refuge, and are separated in the flight. The soldier finds the girl and takes her to the city. Mother finds Pro-busqueda staff, who accompany her in search of her child.

When the characters were asked to share how they felt within their roles, the line between professional and client blurred. The "soldier" spoke of feeling role confusion within his character, as he was suddenly required to shift from fighting soldier to caretaker of a small child. The "mother" of the scene cried as she shared that she, too, is searching for her disappeared children. Members of the "audience" were invited to share the feelings evoked within them. One spoke of being overwhelmed with memories of friends lost during the war. Another shared that her father had disappeared when she was a young child. The group realized that each of them carried memories of the horror of war. Yet they don't allow themselves space to speak of these memories or to cry, fearing that their emotions will be contagious and uncontainable. Many shared a realization that by granting space for the tears, they glimpsed a rainbow of hope. They acknowledged that their work leaves sequelae that they'd heretofore sought to bury. Yet they'd named their fears and now felt more at peace with themselves, and more connected to one another. They could share fear and sadness as strands in a rich tapestry that was also woven with joy and hope.

In my years journeying with Salvadorans, I, too, had developed myths of not being affected by the horrors of war. "I'm a North American," I would tell myself. "I'm a physician." Yet as my Argentine colleagues helped me to realize, we are all affected by the chaos of political violence, which distorts our social ties and robs us of a sense of safety and trust. The challenge that confronts us in the wake of disaster and horror is to build safe space where we can meet again to connect with self and other—to play, to create, to weave meaning, and to keep hope alive.

In the wake of September 11, I returned to El Salvador. During my stay I journeyed with Pro-busqueda staff to meet with a group of searching family members near their rural homes. As we played, groups fashioned sculptures out of newspaper in one game. One group formed gift packages to deliver in gratitude to Pro-busqueda staff. Another group formed a man, whom they introduced as Pinochet, "the father of disappearances" in Chile, who has still not been brought to justice, and who came to power one September 11, years ago. One man invited all to destroy the dictator, and the group eagerly formed a line that trampled on the newspaperman, in a burst of liberated rage. A third group formed two dolls, an infant and a young adult. They later explained that the infant represented their memory of their children at the time they "disappeared"—an image frozen in time. The young adult represented the person they would encounter should their search prove successful. Much time has passed, and the hope for reunion remains.

With time, I have been graced with encounters with Salvadorans struggling to keep such hope alive. Ex-combatants entering a new civilian police force, searchers for the disappeared. I have struggled to create safe
space for the caregivers, so that they might keep on keeping on. In a recent
workshop, I gathered with social workers, psychologists, and teachers,
who work in various contexts, healing wounds and promoting growth in
the wake of El Salvador's many disasters. Small groups created stories out
of two randomly chosen words. I share one such story, crafted with the
words *planet* and *deprivation*.

> There was once a planet named *Deprivation*, where the people were al-
> ways dwelling on the past—problems, war, poverty. But one day peo-
> ple arrived with the notion, "If I change, the world will change as well,
> and one day there will be peace, harmony, tranquility, and happiness."

I share this story as a metaphor for the challenge that confronts me as a psychiatrist journeying in the wake of disasters. Although disasters are earth
shattering, horrifying experiences that threaten chaos, fragmentation, and
isolation, they also inspire many to gather in search of healing, meaning,
hope, and reparation. In workshops of creativity and play, I have found vehicles to transform the silence of speechless terror into a rich tapestry of symbol,
story, image, and song. In playspace, I have enabled survivors to meet in our
common vulnerability, where we discover great richness and strength.

References

American Psychiatric Association (1987), *Diagnostic and Statistical Manual Mental
    Disorders*, 3rd ed., rev. Washington, DC: American Psychiatric Association.
Danner, M. (1994), *Massacre at El Mozote: A Parable of the Cold War*. New York:
    Knopf.
Martin-Baro, I. (1990), War and mental health. In: *Social Psychology of War*, ed. I.
    Martin-Baro. San Salvador, El Salvador: UCA Editores, pp. 23–40.
Solidarity Movement for Mental Health (1987), *State Sponsored Terrorism: Psycho-
    logical Impact on Children*. Buenos Aires: Paidos.
Terr, L. (1985), Psychic trauma in children and adolescents. *Psychiat. Clin. North
    Amer.*, 8:815–835.
Winnicott, D. W. (1971), *Playing and Reality*. New York: Tavistock/Routledge.

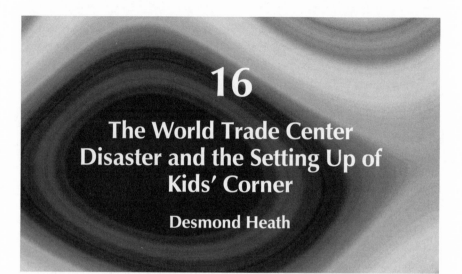

16

The World Trade Center Disaster and the Setting Up of Kids' Corner

Desmond Heath

My immediate personal response to the TV image of planes crashing into the World Trade Center was of a disconcerting lack of feeling, which changed dramatically when I went to the 19th Street Armory DNA matching center as a Disaster Psychiatry Outreach (DPO) volunteer four days later. There a lack of individual response turned into participating in a group response, which I describe in following the stages of the development of Kids' Corner.

Kids' Corner was, at first, a safe haven for children that ended up on Pier 94 as a nursery where children could receive brief psychotherapy. The real spirit and energy that came together to create Kids' Corner arose spontaneously in a group of volunteers and it was overwhelmingly determined by the time and place. They were a group response. The time was early on the Saturday morning four days after 9/11, and the place was the armory.

By 10:00 a.m., Kids' Corner was a cozy, carpeted 15- by 12-foot space separated from the milling crowd by two sofas on one side, a sofa and a table enclosing the two ends, with two tables against the wall to make the fourth side. Multicolored Magic Marker letters on typing paper pinned on the wall announced *KIDS' CORNER*. It was the only bright, welcoming spot in the whole armory.

An hour before, I had found myself a little at a loss standing in a vast hall full of people, many looking official but most looking as if they were trying to figure out where to go or what to do. This was the DNA matching center, the place where relatives came with samples of victim's hair and their own

DNA samples to help in the identification of hundreds of body parts emerging daily from the rubble at Ground Zero. The hope that persons missing
might still be found remained, but that desperate wish, by now, was almost
extinguished and beyond reasonable expectation. An urgency for closure
against terrible individual conclusions strained those in the armory, the
city, and the nation.

I had been told at the DPO desk that as a doctor trained in adult, child,
and adolescent psychiatry and psychoanalysis I might help by making myself
available to respond to persons in distress. In a sea of grown-ups were families with children—toddlers and babies in arms, but no one clearly in such
distress that I could approach to offer help. The children seemed out of their
depth in this urgent, adult world.

We needed a nursery, I thought, and when I communicated this need to
another Red Cross volunteer, the project took off. Volunteers asked:
Where should it be? What do you want? We needed sofas, toys, carpets. We
approached the nearest official and asked if we could use the only sofas in
the armory to make a small nursery area. "Ask that woman in the white shirt
over there. She's the chief of police running the whole place." The police officer immediately understood the need but said that we should clear this
with the Red Cross. I returned to her saying that the Red Cross had an Aviation Disaster child care outfit coming and that the Red Cross officials had
asked us to wait until tomorrow to help with that group. The police chief responded, "Do it now." As we turned to start, she stopped me and said,
"Don't you do anything." And called over three large policemen and said to
them, "Do whatever he says."

While the policemen were forming sofas into a square, we were writing a
shopping list for carpets, paper, pencils, crayons, toys, and other supplies on
the only paper I had—my prescription pad. Volunteers felt this use of prescription pads was good because it might encourage stores to donate. When
I wrote building blocks and airplanes, however, there was an immediate
negative reaction—no planes. We explained that the idea was to set up a
playspace that provided the children with suitable toys to play out their fantasies and traumatic experiences. So we decided to ask the two volunteers
who were to go to toy stores to indicate in the store, "Some of these, some of
those, and some of these." But be sure to get planes. Building blocks to make
towers were not a problem for the other volunteers. Of course, we certainly
should not confront the kids with only Twin Towers and airplanes. Rather,
kids should find a variety of toys that would facilitate their play. Either way,
they would create for themselves whatever they needed. Paper and

Magic Markers are perennially the best materials for the expression of fears and fantasies.

Eight eager-to-help volunteers descended on the first child who entered the space, enclosed by the long tables and the three foam, low-backed sofas. All of us saw the lack of wisdom in this. The boy asked for candy and left with his mother and with a general invitation to come back. The next visitor was a young, very sad-looking Asian woman clutching close her year-old toddler. She asked for and was given a teddy bear—that, too, was clutched tightly by the child. They returned later, and the child's mother talked of her loss. Many bears and beanbag toys had arrived. Masses of donations were to come. All were given out freely.

A feeling of tragedy and loss was in the air along with an energy to do anything that would help. The volunteers needed to come to terms with their own and the national loss. Among the volunteers who, out of nothing, created the bright, colorful, and comforting nursery filled with donated toys were persons experienced in child therapy. It was not easy to engage a child in one-to-one play, however, and even harder to insulate that therapeutic moment from jarring distraction.

My initial response to 9/11 had been a certain disconcerting numbness that came with a feeling of inferiority and personal lacking. I have experienced this before connected with sad losses and traced it to how I dealt with such feelings in childhood. It is akin to sangfroid—a cold-bloodedness and intrepidity that became further established in me through military pilot training as a young man. This persistent absence or attenuation of feeling on seeing the TV images of the planes striking the buildings and the knowledge of the terrible loss of life, remained unbreached by my eldest son's ordeal—he had survived. As a cardiac transplant anesthesiologist he had arrived soon after the second plane hit to set up an intensive care unit. I had seen his videotape, the first on CNN. It showed the falling tower and the utter blackness surrounding him and his camera. Seeing his uncut tape and the CNN version had made me aware of the danger he had been in but it did not, somehow, change my uncomfortable feeling of insufficient response. He had, after all, survived unhurt. At that time I did not personally know anyone else who had been in danger or who was missing. I clearly knew of the meaning of the disaster, but its full emotional impact did not hit me until that Saturday morning when I first saw the faces of missing New Yorkers. The fence round the armory was covered with posters of the missing—every race, nation, and creed was represented—just what I had come to love about this country that had accepted me. The sadness, the pain, and the bewilderment. How had we harmed? How had we hurt that we should be so hurt in return?

I had arrived at the DNA matching center with a group of psychiatrists from Mount Sinai Hospital where I am a voluntary attending. (I have often joked that I trained at Mount Mary's in London and attend at Saint Sinai in New York!) The emotional impact of all those posters and the crowds of people allowed in me a full appreciation of the emotional impact of what had happened. I was relieved of my numbness, though I can still remember the serene state of insufficient feeling. At this point in my personal response to 9/11 my characterologic desire to help got the better of me, and that de-sire to help still powers my interest in the future of Kids' Corner, as this con-tribution, I hope, will show.

The provision of a nursery playroom area was an immediate response to the needs of children and their parents. A conflict was clear from the start and remains essentially unresolved to this day. The conflict is between an imme-diate heartfelt response to make a warm, cozy, child-centered place with food, toys, and presents of teddy bears and other cuddly toys, staffed by generous, caring, supportive persons and the construction of a setting where trauma-tized and bereaved children may tell of their experience by play, drawing, and other behaviors without distraction. That is, a conflict between the setting up of a cozy corner and the provision of a child therapy room.

As those sofas were being moved at the order of the understanding police official, a table of food appeared—candy, sodas, cookies. I immediately wanted that removed but was overwhelmed by the spontaneous opinion of the Red Cross volunteers who had coalesced around the making of a Kids' Corner. Candy prevailed for the first two days until the whole DNA match-ing operation was moved to the Family Assistance Center at Pier 94. There we had no candy or soda, although there was plenty freely available for vic-tims and volunteers alike.

Now, more than a year later, I want to show that even a brief psycho-therapeutic encounter with a child has value. How to set a stage so that a child can tell of his or her intimate experience and how to document the value of this as an effective therapeutic intervention is a persisting issue. The current challenge for the DPO Kids' Corner committee is to figure out how to provide such help and at the same time conduct a psychiatric evalu-ation that might gather data for research into efficacy of intervention.

I can best address these conflicting issues by offering a few clinical vi-gnettes, each of which came from and illustrates the benefits and problems inherent in the stages of development of DPO's Kids' Corner response to the 9/11 Twin Towers disaster.

I hope this description, with clinical examples, of four stages of response will show how an individual child psychiatrist's personal response to the disaster combined with the group response and led to the development of Kids' Corner. The four stages are as follows:

1. *Immediate response*—a cozy, nurturing respite with food and candy and gifts of toys.
2. *Early development*—brief therapeutic interventions possible with diminished distraction.
3. *Consolidation*—more protracted interventions still in a nurturing setting.
4. *Late stage*—a setting in which complex therapeutic intervention could be maintained.

Immediate Response

On the Saturday morning at the Lexington Armory Site, there were no provisions for children and no place where a child psychiatrist could reasonably expect to set up, conduct, and maintain a child therapy encounter. The boy wanting candy and the young Asian woman wanting a teddy bear for her child were followed by children coming to play and be attended to by volunteers. Just the sight of these children playing made evident the immediate need for a cozy, comforting respite for parents and children.

Early Development

In addition to serving children, this phase saw parents of victims, along with police officers and other volunteers, come to find out how to discuss the disaster with their children. The mother of an eight- to 10-year-old boy did not know whether his father had been lost or not and had not been able to tell him anything. She was overwhelmed and distraught. A volunteer went to find a Spanish-speaking adult psychiatrist for her. The boy stood still with a blank expression on his face. I indicated to him that he could play in the Kids' Corner. He went from this item to that item, scattered across the play carpets among other children, considering and then purposefully rejecting this and then that. I offered paper and Magic Markers. He shook his head. He then lighted on a magic drawing pad—a black pad with a page of plastic over it that marks when drawn on, but the lines disappear when the plastic is pulled up from the black base. He immediately made a picture of a plane and then what I thought was going to be a tower, but that was in my mind. He drew another plane and quickly stripped up the plastic, making the picture disappear. He drew figures, and each time no sooner than completed he erased them with purpose and dispatch. I mused that the disappearing so fast seemed important. He nodded and continued with renewed vigor. I wondered if that might be connected with why his mother was so upset. He half turned to me with a gesture and expression of much relief amid his distress. He clearly had felt understood. This illustrates how, surrounded by chaos, a child will determinedly communicate by behavior his inner conflicts of thought, feeling, and expression. Children are good observers but poor interpreters. Their thoughts and feelings are often expressed in behavior and play more readily than in speech. I helped him express his feelings in a mode closer to speech—speech that communicates more clearly and is more readily understood. The purpose of each therapeutic encounter is to bring behavior closer to verbal processing and understanding. Also, such reflective, empathetic interactions foster protective affect-regulating bonds between parent or caretaker and the child.

Consolidation

At Pier 94 in the first Kids' Corner area, bigger than the nursery at the armory but still confined and full of activity and distraction, one 11-year-old girl whose father was missing was engaged in drawing the Twin Towers and describing how her sister and mother missed her father. But she was mad at him because he would not be keeping his promise to take her to stay with his family. Her disappointed sadness she had turned into madness. In the middle of this good therapeutic engagement, a boy, leaping up from a heap of cuddly toys, suddenly distracted her. She immediately joined this boy in a play of taking turns burying each other, lying quite still, but suddenly leaping up. They were playing being dead and buried but also, as the little boy agreed, showing that they were still very much alive. This play may have been more important and helpful to this child than her continuing the session with me. She had told of how she felt she loved her father more than her mother and sister did so she could not only miss him, as they did, but be mad at him as well. "He broke his promise." Without separate playrooms close engagement with a child may well be diverted as this was. Here we can see how a confined space, open and available to all for nurture, is not well suited for child therapy.

The problem of trying to keep a distraction-free therapeutic area remained. One morning, at Pier 94, there was a TV set dominating Kids' Corner, riveting several children to its flashy excitement and drama. We tentatively inquired of the Red Cross child care area if they might have use for a TV set and were told warmly that they had turned down four such offers and were glad to hear the we had the same understanding—that children needed to play their own mental tapes.

Late Stage

At the relocated 70- by 40-foot space, where small chairs and tables, well removed from each other, enabled continued therapeutic interaction, one therapist, concerned about the fears a nine-year-old girl was expressing about watching TV, asked me to help. The child drew a picture of herself with her mother telling her to go watch TV. Watching TV and seeing the plane hit the tower made her more scared. She said that her mother had told her not to talk about the Twin Tower disaster. I apologized for getting her into something her mother had told her not to do. This helped her go on to tell all about her terrifying dreams and hypnagogic experiences of seeing the people of her dream in her room after she woke. She was so scared that she wanted to sleep in her mother's room and would keep waking her in the night. She also had glimpses of a person running out of the wall and across her room when she was wide awake. I asked her if one half of her mind thought this was real and the other half thought it was her imagination. She confidently said, "Both halves of my mind think it's my imagination." She was afraid that an airplane would come and hit her apartment building. This, plus the nightmare experiences, made it hard for her to sleep alone. She knew that the people in her dream were imaginary, even when she saw them in her room but, of course, the fear was real. She also knew that the idea of the plane crashing into her room was also imaginary. These frightening experiences she now understood as coming from the same place as her dreams. As with the hallucinations, they often appeared to be more real than real. Her fear was very real to her, but there was little likelihood that the bad men—as she called them—would fly a plane into her apartment house. She was happy that she had talked and wanted to show her pictures to her mother who on her return was able, with the help of her daughter's therapist, to understand the nature of her child's upset state and her trouble sleeping.

More than a year later we are still struggling with how to provide child-psychiatric response to disaster. Should we, as bare minimum, collect names and addresses for follow-up to measure the effects of our interventions? There is no such information on any of the cases described here. Should a full psychiatric evaluation be conducted? As far as I know, none was done and none seemed appropriate with these four cases, even though at Pier 94 separate rooms at some distance from Kids' Corner were available, though not set up with play material. The last case with hypnagogic and daytime hallucinations may have been followed up by the social worker therapist and, I think in retrospect, should have been referred for full evaluation to rule out a prodromal psychotic condition.

Without more data we cannot approach a scientific study of the various therapeutic interventions. Neither can we conduct a full structured-interview evaluation—such as the Kiddie-SADS (Schedule for Affective Disorders and Schizophrenia for School-Age Children), a diagnostic research instrument—at a disaster site. Our sense of urgency for providing nurturing care and the need for measured psychiatric response remains an unresolved conflict. Superimposed on this conflict is the pressing need for an evidence-based approach to those traumatized by disaster.

I admire the DPO leadership for maintaining an interest in a response to disaster after a disaster is over. Disaster is like a nightmare or a psychotic break—we phobically avoid thinking about it and generally want to put such things clear out of our minds. Like child and domestic abuse, for example, disaster does not create an economic environment that funds research and treatment. Such painful subjects need public, legislated funding of research—research that might lead to the development of effective treatment. I have no evidence, but it seems to me that even a brief moment of understanding and being understood has therapeutic value. Kids' Corner made such moments possible.

Acknowledgments

I thank Mount Sinai Hospital, Disaster Psychiatry Outreach, the Red Cross, the New York City Department of Mental Health, the Federal Emergency Management Agency, and stores such as Toys-R-Us, FAO Schwartz, and others for immediate help and sustaining support. I don't know about the kids and families, but you sure helped me—helped me turn a posttraumatic military response into a psychiatric waging of peace.

17

Working with Fatherless Children
After September 11, 2001

Margaret E. Tompsett

I was in my private office on an ordinary Tuesday morning, when a patient came in saying she heard that a plane hit the World Trade Center. She was anxious, but both of us discounted it as some curious accident and continued with the session. Then another woman came in, this time a mother who was worried about her children and wanted to pick them up from school. It was becoming clear that a terrorist attack had occurred. A little later the Red Cross called me to go down to our town railway station to meet people coming home on the trains from New York City. Three of my afternoon patients had already cancelled, and I called the other two to cancel their appointments and left to change and go to the station.

There were three of us from the Red Cross Disaster Mental Health Network, ready to speak to people as they came off the train. In addition, other members of the Disaster Network and the local rescue squad were there. It had been decided by the Occupational Safety and Health Agency (OSHA) that the people, who had been covered with dust from the collapse of the towers as they left New York City, needed to be decontaminated. As they came off the train, the people were directed to a tent where they were hosed down and given alternative clothing. While they were waiting for this, there was an opportunity to speak with them and to hear their stories. Most were people in their 20s and 30s who worked in the city and were still in a state of shock over what had happened. One woman was shaking with fright and clinging to her boyfriend, refusing to talk to anyone but him. I reassured them that they were now out of harm's way and would shortly be in the safety of their own home. There, if the symptoms did not improve her boyfriend was advised to call their family doctor. There was one woman with two young children who lived in an apartment near the World Trade Center. They were trying to get to a country home in northern New Jersey. Both mother and children were relieved to share a little of their scary experience of the cloud of smoke and dust and their struggle to get to the ferry. One of the rescue squad workers volunteered to take them home.

Late that evening, emotionally and physically exhausted, I retreated to the warmth of my home where my husband and I listened to the radio and tried to make sense of it all. In the next few days, I called many people in the Disaster Mental Health Network, offering to do something useful for the survivors, but nothing materialized. It seemed that everybody was too busy even to get back to me. The Red Cross wanted people but only for two weeks at a time on a full-time basis, and I did not feel that I could abandon my patients for two weeks at a critical time like this. Fortunately, none of them had lost anyone close, and, in the next week or two, I heard many lucky escape stories. Some asked for advice for their children and loved ones. Some with preexisting anxiety and posttraumatic stress disorder called for emergency appointments. I kept looking for some way to help those more closely affected by the disaster and felt helpless, frustrated, and impotent, because no one seemed to need me. Then the call came.

Linda, a school social worker from North Carolina, had been working at our local Red Cross chapter visiting each of the affected families in our area. She was struck by the mothers' concern about their children and wish for some way to help them. The need was readily apparent as she spoke to one or two of the children who had lost their fathers. Linda had run a grief group in her home state and had spoken to all the families with school-age children, who had lost a parent in the disaster, about starting groups for these children. Now she was leaving and was calling to ask me to colead a group with Donna, an art therapist from a nearby hospice. Finally, I could do something useful to help the local families most in need, using the best of my skills, my knowledge, love, and understanding of children. I had never run a group before, although I had worked with children individually who had lost a parent. After talking to Donna, we decided that our skills were complementary because she had extensive group experience.

While I was out of town because of an illness in the family, Donna met with the widows. She found the women shell-shocked and trying to come to grips with the sudden loss of their husbands. Their chief concern was for their children, who were having even more difficulty in grasping the enormity of what had happened. They filled out children's bereavement assessment forms, which showed that the children had a range of symptoms, including crying, worrying, anger, defiance, sleep, and appetite difficulties. All were having a hard time with such a sudden, traumatic loss and needed help to talk about it, cope with their feelings, and deal with their shock, anger, and grief. Some of the women had not been able to accept the reality of their husbands' death and listed them as missing. Donna spoke to them briefly about the stages of grieving and some of what they might expect to experience both in themselves and their children. These sensitive mothers in the midst of their grief and outrage could feel the pain of their children and asked us to help.

Our goals for the group were to help the children develop a better cognitive understanding of death and its impact on them, to enable them to begin processing the traumatic and sad memories, and to acknowledge their feelings and find constructive ways of coping with them so that they could move on with their lives. Thus we hoped to foster their growth and reduce their symptoms, although the latter were not a major focus of treatment. We hoped that by bringing the children together they would gain support from one another as well as from us and would stimulate each other with thoughts and memories. In this way the openness of one child would reduce the resistance of another. We would touch base with the mothers to give them help in handling symptoms such as sleep difficulties.

Traumatic grief differs from uncomplicated bereavement in that posttraumatic stress disorder symptoms are also present, and intrusive traumatic reminders interfere with the child's ability to do the grief work (Pynoos, 1992). We realized that we would have to pay attention to these memories, mainly of the World Trade Center images shown on television, in addition to personal ones. The unusual part of being therapists in this situation is that we, too, had experienced the images and, to a much lesser extent, some of the trauma associated with them. This increased our empathy but also our own pain working with them. Thus, talking to one another about the group after the children went home was invaluable to maintain our own well-being.

Together, Donna and I developed a plan for the group. We had 10 elementary school children ranging in age from 5 to 11. Amy and Judith, both clinicians experienced in hospice work, worked with four adolescents at a separate time. Some of the children were siblings. The staff and volunteers at the Red Cross had done a marvelous job of redecorating a room for us and giving us a table and chairs, lockers for the children to put their belongings in, snacks, and an abundance of Beanie Babies. Alex was the organizer, a young man who experienced the loss of his own father at a young age and worked tirelessly to help the grieving families.

We planned a series of eight weekly groups, starting with an introductory session getting to know the other children and the kind of work and play we would experience together. They would have the opportunity to tell their story. In that session, we would give each child a "Memory Book" to be used both in group and at home. In this book Donna put sheets of paper with various trigger sentences such as "My Favorite Memory" or "Something Important I Learned From My Dad." This would be followed by some work on identifying their various feelings and how they express them. The reality of the trauma as well as the loss would be recognized, and education about the finality of death would be included. We would talk about ways of coping with feelings so that they would not be so overwhelming or harmful. In one session, we would think together about all the things "We Could Have, Would Have, Should Have"—that is, the unfinished business. Then we intended to focus on how their lives had changed and how their lives would go on, emphasizing both the people around them and their own inner strengths.

Needless to say, all these themes would be interwoven throughout the meetings. We realized that our eighth session, saying "Good-bye," would be right before Christmas, so we planned a follow-up session in January and one before Valentine's Day focusing on those whom we love now, especially our mothers, while remembering those we have lost. We found additional resources in the *Mourning Child Grief Support Group Curriculum: Early Childhood Edition* (Lehmann, Jimerson, and Gaasch, 2000).

We met all the children for the first time on October 23, and it was chaos! Two children from one family did not want to be there and were angry about being made to come by their mother and aunts. Despite intensive work with them and empathy for their anger, they did not come back. One young boy found the group overpowering and stayed with his mother in the widows' support group run by Joanne, a seasoned disaster mental health specialist and Brenda, who had extensive experience with hospice work. This six-year-old boy, Michael, had lost his father at the Pentagon and did some expressive pictures of the plane hitting the Pentagon while he was with the adult group.

Despite all the games and activities we planned, it was hard to calm the children and begin to develop a group sense. Donna and I discussed it afterwards and decided to split the group, so that each subgroup would be geared to a different developmental level. She took the third through fifth graders, and I took those from kindergarten through second grade. I had four children in my group, two of whom, Mary and Kenneth, were sister and brother. Of the other two, Michael has already been mentioned. He was the older of two boys. The fourth was Enid, a bright, engaging six-year-old who was a gifted artist and talked continuously. She had a brother in the older elementary school group and two younger siblings.

Donna's group consisted of Rebecca, an unusually expressive 10-year-old girl with a remarkable capacity to put on a smile to cover her sadness, and Adrienne, the only child who always arrived punctually for the group, eager to be a part of it, and who was very verbal about missing her father. Mark, Enid's older brother, felt the responsibility of being the oldest son. He had great difficulty talking about his tragic loss, but clearly thought about things very deeply, at times sharing some of the profoundest thoughts. Richard was an energetic boy, whose face showed his deep sadness. He used sports as an outlet. Adrienne, Rebecca, and Richard all had older siblings in the adolescent group.

We developed a pattern of an opening ceremony in which we all held hands. Then Donna would read a story, we'd talk about it a little and then split into the two groups. I would take the younger ones out, and we would do our activities before returning for a closing ceremony, once again holding hands. This worked much better because the younger ones needed a lot of activity and movement, whereas the older ones were more ready to sit around and talk about memories, feelings, and fears while working with clay. Stories that we read included "Where the Balloons Go," "Lifetimes," "I Feel Silly," and "Sam's Dad Is Dead." These provided varied ways of talking about memories, feelings, and the reality of death. For example, when we were talking about balloons, Mark told us excitedly about how once he and his father had written their name and address on a card and launched a helium balloon. Weeks later they received the card from Germany! We also used balloons to play with, each child blowing one up, writing a feeling on a piece of paper and putting it inside. After playing with the balloons each child burst one balloon and talked about the feeling.

In the older group, much time was spent working with clay. The children loved the work, but most did not save it. Rebecca made some beautiful beads, which she continues to treasure. On one occasion, about five weeks into the group, Mark and Richard spent almost the entire session lining up all the Magic Markers on their ends in a compulsive manner one next to the other and making sure that they did not fall over. The symbolism was evident, as was their yearning that the destruction of the World Trade Center had not happened, or that they had the power to make it not happen.

It was not easy to work with the younger children, because both the boys were very active, avoiding verbalizing their feelings. I brought in a box of Legos, which the boys loved because they could make houses and planes, crash and rebuild things. Both Mary and Enid were artistic and were remarkably expressive through their artwork. Mary was noticeably more mature and was a leader in talking about feelings and memories and ongoing difficulties. When we talked about the last time they had seen their fathers, both she and Enid expressed the idea that they should have stopped their fathers from going to work that day. Working with that sense of responsibility was vital to help them stop blaming themselves or their fathers and accept the reality that bad things happen that no one can foresee.

All the families were Christian, and for some the church played an important part in their lives. The younger children translated their beliefs into a firm conviction that the bad terrorists would go to hell, whereas their good fathers would be angels in heaven. They could derive some comfort from the thought of their being in a better place. The older children had more doubts, and one started refusing to go to church. This was partly a rebellion against her mother and partly some genuine doubts about how a good God could allow such a bad thing to happen. Later she refused to give up anything for Lent as she felt she had given up her father and how could more be asked of her?

The authors of the grief group curriculum were extremely helpful when I reached out to them. I started using some of the material from the preschool curriculum in addition to the early childhood one because it was more suited to this group of children. We talked about having many different feelings and went on a journey through various rooms of the Red Cross building to the Moody Mountain Range. We started at Happy Mountain where the thing that made them happiest was having a play date. We went on to Creepy Cave, a dark room where we lit a candle and talked about some of the things that made them scared. From there we went to Teary Valley where they drew pictures of things that made them sad, and then on to Mad Canyon where they worked with Play-Doh. Michael made a green dragon to breathe fire and destroy the terrorists, and both the boys were able to express some of their anger.

Another activity, which appealed to all the children, was taking turns being memory king or queen. Each child was asked to bring in a photo of his or her father and took turns putting on the crown and the red velvet robe and talking about their picture. They each chose happy memories of being with their fathers on vacation. This was the first time that Kenneth had spoken of his father, and he chimed in excitedly when Mary, his sister, started talking about a vacation episode when they went swimming together.

There were many touching moments in the group. As time went on, the children showed caring and concern for one another. Enid was worried about Mary when she missed a session because she was sick and drew a beautiful picture for her. Kenneth followed Michael out of the room to bring him back when the feeling was too intense for him. Some of the things the children said made our hearts melt. For example, Enid once said as she was drawing, "Sometimes I think I'll stop eating so that I can go and be with my father in heaven."

We were with the children through Halloween and Thanksgiving and arranged a follow-up group after Christmas. Fortunately most of the families spent time with their extended families, so that the children could begin to turn to uncles, grandfathers, and other relatives. Early on we had asked that each child bring a shirt of his or her father's to be made into a pillow. Donna's mother and a friend very kindly sewed these into pillows made according to each child's design. Rebecca asked for a big pillow that she could hug like she used to hug her father, and it was important to her that the shirt not be cut. Enid asked for one of her father's ties to be included and make a cross on the pillow. At the follow-up group we gave out the pillows and the children were thrilled. Each hugged his or her pillow with a smile and one commented on how it still smelled of her father.

By the end of the group sessions the mothers were feeling stronger, and the children's symptoms were reduced, but the women were anxious to continue. They decided to meet on a monthly basis and bring snacks and videos for the children. It has been, and continues to be, an important support for both the mothers and their children. In this area, only one or two families in each school lost a loved one, and the children would have felt as if they were "the only ones" affected by this tragedy if they had not been brought together with their peers. It helped them to start on the long process of grieving for their fathers and deal with some of the shock, pain, anger, and loss. It was also important that the grief group was held at the Red Cross rather than at a local mental health clinic because they were already in contact with the organization so they did not have to start over. In addition, this normalized the grieving process. Some are now in individual therapy, and all seem to be coping well. This is a tribute to their resilience, as well as to continuing family and community support. All commented on the importance to them of their pillows, which they sleep with every night.

Closure has been especially difficult for the families because of the lack of a body. Gruesome though it is, the recovery of even some small body part was helpful in finally accepting the reality of death. Once the mothers could accept death, it became easier for the children to do the same. As Donna and I have talked about their struggle to come to acceptance of death, we have felt that by making their husbands into heroes this in some way makes it okay for them to die, but it is not okay. In a sense, this is society's self-protective device from the pain of the bereaved.

This work is very different from other disaster work that I have done, which was solely concerned with the immediate loss or trauma within the first two weeks. In addition, most of my previous work was done with adults. When a disaster hits close to where one lives, one has a special responsibility of ongoing involvement as its shock waves continue to be felt. As a child psychiatrist, I feel I had an important place in the team of those who helped these grieving families because of my greater knowledge of child development and psychopathology and my many years of experience working with children and helping them to express their feelings and be understood. Working with children is a challenge, but having plenty of hands-on activities, being flexible and creative, and reaching out to colleagues for help can make this a successful experience.

I suspect that work of this kind would be helpful following other disasters. The Red Cross family service workers always obtain names and ages of affected children when called to the scene of fires, floods, tornadoes, and so on. The next step would be to contact local workers with the Red Cross, schools, psychiatric associations, and mental health clinics to encourage formation of trauma and grief groups. Both parents and children derive help and support from this type of intervention. An added benefit may be that some adults who would not seek treatment for themselves, despite their need, may be willing to seek it for their children. As we look for ways to mitigate the negative effects of disasters, this is an area worthy of further research. From a personal point of view, this is some of the most meaningful and important work I have ever done.

Acknowledgment

I acknowledge the valuable insight, experience, and warmth that Donna Dandrilli brought to our work together.

References

Lehmann, L., Jimerson, S. R. & Gaasch, A. (2000), *Mourning Child Grief Support Curriculum: Early Childhood Edition*. Philadelphia, PA: Buchanan.

Pynoos, R. S (1992), Grief and trauma in children and adolescents. *Bereavement Care*, 11:2–10.

V

Other U.S. Disasters

The collection closes with three essays about psychiatrists' reflections on their involvement in U.S. disasters other than 9/11. Perhaps no other domestic disaster has drawn public attention to the psychological and emotional dimensions of disasters as did 9/11. This can be counted as a silver lining in the otherwise dark, dark clouds of that day. But even though 9/11 still reverberates through two of them, the following essays remind us that disasters indeed struck the United States prior to 9/11 and that psychiatrists have made skilled interventions during these earlier disasters. Psychiatrists have been addressing the trauma of the Vietnam War both as military officers during the war and as Veterans Affairs employees since that time. Arthur Meyerson's essay offers a glimpse into the work of psychiatrists during the Vietnam War, and in the process he helps to elucidate the difference and similarity between the relatively well-charted landscape of military psychiatry in wartime and the developing field of civilian disaster psychiatry. At least one domestic civilian disaster, the Buffalo Creek tragedy, has been studied by psychiatrists in some depth over a long period of time. Nonetheless, as the essays by David Lindy and Donald Rosen indicate, most psychiatric responses to disasters are of much smaller scale, often requiring tremendous improvisation by the clinicians. One wonders whether much needed mental health resources directed toward survivors of the 9/11 terrorist attacks have ever before been so comprehensively provided to victims of lesser known civilian tragedies. What streams of emotional suffering have poured from natural and man-made disasters into the U.S. landscape without being stanched or even identified?

Perhaps more dauntingly, will the lessons of 9/11 be applied to future tragedy? Lindy's essay makes excellent note of the importance of disaster psychiatrists' being able to work within the hierarchical system of disaster response. Will that system now welcome psychiatrists and other mental health professionals around the planning table for future disasters? Or must they integrate themselves after the fact, as reflected in the experiences that Rosen lays out in Kansas and Oklahoma City? In an essay earlier in this book, Beverly Raphael described how a disaster mental health plan has been incorporated into Australia's countrywide disaster response system. Despite the fact of many natural and man-made disasters right here on U.S. soil and of the unprecedented magnitude of 9/11, no such system has been erected in the United States.

Today it is still left to energetic mental health professionals in the United States to be advocates for their role as much as they are practitioners after disasters. As the experience of so many writers in this book attests, psychiatrists are often consigned to serving as consultants and educators on disaster mental health to disaster response leaders and agencies after disasters rather than before them. The ad hoc nature of their involvement limits them to the periphery of disasters rather than being able to work at the heart of the situation, where they can apply their expertise directly to the mass human suffering. As a consequence, many psychiatrists have missed the opportunity to practice the uncommonly rewarding psychiatry that Lindy and Rosen describe and thereby to benefit their communities on a level and with a poignancy not routinely approached in other areas of their field.

It might seem that 9/11 casts a wide shadow over this book. But perhaps it has, in fact, shed light on a previously unheralded role for disaster psychiatrists and other mental health professionals within the panoply of response functions commonly laid out in disaster plans. As this book concludes, we express the hope that it has motivated psychiatrists and non–mental health professionals alike to think about how to avoid or at least to mitigate the invisible wounds of future disasters.

18

Debriefings in Kansas and Oklahoma

Donald E. Rosen

My involvement in disaster psychiatry occurred more by accident than design. The first exposure I had occurred in response to a siege by a gunman in the Frank Carlson federal courthouse in Topeka, Kansas, in 1994. The second, and most widely known, was the bombing of the Alfred P. Murrah federal building in Oklahoma City in 1995. Before these events, my primary involvement with victims of trauma was in a standard treatment setting. During my 15 years at the Menninger Clinic (1984–1999), I provided treatment to survivors of trauma in individual and group therapy, both as outpatients and inpatients. Some were survivors of shared tragedies, but most were victims of individual trauma. All were designated as "patients" who came seeking "treatment." None of their specific trauma was also my own. During my time at Menninger, I had extensive experience with survivors of several types of abuse—by loved ones, strangers, and groups. Some were recent traumas, many were not.

In the spring of 1994, a convicted felon laid siege on the federal courthouse in Topeka. Gary McKnight was awaiting sentencing on a drug charge. He drove his car to the courthouse as it was opening, rigged his car with explosives, and entered the building. The car exploded. He shot a security guard and headed to the clerk of the courts' office. Having heard gunshots, the employees in the clerk's office scattered. Some went to other parts of the building and found peers from other federal departments. Others hid sitting on pipes above the suspended ceiling. For nearly eight hours the siege

221

continued. McKnight ultimately blew himself up with a pipe bomb. When police and FBI entered the area, those in hiding weren't sure if the agents were to be believed, suspecting that the assailant(s) could be trying to lure them out in the open by reading the nameplates from their desks. Finally, in the late afternoon, a supervisor came in and her voice was recognized. All employees were accounted for. There was one death other than the assailant, and a couple of injuries.

The idea to develop a community response gelled quickly. As the tragedy unfolded, a reporter from the local newspaper called wanting to know about the anticipated effects of trauma on the survivors. I had given several interviews on a variety of subjects for the media and was contacted more for being known to the reporter than for a specific expertise in community tragedy. There was an obvious need to do more, and Menninger supported the effort. Late in the same day, I met with a colleague, Dr. Bonnie Buchele, who had extensive experience with survivors of sexual trauma and in group therapy. In addition, her then-husband and my brother were both Kansas district court judges less than four blocks away.

Soliciting and coordinating the volunteers were straightforward. All the volunteers were Menninger or Veterans Affairs clinicians who were willing to do whatever was needed. All agreed to help with the Critical Incident Stress Debriefing (CISD) and donate three additional clinical hours if necessary. The newspaper and TV stations informed the community of our intent. We were contacted by the Federal Emergency Management Agency (FEMA) and met with their representatives, who were somewhat apprehensive about our plans. They explained that this was their area of expertise, that they had seen several communities respond poorly and that locally organized CSIDs might exacerbate the effects of trauma rather than soothe them. They explained their protocol (essentially no different from our own), and we invited them to join us. Their participation was a beneficial addition to our program.

Approximately 150 to 200 people attended, including two friends of the assailant, who came because they were shocked he could do such a thing and felt alone and confused. The CISD went according to protocol. We welcomed everyone and described how the evening would unfold, including availability for follow-up appointments. We didn't want anyone to feel on edge about what we were going to do.

After an opening nondenominational prayer, FBI agents gave the official account of the event and the ongoing investigation. They talked about who the assailant was, his court case, his history, and what actually happened that day. They described where he entered the building, where he went, and what he did. Other officials talked about when the building would be open, how people could get their belongings and return to work schedules, and how subsequent information would be communicated to them. Dr. Buchele and I talked about the impact of trauma and some responses that may occur. We were careful not to prescribe reactions that people "ought" to have, because we didn't want to encourage their emergence or have people think something was wrong with them if they didn't have some of the common reactions.

After we answered questions from the larger group, we broke up into small groups so attendees could talk about their experience with professionals present. Groups had a set structure. There were coleaders to each group, so if someone left, a professional could go with them, and the other could stay with the group. The coleaders were instructed to assure confidentiality and ask the participants to describe their individual experience of the events—where they were, what they heard or saw, and so forth. After everyone in the group had the opportunity to do this, the coleaders went around the group again and asked them to describe their feelings during and after the event. At the end of the group, the leaders reminded everyone of follow-up availability, through their Employee Assistance Program (EAP), FEMA, and Menninger. The FEMA representatives were pleased with the way the CISD went.

Dr. Buchele and I co-led one of the small groups. Because I knew the assistant U.S. attorney from a prior context, he brought the employees of the clerk's office to our group. We met for twice as long as scheduled. The group members described the experience of sitting on pipes in the dark above a suspended ceiling, being careful not to make any noise. Supervisors felt they had abandoned their friends and supervisees. Those who were not there that day felt guilty. All were struggling with intense reactions. Outside our room the other groups had drawn to a conclusion, and our colleagues wondered what was going on with us. Dr. Walt Menninger, president of the Menninger Clinic, knocked on the door and poked his head in the room to "make sure we didn't need anything." He recognized these were the employees from the clerk's office and excused himself. We decided to end the group shortly after and agreed to reconvene the next day.

I continued to work with the employees of the clerk's office for nearly a year. We met every few weeks for two months, then monthly for three months, then quarterly. Some had lingering symptoms, but all showed substantial improvement from the symptoms they had shortly after the siege. Those who were more socially isolated or had a history of prior trauma had a more difficult time than the others. Some got into individual treatment. All were pleased at the community's support of them and grateful for the ongoing availability of a forum to discuss their experiences. I had learned much from the experience and felt that I had done a service to my community and family. I returned to my duties as director of the Professionals in Crisis program and associate director of the C. F. Menninger Hospital, in charge of hospital education.

The Oklahoma City bombing of the Alfred P. Murrah federal building occurred less than a year later on April 19, 1995. Before the September 11, 2001 attacks on the World Trade Center and the Pentagon, the bombing of the Murrah building was the largest single terrorist attack made on domestic soil. It remains the largest bomb ever used against Americans in this country. I did not expect to be asked to be of assistance. As the day unfolded, a few colleagues asked if I had heard anything or would I be going. The newspaper reporter I had spoken to after the courthouse siege called, and I spoke with a few of the employees at the courthouse. We are all familiar with the increased risk of vicarious retraumatization after subsequent traumas, even if they occur far away. I spoke with the supervisor in the clerk's office, and we agreed that she would see how her employees were doing and likely offer another meeting with me. What I did not know was that officials from the U.S. district court of eastern Kansas had contacted their colleagues at the federal court of western Oklahoma and suggested they invite me to come to Oklahoma City to do similar work with them. The Murrah federal building was adjacent to the federal courthouse and they used a common garage, cafeteria, and other facilities.

During the afternoon of April 19, I received a phone call from the U.S. Department of Justice asking me to come and organize a similar response for the employees and their families of the federal courthouse in Oklahoma City. I asked for and received permission to bring a colleague with me. This helped tremendously both with the planning of the intervention and with easing my anxiety. I was apprehensive about going into such a novel and intense situation without someone I knew to help plan and process the experience. Dr. Buchele had left Menninger, and I asked Dr. Jon Allen to accompany me. Dr. Allen was in the process of finishing his book, *Coping with Trauma,* and was an acknowledged expert in the field. We left the next morning.

The situation in Oklahoma City was dramatically different from what I had encountered in Topeka. At the time of our arrival, many assumed that this was the work of foreign terrorists. Timothy McVeigh and Terry Nichols, who were later convicted of the bombing, hadn't yet been connected to the crime. We were met at the airport and taken to a 10:00 a.m.

meeting with the federal judges, the U.S. attorney for Oklahoma, the federal public defender, and investigators from the FBI. The meeting took place in the storeroom of the main post office downtown; a clear statement of how much logistical scrambling had to be done. The folding metal chairs on the concrete floor were a far cry from the chambers and conference rooms of the federal courthouse.

At the conclusion of that first planning meeting, eight of us were taken to the remains of the Murrah building. As the van got closer the signs of destruction became more obvious. Blown-out windows, fractured facades, and empty streets became more prevalent. There were three security perimeters set up around the site. Immediately outside the outermost perimeter was the press area. It was a parking lot crowded with RVs from which reporters would emerge when people left the secure area. Almost all the photographs of the Murrah building were taken from this spot, approximately three blocks away. Inside the outer perimeter was FEMA's on-site headquarters, with supplies of rescue equipment, food, and clothing. It was well staffed with dedicated public servants. We went through two more checkpoints and then we were in front of the Murrah building. We were briefed by ATF (Alcohol, Tobacco, and Firearms) and FBI agents about the events, how ammonium nitrate bombs work, and how the rescue-and-recovery operation was organized. Rescue workers were finding bodies but not survivors.

While talking to an ATF agent, another agent put a piece of black tape on each of our name badges. I looked at the agent, and he said "fallen officer." The body of a fellow ATF agent had been found. They had worked in the same office. It was not the first time since the bombing that this had happened to this man. Helpful words were at a minimum. Presence was more important. I became increasingly less aware of my own feelings as the day wore on.

The crater left by the explosion seemed large, approximately 20 feet long, 15 feet wide, and 12 feet deep. Cars in the parking lot across the street were unrecognizable, burned-out shells. Buildings looked precariously close to falling and would obviously have to be razed. Around the corner the parking garage was a temporary morgue. The federal courthouse behind the Murrah building sustained significant damage.

We were brought back to the outer perimeter after our tour and interviews with the officers and recovery workers concluded. The press emerged en masse to hear our story. Except for the BBC and *Der Spiegle,* our comments held little interest for the media. They seemed to flee back to their RVs as quickly as they came out. There was a complete disconnection between the power of our personal experience, the magnitude of our task, and the interest the press had in our experience. I was disappointed and relieved. I suspect they had news stories they were working on and were not interested in the information or perspective we could offer.

The interplay of logistical planning, personal experience, and providing counsel was interesting. Over the next few days, our task was to plan the event, make sure that volunteers were available and capable, and provide counsel to our sponsors and each other regarding our own reactions. Volunteers were screened for experience in the field, with CISD, and with group therapy. Some volunteers were not asked to participate if they were assessed to have insufficient experience. We had a great deal of support from Red Rock Community Mental Center, the federal EAP, and a host of local Oklahoma City mental health providers. We were given the use of a large church downtown. It had a large sanctuary and several classrooms for us to use.

I was asked to meet with one of the attorneys in the evening. The meeting did not occur, and when I saw her the next morning, I was informed that she had been called to represent Timothy McVeigh in his first appearance. The attorney had lost friends in the bombing and had the responsibility to represent the accused bomber just two days later, as it began to dawn on Americans that the terrorists were also American. Almost without exception, the level of professionalism and utter human decency shown by the attorney and the ATF agent was demonstrated by everyone we met during our stay. There was little denial or minimization of the profound psychological circumstances they (and we) found themselves in. Everyone rose to the occasion and supported each other through this unchartered territory.

Approximately 600 courthouse employees, Murrah building employees, and family members attended the CISD, held three days after the bombing. The process unfolded similarly to the one described earlier, with one significant exception. The small discussion groups did not materialize as they had in Topeka. The chief judge of the western district of the Oklahoma federal court welcomed everyone, and a minister led a prayer. FBI Agent Ricks described the events and the state of the investigation and announced McVeigh's arrest. FEMA officials described the logistics of the operation: how people could get their car, where personal items found in the wreckage would be sent for claiming, and so on. People felt isolated, bombarded by the inability to escape the news coverage, and unsure of what to do. Many wanted to return to work, not so much in an effort to deny what happened but for a sense of efficacy and productive diversion. They didn't know what else to do and wanted to do something. After the bombing, employees were sent home and had done little verbal processing of the tragedy. Many felt isolated in their experience. Phone trees were set up for communication and support.

There were two major differences in the CISD of the two tragedies. Press coverage of the bombing in Oklahoma City was unavoidable. One could not watch TV, listen to the radio, or read the paper without being flooded by all aspects of the news. Being dubbed by the media as "Terror in the Heartland" highlighted the sense of betrayal of a sense of safety that we all would like to think we have working in a federal building in a medium-sized Midwestern city. Some complained that the phrase sounded patronizing, that it attempted to bring a distinction to a terrorist attack occurring in Oklahoma City as being different from one that happened outside "the Heartland."

The other major difference was that the large group did not break up into smaller process groups. After having been sent home and not having seen each other for three days, the large group wanted to stay that way. They did not want to be sent anywhere. They wished to stay until they were ready to leave. This much larger group (approximately 600) talked much more openly in the large forum than the Topeka group had. People wanted to know who survived. Many knew other people's names or faces but often not both. "Did the woman with long brown hair in Health and Human Services [HHS] make it?" "What about the guy with the curly hair, mustache, and those funny ties?" We had lists of known survivors from various agencies, but people needed descriptions to go with the names. People seemed to be trying to piece together what they could, as most trauma survivors do. I was the emcee for the event, introducing the speakers and leading the discussion. The presenters did a superb job at detailing the events, logistics, and plans for ongoing contact. Services for ongoing support were available through the federal EAP and Red Rock Mental Health for employees and their family members. Dr. Allen's discussion of what might happen to people following trauma was excellent, and the discussion that he and I led seemed useful.

The event was well received at the time and in follow-up review by the federal EAP and FEMA. It helped to bring together those who had been isolated from each other (both physically and emotionally) after the bombing and to provide a frame for survivors to hear about the event from people they knew and from the experts brought in to assist. The CISD allowed for a systematic processing of an event that had been overwhelming. The process began with the facts and progressed through to individuals' experience. Information was provided from multiple sources, because life was interrupted in multiple ways.

The format of the CISD provides a guide to the management of trauma for both victims and treaters. It is clear, but not formulaic. Follow-up is a crucial component and proved to be in the Kansas and Oklahoma cases as well. Clear descriptions of services available to aid in anticipated and unanticipated sequelae proved important. The quick intervention by skilled workers using a CISD format with available follow-up has been shown to decrease morbidity and mortality following several types of trauma in military, industrial, group, and individual settings. Having a working knowledge and experience with disaster psychiatry helped me in my work with posttraumatic stress disorder (PTSD) patients whose trauma happened long ago. I had a heightened appreciation for what their immediate reaction to trauma might have been. My previous work with victims of PTSD proved invaluable to being effective in disaster work. My work in Oklahoma City and Topeka was in the paper and on local television, and I told several patients that what I had learned from them helped me to understand my task in the CISD and to do it better.

Follow-up between me and the federal judges and Red Rock Mental Health Center was sporadic. Our contact with the center was felt to be useful both to them and us, if for no other reason than to discuss what we had been through. I continue to feel a close tie with those involved. We returned home Sunday, April 23, 1995, and the typical sight of kids playing in the street on a clear spring day made me realize how traumatizing the event was. The degree of abnormalcy in Oklahoma City was a powerful contrast with the bucolic scene in my neighborhood. Each reinforced the meaning of the other. The experience was at once draining and immensely rewarding. I came away an advocate for CISD and with the conviction in the capacity of well-trained professionals to take their skills to new areas of work and do an admirable job. Disaster psychiatry is not something I have chosen to specialize in, but I would gladly do more of it. The experiences left me optimistic about the basic goodness of the vast majority of people and our capacity to rise to the occasion in the face of unspeakable cruelty. For me, what started as "accidental involvement" became one of the most meaningful experiences of my professional life.

19

Upheaval of the Stars

From Happy Land to the World Trade Center

David C. Lindy

The Psychological Impact of Disasters

Although disaster psychiatry is currently receiving a great deal of apparently new interest and attention, it has, in fact, been around for a long time. Numerous trauma experts (e.g., Herman, 1992; Ursano, Fullerton, and Norwood, 1995; van der Kolk, Weisaeth, and van der Hart, 1996; Leys, 2000) relate its history. For example, Civil War soldiers with unusual distress were said to suffer from "nostalgia." Victorian physicians described "soldier's heart" in 1870 as a form of shell shock (itself a term from World War I) and "railroad spines" as the psychological symptoms that developed in survivors of train and other accidents of the Industrial Age. Military psychiatrists dealt with combat-induced psychological syndromes in both world wars, as well as the Vietnam War. What is new, however, is the now commonly held assumption within the disaster response community at large that psychiatrists and mental health personnel perform integral functions in disaster response. The psychological responses of trauma victims have come to be regarded as basic needs requiring attention in the disaster situation, along with such fundamentals as physical safety and appropriate governmental intervention. The disaster psychiatrist, and all mental health personnel working in disaster response, must therefore understand these reactions and their sequelae on two levels. We must understand their clinical dimensions as they affect victims and loved ones, and we must understand the complex organizational and social contexts in which these responses occur.

Indeed, an examination of the etymology of the word *disaster* shows that it touches on both of these personal and social aspects at a very basic level. According to Webster's *Third New International Dictionary, disaster* comes from two Latin roots: *dis,* meaning "away," "separation," "negation," and *astrum,* "star." Something creates a separation from the stars, a negation or disturbance in the heavens. As noted disaster psychiatrist Jack Lindy (personal communication) has observed, the etymology of disaster reflects a disruption in the fabric of the usual, expectable order of our universe. In other words, disaster refers to a destructive event that changes our relationship to the world. It affects what psychoanalysts call external reality. But that speaks to our *experience* of that external reality, what it means to each of us individually and what we do with that meaning. If a star goes out in the distant heavens without affecting us here on Earth, we would probably not call that a disaster, whatever the impact in its local part of the universe. The event is a disaster when it changes *our* world. This external reality leads to changes in our internal reality. The two are inextricably interwoven. In a sense, external disaster creates an internal disaster, an overwhelming, intolerable internal reality. This reality is intolerable because we are helpless in the face of its terrifying, horrible, dangerous effects. Helplessness induces deformations in internal reality because it renders us helpless to influence external reality. Depression, panic, dissociation, and suicidal behavior can be manifestations of traumatic injury in the mind, and, as indicated by a growing body of research, most probably the brain. (See Brockman's excellent 1998 review, for one example among many.) Disaster often causes mental scarring; with the right conditions, there may be healing.

Psychiatry attempts to understand and heal inner pain, including traumatic interactions with an external world that cause or exacerbate suffering. Disaster psychiatry can be understood as a more narrow aspect of psychiatry's interest in trauma. However, in so far as disasters are social events, often on a large scale, disaster psychiatry has a much broader scope than traditional clinical psychiatry. Disaster psychiatrists must work in situations that are essentially nonclinical, often reporting to nonphysicians, and dealing with a wide variety of government, law enforcement and other emergency agencies, and pastoral and media personnel. Psychiatry deals with patients; disaster psychiatry deals with victims. Accordingly, mental health training and experience must sometimes be subsumed to the greater needs of the disaster response. It must also be flexibly adjusted to the needs of victims who do not see themselves as patients and will not respond to standard clinical interventions in the usual ways. I discuss this further later. The important point here is an idea called *countertransference,* a concept that is well known to mental health clinicians but really basic to human psychology. Countertransference is related to transference, a psychoanalytic concept that describes how patients react to their therapist in terms of important people from the past. These reactions exist in a dynamic relationship to re-actions based on the present, a "new edition" of the old relationship, as Freud (1901) described it. Countertransference refers to the same process going on in the therapist and is understood as an important source of infor-mation regarding the patient's state of mind. Clearly, disaster's powerful ef-fects on internal and external reality make countertransference a critical is-sue for mental health disaster workers (Wilson and Lindy, 1994).

I have been privileged to serve as chief psychiatrist and clinical director for the Visiting Nurse Service of New York's (VNS) Community Mental Health Services since 1986. In this role, I have been involved in the relief efforts for such disasters as the Happy Land Social Club fire (1990), the first World Trade Center bombing (1993), the TWA 800 crash (1996), and the September 11 attack on the World Trade Center (2001). VNS Community Mental Health Services treats seriously ill patients, fre-quently in crisis situations, and, building on VNS's 100-year-old tradition of home care, we provide all services on an outreach basis. This has pre-pared our staff for the kind of crisis-oriented field work required in disaster relief projects. In addition, I have found my experiences with disaster work greatly enhanced by psychoanalytic training, particularly in regard to my interest in the intrapsychic defenses used by disaster victims to cope with their experiences. Here I draw on my work with VNS to compare aspects of my first disaster experience with the Happy Land Social Club fire to my most recent, the attack on the Twin Towers. This will set the stage for a discussion of identification with the victim, a trauma-induced defense that I suggest is a normal and ubiquitous defense against the experience of vicarious traumatization, much the same way that the well-known de-fense of identification with the aggressor (Freud, 1936) defends against the experience of helplessness.

The Story of Rosa Sanchez

We first met Rosa Sanchez at the Relief Center set up at Pier 94 after 9/11. She was frightened, agitated, and confused. Initially unable to tell anyone her name or address, she was brought over to the mental health area. With the help of a Spanish translator, we eventually calmed her down and she was able to say that she was 46 years old, had emigrated to New York City from

Honduras about 20 years before, and had worked as a cleaning lady in the World Trade Center. She was at work the morning of September 11, and even before anything happened, an "eerie feeling" had been bothering her. Suddenly there was an explosion and lots of black smoke. In the commotion people were saying that everyone should remain where they were. Instead, she panicked and ran, running down many, many stairs, emerging from the building with her hair on fire. She told us that many sad things had happened to her, like leaving her country to come to New York and losing 12 members of her family when Hurricane Mitch hit Honduras in 1998. In addition, 9/11 was not her first experience with fire. There had been another, far worse. And even though it had not happened directly to her, she had never gotten over it.

On March 25, 1990, Eduardo, Rosa's 17-year-old son, was enjoying a Saturday night at the Happy Land Social Club in the South Bronx with friends on his soccer team. As related by Ray Bromley in his in-depth review of the Happy Land fire (Bromley, 1992a), there is a long-standing tradition of social clubs in New York City that serve as comfortable, inexpensive gathering spots for its ethnic, religious, and immigrant communities. Scattered throughout the boroughs, the clubs are places of respite from a foreign land where people can feel like they are back home. The Happy Land, specializing in Honduran *punta* and other types of Latin dance music, was a favorite local spot, catering especially to the neighborhood's many Honduran residents. It appealed to a wider audience as well. The night of the fire, "the 94 people inside formed a typical mixture of club regulars, . . . employees, . . . and first-timers, including such tragic cases as a 14-year-old on his very first date, . . . [and] a married couple from Boston sampling New York Honduran night-life" (Bromley, 1992a, p. 7). Four birthday parties were being celebrated. Significantly, the club was illegal because the city had ordered it closed 16 months before for fire safety and other building-code infractions. This technicality did not deter Eduardo and his friends. Indeed, city officials seemed content to allow the club to function openly.

Julio Gonzalez, a Cuban refugee and alumnus of the infamous 1980 *Mariel* boatlift, had recently lost both his job in a warehouse and Lydia Feliciano, his girlfriend of six years. She was working that night, checking coats at the Happy Land. Julio went to the club to plead with her to take him back, but she had him ejected by the bouncer. As he was thrown out, he screamed, *Regresare, ha cerrar esto!* ("I will be back, I'll shut the place down!") Humiliated and enraged, he bought a dollar's worth of gasoline from a nearby gas station. That, plus a match, was all he needed to start the deadliest fire in New York City since the devastating Triangle Shirtwaist fire of 1911, exactly 79 years before. As reported the following day in the *New York Times*, "[Gonzalez's] girlfriend and at least three others survived. But the flames quickly cut off the only open door and almost instantly filled the club with smoke. Some victims suffocated so rapidly that their bodies were found with drinks in their hands" (Blumenthal, 1990). In fact, seven people survived, only one of whom was significantly injured. But 87 people died, including Rosa Sanchez's Eduardo and his soccer mates. The Happy Land fire was the worst mass murder in the history of the United States committed by a single individual.

After September 11, of course, the significance of that statistic changed profoundly. For Rosa Sanchez, it changed in a way particular to her. Rosa is part of a select group of people who were directly affected by both the Happy Land fire and the World Trade Center bombing. This is a group that no one chooses to belong to. It chooses you, according to the terrible calculus by which trauma selects its victims. The attack on the World Trade Center changed the world. Rosa's world had changed when she lost her son in the Happy Land fire and her relatives to Hurricane Mitch. With 9/11, the defenses that she had developed to cope with her losses broke down, leaving her helpless in the face of a world that wanted to kill her—again. It is well known that survivors of previous trauma and disaster are more vulnerable to subsequent trauma, as shown by higher rates of psychiatric symptoms and posttraumatic stress disorder (PTSD) compared with victims of single events (Breslau, 1999). There may be an adaptive aspect to this vulnerability as well, however (Card, 1983). Many of the people who experienced the first World Trade Center bombing immediately left the buildings when the first plane hit the north tower, although they had been told to stay at their desks. Like Rosa, running down the stairs with the memory of the Happy Land fire rekindled in her mind, they survived while many of their less traumatized coworkers complied and perished (Goode and Pogrebin, 2001). The 9/11 attacks affected the world, but, like all disasters, its traumatic effects have to be psychologically metabolized by each of us individually. For Rosa, this meant experiencing 9/11 in light of her memories of Happy Land.

The Happy Land building still stands. It is located at 1959 Southern Boulevard, just off of East Tremont Avenue in the South Bronx, close to the Third Avenue exit from the Cross Bronx Expressway. The Cross Bronx bisects the South Bronx, one of the poorest areas in New York City, and people drive through on their way to the suburbs of Westchester or New Jersey. Many Honduran immigrants live in this area, and the Happy Land Social Club provided them with a place to relax and have a good time. There is a barren little park across the street from the Happy Land where a monument to the victims stands today. A few blocks to the north there is a Catholic church, St. Thomas Aquinas. A few blocks to the south stands an elementary school, P.S. 67. The morning after the fire, ambulances, police cars, and fire trucks were parked all over the place; body bags covered the sidewalk in front of the building housing the club. Media people bustled around everywhere and thousands of curious onlookers lined the streets. A "command post" had been set up in the school to function as the center of operations and a makeshift morgue. Family members, friends, and neighbors waited to get any available information regarding missing loved ones from disaster relief workers who took names and descriptions from them. They reviewed photographs of the faces of the victims to identify the dead. Friends and staff comforted wailing mourners.

To a psychiatrist, the scene was striking for several additional reasons. Like an emergency room, a disaster scene is a paramilitary situation in which an operational hierarchy is used to structure an otherwise chaotic, overwhelming environment. The Happy Land scene was characterized by a charred building, dead bodies, uncertainty, confusion, and panicked loved ones. But unlike an emergency room, at the disaster scene the physician is not in charge. Although the exact relationships are worked out on a case-by-case basis, primary responsibility for managing a disaster is usually shared by the Red Cross and fire and police departments. At Happy Land, aside from helping with acute grief reactions, little medical work was required. By the time most disaster relief workers arrived on Sunday morning, the bodies had been dealt with and the seven survivors examined in local emergency departments. Only Ruben Valladarez, one of the two deejays working at the club that night, was actually physically injured, with serious burns to 40 percent of his body. The medical work was under control. Nevertheless, many critical administrative responsibilities remained, for example, organizing a place and a means for loved ones to identify bodies, making funeral arrangements, determining benefits, dealing with immigration issues. Many years of medical education offers little preparation to psychiatrists for most of this work. Indeed, some psychiatric training is in fact counterproductive in this setting because disaster relief workers must follow orders within the hierarchy of the disaster scene rather than the doctor-controlled hospital. The disaster situation is no place for doctors who believe they always know best and who would never dream of taking orders from anyone without an MD.

With the World Trade Center bombing, loved ones of victims felt fortunate if any physical remains, much less an intact body, could be identified. The Happy Land fire sucked the air out of the crowded building so quickly that most of the 87 victims died of asphyxiation and were untouched by the fire. Many looked as if they were sleeping. Out of this developed a creative and effective administrative process, born in the crucible of the disaster. I have been unable to discover who deserves credit for this (perhaps the medical examiner), but someone in the early hours of responding to the disaster realized that, because of the intactness of most of the bodies, photographs of the deceased could be used for purposes of identification. This spared loved ones the gruesome process of identifying bodies, typically required in disaster situations. None of the sources I reviewed documenting the Happy Land fire (American Red Cross [1990]; *New York Times* [1990]; New York City Department of Mental Health [1991]; Bromley [1992a, b]) gave any detail about how this procedure came about. But soon after arriving on the scene, someone had the presence of mind to come up with the idea, take the photographs, get them developed, and put them up in the school's gymnasium. By the end of the day on Sunday, 77 of the 87 victims had been identified.

In addition, there was a new level of integration among the many agencies responding to the disaster, including mental health providers. In many ways, the Happy Land fire marked the beginning of New York City's effort to create an organized mental health disaster relief system. Various aspects of a system had been in place for many years, including the Red Cross, the police and fire departments, emergency medical workers, victims services agencies. These agencies did not necessarily see themselves as components of a larger disaster relief system, however, and mental health was not seen as playing a key role in disaster response. At least two factors converged to contribute to Happy Land's importance in changing that. First, trauma had reemerged as a topic of interest within psychiatry. Although its importance had never been entirely forgotten, work with Vietnam veterans with PTSD and with victims of sexual trauma made mental health workers more cognizant of the psychological sequelae of traumatic events such as disasters. Second, in 1986, the New York City Department of Mental Health, Retardation, and Alcoholism Services (DMH) initiated a citywide mobile crisis service to provide on-site mental health assessment, treatment, triage, and support to persons experiencing psychiatric crises. Through DMH contracts with various agencies operating throughout the city, a loose network of teams developed to cover a wide area of New York. This network possessed a capacity for acute response to traumatic events occurring throughout the five boroughs. The Happy Land fire created a first unfortunate opportunity to deploy mobile crisis teams functioning in a large-scale disaster capacity.

Responding to DMH's directive, VNS's Bronx Mobile Crisis Team got involved with the Happy Land crisis from the beginning. Although we had never done disaster relief work before, our mental health background, mobile orientation, and familiarity with the area provided a solid starting point from which to build experience. In addition, because every disaster is different, there is always a lot of on-the-job training for everyone. Even the most seasoned disaster workers have to learn what the specific issues are with every new event. With Happy Land, many of the people requiring services spoke only Spanish. Our bilingual staff members provided an important service in speaking with distraught relatives and interpreting for other workers in situations of great emotional intensity. As the first week following the fire ended, the P.S. 67 command post was disbanded and, with the loss of this central location, people drifted back into the neighborhood. Importantly, DMH understood that the flexibility and availability of mobile crisis teams enabled them to serve a critical role in the acute phase of a disaster, but also that they could be uniquely helpful in engaging victims in the ensuing weeks. Many of the agencies initially involved with Happy Land, including the Red Cross, provide primarily acute disaster services. (The Red Cross remained deeply involved, however, with the 9/11 response for many months.) Disaster's victims, defined for these purposes as those affected directly and indirectly, continue to suffer beyond the first days. PTSD cannot be diagnosed until symptoms have been present for at least one month (American Psychiatric Association, 2000). Yet successfully engaging members of this population despite their need for treatment can be challenging.

There are many reasons the Happy Land families were difficult to engage. First, as noted earlier, most disaster victims are not psychiatric patients and do not think of themselves as such. When approached by well-intentioned mental health workers, however sensitively, their typical response is, "I'm not crazy!" They see no need for mental health services and do not want to be associated with the stigma of mental illness. They will often reject help because accepting it is seen as an acknowledgment of weakness. Sometimes loved ones surround the victim with a "trauma membrane" intended to keep out potentially hurtful influences from a dangerous outside world (Lindy, 1981). Important cultural factors played an additional role with the Honduran victims of the Happy Land fire. (It should be noted that almost 30 percent of the Happy Land victims were not Honduran, but came from the Caribbean, Britain, and the United States.) Concerns about stigma and the perception of weakness, especially among the men, were very strong. In addition, some of the Hondurans were illegal immigrants or had other legal or financial problems and therefore were suspicious of anyone who could be a government official. A knock on the door by a stranger identifying herself as a member of the VNS Mobile Crisis Team was not a terribly compelling reason to open up. In addition, relief personnel, such as police and firefighters, often require support, and occasionally treatment, from their disaster experiences. This group also tends to reject mental health services because they are acculturated to believe that they "don't need it, stress just comes with the job."

The problem of how to engage populations affected by disaster, including relief workers, is one of the most difficult and important issues in this field because they experience significant psychopathology. DMH sponsored a study (1991), completed one year after the fire, in which "representatives of 72 relatives (people who lost someone in the fire) and four survivors' households" were interviewed using a structured questionnaire called the Case Management Profile. It showed

> a picture of estranged, despairing, lonely relatives and survivors experiencing extreme stress and negative psychiatric symptoms in response to the loss of their loved one(s) . . . Some of the most common symptoms found . . . have been guilt, depression and post-traumatic syndrome, including insomnia, withdrawal, and disorientation. . . . [Some] confessed frequent thoughts about suicide, and others reported long periods of confusion and disorientation: staring blankly into space; not being able to follow even simple instructions; forgetting where they were going; and, in several cases, having to give up driving a car because of blackouts, fears, and lost sense of direction. . . . Depression has been a major cause of problems . . . sometimes resulting in the loss of jobs and/or housing, or in dropping out of school [Bromley, 1992b, pp. 13–14].

Clearly, posttraumatic syndromes can create enormous suffering in the aftermath of disasters like Happy Land, and on a wider scale, the Twin Towers. Reaching the victims to provide treatment and support in both acute and chronic phases is a critical function of disaster psychiatry. One month after the fire, we were following only two of the 14 families originally assigned to VNS, as reported by Linda Sacco, director of the Bronx Office of VNS Community Mental Health Services. Of approximately 60 people referred to local mental health clinics, most showed up only once or twice, although the treatment was offered without charge. Some felt therapy was inappropriate for grief, and some could not afford transportation costs, get off work, or arrange for child care.

It became clear that traditional ways of offering mental health care were not going to work in this setting. As mentioned earlier, mistrust of "officials" often prevented us from getting inside the door, even with the mobile crisis approach. We could visit clients in their homes, saving them the trouble and expense of a trip to the clinic, and we arranged evening visits when people needed to be seen after working hours. We could stop by repeatedly if people were not at home, or if we felt that they were avoiding us. These strenuous efforts, however, often failed. The critical step forward occurred when we connected with the Hope Line, a grassroots community group that had been organized to respond to the needs of people affected by Happy Land. Located in the basement of St. Thomas Aquinas, two blocks down the street from the Happy Land site, this group possessed the natural trust of the community because they were part of it. With their introduction, we could get past initial rejections and begin the delicate process of establishing rapport. We learned that the most important first step, once we got in the door, was *not* to talk about therapy or mental health issues. The Happy Land families usually had pressing concrete needs with such issues as food, housing, entitlements, and immigration. Sometimes they were embroiled in battles with relatives over who should have custody of children orphaned by the fire. (At least 99 children lost one or both parents; seven more were subsequently born fatherless.) These needs were their greatest concerns, and when we could help, we were providing a service for which they were very grateful. As trust developed, walls came down and we began to hear about Grandma's sleepless nights or Juan's drinking and fighting. Operating outside of the formal treatment setting, we could initiate treatment, sometimes continuing it in the home, sometimes making a referral when that was acceptable to the patient.

Eighteen months after the tragic night, VNS was working with about 40 people whose lives had been changed by the Happy Land fire. We had been with them through the trial and conviction of Julio Gonzalez, we had been guests in their homes. In the end, we received this invitation from Comite de Familias de las Victimas del Happy Land.

September 16, 1991

Dear Friends,

The families of the victims of the Happy Land fire invite you to attend a mass on Sunday, September 22, 1991, at 12:00 noon. The mass will be followed by a Lunch Buffet. At this time we will give thanks to all those individuals and institutions that supported and helped us. . . .

Sincerely,

Committee of Families

I had never been inside St. Thomas Aquinas before. It is the size of a cathedral, as I remember it, and on that beautiful September afternoon the sun poured through its huge stained-glass windows. The charred remains of the Happy Land building nearby, the church was filled with people remembering the tragedy, but also reaffirming life and connection. I sat between two people from the community, probably Honduran, smiling and polite, speaking little English. I felt uncomfortable, out of place. But as the service proceeded, its warmth and spirit washed away my feelings of strangeness and discomfort. Music played on guitars and wooden flutes filled the church. We stood, arms linked, swaying, my neighbors singing happily to familiar songs, me humming along as best I could. The lunch took place in the basement following the service. It was actually a feast and every time I finished my plate of roast pork, rice and beans, and fried plantains, someone with a big smile filled it again. I was moved by the kindness and gratitude I experienced that day, and the memory of why we had all come together.

The Mayor's Interview

Almost 10 years later to the day, the world watched in horror as two commercial airliners flew into the Twin Towers of the World Trade Center. Although approximately 2,000 people were estimated to have had a direct connection to someone lost in the Happy Land fire, millions of us have been directly touched by the events of 9/11. Almost 3,000 people were killed, and tens of thousands of others, at the least, witnessed the attack, either directly or on television. In addition, in so far as this disaster, this "upheaval of the stars," potentially threatens the way of life of millions of people throughout the world, its traumatic impact is even greater. In his classic paper "Mourning and Melancholia," Freud (1917) suggested that the loss of an ideal could create depression. Similarly, we can hypothesize that the fear of the loss of freedom and security might cause symptoms on a traumatic basis. This could further enlarge the pathological impact of 9/11. While few of us remember

Happy Land 10 years later, it is safe to say that the story of 9/11 will be told for many years to come. Like the images shown and reshown on television during those first days after the attack, we have returned again and again to the telling of this story. This is part of how we perform the crucial psychological task of coming to terms with an event that defies comprehension in its traumatic assault on our sense of reality, that pushes the stars out of kilter. We work it over, again and again, as if repetition will wear it down to a size and shape that we can manage. Often, as Freud (1920) tried to convey with his notion of the repetition compulsion, this process leads to illness instead when the trauma remains unmanageable.

Within two days of the World Trade Center attack, a family relief center was established in the Lexington Avenue Armory at 28th Street. Like the P.S. 67 command post for Happy Land, this site was the disaster response center of operations, but on an entirely different scale. The scope and complexity of the makeshift facility, as well as the speed with which it was set up, were impressive. City, state, and federal agencies with little history of cooperation worked together as team members. Police officers who might typically regard mental health professionals with suspicion came to appreciate the help when faced with telling a nine-year-old about a DNA match with remains that turned out to belong to her father. Military personnel, Red Cross workers, clergy, and many other people offering their help all worked together within the huge, hangarlike space of the armory. Although we were all stunned and grieving, these were the amazing days following 9/11 when everyone in New York was being nice. We were all particularly sensitive to the thousands of family members, friends, and coworkers lined up around the block outside the armory and winding their way through the building inside, hoping to get information about missing loved ones. They were quiet, focused, determined. Mental health staff, Red Cross, and clergy were available for counseling and support, but most people got their information and left. Overnight, the armory building and surrounding streets were plastered with thousands of papers with names and photographs of the missing. "Last seen 9/11, working in Tower 2, 98th floor. John, we love you." They were taped to the walls of buildings, mailboxes, street lamps. People stood around, reading them sadly. At Happy Land, loved ones identified victims from photographs of their dead faces. At the armory, they searched for them with photographs of their living faces.

That day at the armory, I saw colleagues I had first met at the Happy Land disaster and met others for the first time. Tony Ng, medical director of Disaster Psychiatry Outreach, was deciding how to best deploy a group of eager and anxious medical students. We were all feeling our way, trying to figure out how best to proceed. Like at Happy Land, there was a lot of confusion in the early days of the disaster response effort. DMH staff directed me to a secluded room off to one side designated as a place where grieving loved ones could have some privacy and avail themselves of support if they wanted it. It was a large, old, paneled room with 20-foot-high ceilings, Civil War prints on the wall, and empty paper cups and pizza boxes littered about. It was also filled with mental health people, several of them colleagues from VNS. The line continued to flow through the building, but no one came to our room. We waited. There is a lot of waiting in disaster situations. It is often accompanied by an ambivalent hope that no one will show up while still wanting something to do. Suddenly, there was a spasm of excitement, "The mayor is coming!" By this time, Rudy Giuliani was already well on his way to becoming the hero of 9/11. His resolve, compassion, and leadership in the face of the disaster had made him a household name across the country. Guys in windbreakers closed the doors, securing the area in anticipation of the arrival of his Honor and his entourage, with the command, "Don't leave these two rooms."

I was coming back from the room next door loaded down with cups and soda bottles when the mayor's group reached us. They caught me standing inside the door as they entered. Rudy came right up to me, hand extended, and said, "Thanks so much for the great work you're doing." At that point, all I had done was bring soda to my coworkers but his sincerity moved me. I felt a desire to *do* great work, to try to make some contribution worthy of his tireless efforts. The FEMA representative accompanying the mayor next accosted me, "Thanks! Your work means so much to all of us!" I started to introduce myself, but he grabbed my shoulder and said, "I know who you are." I am sure that he did not, but I learned an effective way not to have to learn people's names, while leaving them feeling important and good about themselves. I guess they know how to do these things in Washington.

Shortly after the mayor left, two Red Cross volunteers brought a sobbing group of people into the room. This was Mr. and Mrs. Ferguson, their 20-year-old son, and four or five friends of their daughter, Patricia. Although most of the people going through the line were receiving inconclusive information, the Fergusons had just been told that Patty had died and her body had been found. We did not know at this point how infrequently that outcome would occur. Everyone was crying, and the Red Cross volunteers and a Protestant chaplain got right in there with them, hugging, consoling, trying to help. Most of the mental health people, including me, held back. I felt envious of these laypeople who reflexively hugged someone stricken with grief while I felt anxious and unsure of what to do. In these situations, psychiatrists may need to unlearn part of what our training has taught us. Disaster workers hold the hands of traumatized people, hug them, share personal stories. Many psychiatrists have been trained to regard such interactions as countertherapeutic—that is, potentially harmful to patients. In the classical treatment setting, the transferential feelings and ideas discussed earlier can become intense, providing opportunities to better understand the patient's illness. To touch a patient who is desperately longing for her father's love can lead to explosive and unworkable treatment impasses. But *not* to touch a dazed or terrified disaster victim can be a dreadful rejection or abandonment. Mental health disaster workers must be able to ascertain the most appropriate response for the circumstances, even under circumstances that are extremely stressful for the workers themselves.

Suddenly the mayor was there again. He had been told about this family, and he came back to our room to see them. He sat down next to Mr. Ferguson, implicitly conveying his respect for the head of the family and his recognition that this was appropriate with this family. He leaned forward, looking directly at them all, and said, "I'm so sorry. Tell me about your daughter." They all started to cry. Someone said that Patty did not work in the World Trade Center, she was just dropping something off. The news was full of stories about people who were alive because they went in late that morning. Patty was dead because she just happened to be there. She had only recently moved to New York, but she loved it. Her friends described what a wonderful person she was. Patty's mother and brother hugged each other, unable to speak. The mayor told them that he had narrowly missed getting killed himself, having just left a spot near one of the towers right before it collapsed. But Father Mycal Judge, the chief chaplain of the fire department, his friend to whom he had just said good-bye, was killed in the collapse. Giuliani has subsequently told that story in many interviews, but at that time the wound was fresh. He shared this story about himself with perfect timing, deepening his empathic connection with their grief rather than drawing attention to himself. He could not bring back their child, but he gave something of himself that I am sure they will always remember.

Identification with the Victim

Hearing these exquisitely painful stories, I realized that I literally could not listen to them. Although it sounds awful, I became aware that I wished that these people would just be quiet and go away. I looked at the Fergusons in their grief and felt a pain so deep that I could not stand it. At the same time, I wanted to reject their grief as I identified with it and their inability to escape its pain. I remembered losses of my own and saw that they were part of my reaction. Observing my countertransference to this encounter made my own feelings more tolerable. I was then able to be more open to the needs of this grieving family and try to be helpful to them in whatever ways might be most appropriate under these terrible circumstances. After the mayor left, I talked with Mr. Ferguson. I think that I was of some help to him, although he was the kind of guy who was so thoughtful that he would have told his painful story if he felt that that was what I needed. As we spoke, I found myself remembering a recent conversation I had had with my sister—a conversation that, until that moment, I had forgotten.

Earlier that summer, on August 9, 2001, a Palestinian suicide bomber blew himself up in the Sbarro pizzeria at the intersection of King George Street and Jaffa Road, one of Jerusalem's busiest shopping areas. The blast occurred at 2:00 p.m. when the two-story restaurant was packed with families and kids enjoying summer vacation. According to *Ha'aretz*, Israel's daily English-language newspaper, "a 5- to 10-kilo bomb" filled with nails and screws exploded, killing 14 and injuring 132. The injured and dead included many adolescents. My sister, who lives with her two teenage daughters in a suburb of Tel Aviv, knew the father of one of the injured kids. Shaken, she called me, her brother the psychiatrist, to ask about the impact of living with the constant threat of terrorism. I remember feeling a little distracted in response to her question. I said something to the effect that people probably become hypersensitized to particular stimuli, like sirens and loud noises on one hand, while on the other they become partially numb, shutting down psychologically in response to chronic fear. She said that sounded about right and the conversation moved on.

Talking to Mr. Ferguson that day in the armory, I realized that I had shut down in response to her question, as I had initially shut down in reaction to his grief. It struck me that, despite our best intentions, many of us cannot fully consider the terrifying, painful nature of such realities. Indeed, our impulse is to reject and deny these realities most actively when they actually touch us. My sister and I had been discussing the chronic threat of grave danger to my nieces and herself. I had been concerned but also removed. I wondered if this might be conceptualized as a specific intrapsychic defense. In her famous book, *The Ego and the Mechanisms of Defense*, Anna Freud (1936) described a defense she called identification with the aggressor. She suggested that people who are treated with aggression can identify with the sadistic and aggressive characteristics of their terrorizers as a defense against their own helplessness and rage. Within this frame of reference, identification is understood as a psychological process in which we take positive and negative aspects of important others into our own identity or subjective experience of ourselves. Through identification with the aggressor, victims of aggression become aggressive themselves, brutalizing those weaker than themselves. The classic example is the Jewish inmates in concentration camps who worked as police for the Nazis and were often just as brutal to their fellow prisoners. A more pedestrian example would be the older sister who yells at her younger brother after her father has yelled at her.

If we look more closely at identification with the aggressor, we see that it has two parts. First, there is the experience of sadistic brutalization with its fundamental component of helplessness. This helplessness stimulates the need for defense because it is intolerable and at the same time inescapable. Second, identification serves a defensive function here because it creates a fantasy of escape where in fact none exists. It is as if we say, if I feel like I can be sadistic, and if I can even act that way toward others, I can feel like I am not helpless, even though I have done nothing to alter the basic relationship to my tormentors. Through identification, I have instead altered my relationship to my "self." My reaction to my sister and Mr. Ferguson could be seen as a defensive process for preserving my relationship to my self as not helpless while threatened with helplessness. We might call it "identification with the victim."[1] Here the danger is the *threat* of helpless victimization or loss. As noted earlier, this defense can be seen as a form of countertransference and therefore of particular importance for disaster workers. Like identification with the aggressor, identification with the victim is also a two-part defense against helplessness. First, we empathize with someone else's experience of terror that leads to feeling the threat of pain, loss, and inescapable helplessness. Second, we attempt to maintain the empathic connection while at the same time we unconsciously and defensively assert, "This can't happen to *me*, it can't happen *here*." The helplessness we feel in empathically sharing the victim's experience results in a profound, unconscious denial of our vulnerability to that experience; like touching a finger to a hot pan, we instinctively withdraw.

The concept of identification with the victim is useful if it helps us as disaster workers to deal with the impulse to push away the pain of those we seek to help. As a defense, we use it because we cannot tolerate the feelings

---

[1]Macgregor (1991) has used the same term to discuss a very different concept. He sees identification with the victim as an aspect of a universal sadomasochistic wish to both inflict harm and punish oneself for these wishes. I am describing a denial of helplessness stimulated by empathy with the victim's experience.

from which it protects us. As a normal response to the threat of disasters, terrorism, and trauma, it represents a ubiquitous and understandable reaction. Anyone involved in disaster work—psychiatrist, Red Cross volunteer, emergency worker—is vulnerable to countertransferentially identifying with the victim. In my own case, as I identified with Mr. Ferguson's pain and loss, I shut down emotionally to avoid the pain that this created in me. I then became empathically unavailable to Mr. Ferguson and could be of no help to him. All countertransference can interfere with our availability to our patients, but understanding how it interferes can also locate the critical emotional issues evolving between the people involved. Our goal is to become aware of our countertransference so that we can understand how to be most available to meet our patient's needs. As I became aware of how I had shut down with Mr. Ferguson and why, I was able to sit with him, listen to his painful story, and hopefully provide him with some small measure of comfort at an unbearably painful time.

Final Remarks

Thus, identification with the victim can be seen as one way that many of us try to deal with the threats of a dangerous world. For New Yorkers, this defense was shattered as the terrorists' planes brought down the World Trade Center. The psychological distance between us and other, remote victims of terrorism was vaporized, leaving us to contend with the intolerable realities of loss and vulnerability. Of course, the entire country was deeply affected, especially the people of Washington, DC, with the attack on the Pentagon. But in New York, perhaps because of the civilian nature of the targets and victims or the magnitude of the losses and destruction, it was different. Perhaps because it occurred in our own backyard. A recent study published in the *New England Journal of Medicine* found that rates of PTSD and related symptoms rose as subjects got closer to Ground Zero (Galea, 2002). It is almost as if there is a line dividing victims of trauma from people who have not been traumatized. On one side of the line people use defenses to protect themselves from the threat of trauma, on the other they use defenses to cope with the experience of trauma. The closer we get to the site of the disaster, the more we see people cross from one side of the line to the other with more disaster-induced pathology and defenses. For our purposes this might suggest that if we have not experienced trauma we cannot really understand, despite our best efforts. Something stands between us and truly connecting with the idea of the overwhelming nature of trauma. This is reminiscent of Freud's (1920) notion of the stimulus barrier, a psychological membrane separating outside from inside while allowing optimal interchange between the two. This barrier is breeched by trauma, implying that there is a quantitative dimension to trauma. Everyone has their own breaking point. Perhaps we cannot fully, consciously empathize with the victim until we have experienced the breeching of our own stimulus barrier. That is, until we have been victimized ourselves.

For far too many people in far too many countries of the world, life on the other side of "identification with the victim" is nothing new. As many have noted, perhaps the really extraordinary thing is that we have been able to live in this country with the belief that we were safe and secure within our own inviolable borders. The stunning fact that we maintained this conviction despite the 1993 bombing of the World Trade Center seems to support the power of this defense. And now that the world looks different to us, we can see that a naive arrogance, also defensive, has been part of how we tried to tell ourselves that we were immune from this kind of fear. Many of us have been unaware that, even within our own borders, many people have not felt safe or protected. For Rosa Sanchez and other members of the Happy Land community, 9/11 traumatically reconnected them to old wounds. The Happy Land fire, as a tragedy of poor immigrants in the South Bronx, was easy to forget. Ironically, 9/11 connected Rosa to the Fergusons, the community of mainstream, traumatized America. In so far as disaster short-circuits identification with the victim, it can bring us closer together.

Disasters are upheavals of the stars, events that induce helplessness. They also constitute some of society's most significant experiences. Disaster psychiatry attempts to help in the face of these events. This is important in two ways: it is a way to affirm that in fact we are not helpless, and it provides an opportunity to help. My participation in disaster psychiatry has provided some of the most meaningful experiences of my career.

References

American Psychiatric Association (2000), *Diagnostic and Statistical Manual of Mental Disorders*, 4th ed., text rev. Washington DC: American Psychiatric Association.

American Red Cross in Greater New York (1990), *After the Fire: The Humanitarian Response to the Bronx Happy Land Tragedy of March 25, 1990*. New York: American Red Cross.

Blumenthal, R. (1990, March 26), 87 die in blaze at illegal club; Police arrest ejected patron; Worst New York fire since 1911. *New York Times*, p. A1.

Breslau, N., Chilcoat, H. D., Kessler, R. C. & Davis, G. C. (1999), Previous exposure to trauma and PTSD effects of subsequent trauma: Results from the Detroit Area Survey of Trauma. *Amer. J. Psychiat.*, 156:902–907.

Brockman, R. (1998), *A Map of the Mind: Toward a Science of Psychotherapy.* Madison, CT: Psychosocial Press.

Bromley, R. (1992a), Happy Land: Global dimensions of a local tragedy. Presented at annual meeting of the Association of American Geographers, San Diego.

_____ (1992b), Coping and caring: The aftermath of the Happy Land tragedy. Presented at annual meeting of the Urban Affairs Association, Cleveland, OH.

Card, J. J. (1983), *Lives after Viet Nam.* Lexington, MA: Lexington Books.

Freud, A. (1936), *The Ego and the Mechanisms of Defense*, rev. New York: International Universities Press, 1966, pp. 109–121.

Freud, S. (1901), Fragment of an analysis of a case of hysteria. *Standard Edition*, 7:3–122. London: Hogarth Press, 1905.

_____ (1917), Mourning and melancholia. *Standard Edition*, 14:237–260. London: Hogarth Press, 1981.

_____ (1920), Beyond the pleasure principle. *Standard Edition*, 28:3–64. London: Hogarth Press, 1981.

Galea, S., Ahern, J., Resnick, H., Kilpatrick, D., Bucuvales, M., Gold, J. & Vlahov, D. (2002), Psychological sequelae of the September 11 terrorist attacks in New York City. *New Engl. J. Med.*, 346:982–987.

Goode, E. & Pogrebin, R. (2001, September 25), Anguish of recent events can awaken old trauma. *New York Times*, p. F1.

Herman, J. L. (1992), *Trauma and Recovery.* New York: Basic Books.

Leys, R. (2000), *Trauma: A Genealogy.* Chicago: University of Chicago Press.

Lindy, J. D., Grace, M. C. & Green, B. L. (1981), Survivors: Outreach to a reluctant population. *Amer. J. Orthopsychiat.*, 51:468–478.

New York City Department of Mental Health, Mental Retardation, and Alcoholism Services (1991), *The Happy Land Tragedy: Research and Staff Training on Mental Health Issues Affecting Relatives and Survivors.* New York: New York City Department of Mental Health, Mental Retardation, and Alcoholism Services.

MacGregor, J. R. (1991), Identification with the victim. *Psychoanal. Quart.*, 60:53–68.

Ursano, R. J., Fullerton, C. S. & Norwood, A. E. (1995), Psychiatric dimensions of disaster: Patient care, community consultation, and preventive medicine. *Harv. Rev. Psychiat.*, 3:196–209.

van der Kolk, B. A., Weisaeth, L. & van der Hart, O. (1996), The history of trauma in psychiatry. In: *Traumatic Stress: The Effects of Overwhelming Experience on Mind, Body, and Society*, ed. B. A. van der Kolk, A. C. McFarlane & L. Weisaeth. New York: Guilford Press, pp. 47–74.

Wilson, J. R. & Lindy, J. D., eds. (1994), *Countertransference in the Treatment of PTSD.* New York: Guilford Press.

20

Vietnam and the World Trade Center

One Psychiatrist's View of Defining a Disaster and Working with Its Victims

Arthur T. Meyerson

I am 67 years old and have been involved as a psychiatrist in evaluating and intervening for the victims of what can be defined as two disasters, the Vietnam War and the World Trade Center (WTC) attacks of 9/11. One might argue that these events are sufficiently different as phenomena that they should be considered as distinct and not comparable. In the Vietnam War, combatants on the American side were anticipating battle conditions for which they were trained, and one factor which seemed to lead to increased risk of subsequent psychiatric difficulties was exposure related, those serving longer having greater risk. The war was also the province of the young and largely male population. Although these elements might seem to set Vietnam apart from the WTC disaster, the similarities are overwhelming. In both cases masses of people were exposed to great danger of life and limb, suffered injury, and/or had friends and coworkers who were seriously injured or killed. Many firefighters and police personnel spent months going through the wreckage, exposed, like the Vietnam veterans, for prolonged periods to body parts while personally exhausted and mourning their lost comrades. Finally, many of the WTC dead were women and many were elderly, but many were younger men who, though not in the military, were nevertheless trained and experienced in facing dangerous, life-threatening conditions. Of course, in Vietnam, Americans were inflicting a series of disasters on the country and its citizens while undergoing our own traumatic and painful experiences. That is clearly different. Nevertheless, my experience of interviewing dozens of survivors, dozens of family members, and at least 40 firefighters and police officers has led to a conviction of some considerable commonality between the reactions of these persons to those who were exposed to the trauma of Vietnam. This follows if a disaster can be defined as a mass exposure to events that are life threatening. Unexpected was the finding, on reflection, of many similarities of my own reactions to both events and to the persons I attempted to assist.

Vietnam

I finished my psychiatric residency in 1965 and was immediately placed on active duty as a lieutenant in the U.S. Navy assigned as brig psychiatrist at the receiving station at the Brooklyn Naval Yard. For the previous two years, while a resident and reserve officer, my wife and I had been active in the antiwar movement and in Physicians for Human Rights. Becoming an active military officer was thus fraught with mixed feelings. Long-held feelings of patriotism were in internal conflict with a sense that the United States was in the wrong and that, other than World War II, the American Revolutionary War, and the Civil War, no armed conflict had ever appeared morally justified to me.

In the second year of my psychoanalytic training, I could continue analysis and classes (held at night) while on active duty, and so no personal hardship or danger was involved. Over the course of two years of active duty, I interviewed well over 200 persons exposed to combat, and every day felt as if I were caught up in a historic event without any direct sense of what my patients had experienced except what could be gleaned from their descriptions and from images on television. That many were suffering from acute stress reactions or posttraumatic stress disorder (PTSD), as we now label their signs and symptoms, was clear, but a real sense of the horror of their experience seemed alien, perhaps defensively but surely to some degree because I could not imagine anything so singularly different from my own life experience.

Because I was a naval officer (eventually promoted to lieutenant commander) assigned to a marine-operated brig, I was exposed to officers and enlisted men in both services. There were striking differences between the two services. Naval officers and enlisted men believed, much as I did, that the war was tactically and logistically impossible to win for the U.S. forces. Their beliefs were not at root based on moral objections, but they did deplore the futile loss of American lives. They simply felt that we could not win a jungle war against indigenous persons who were supported by the poor

people of their country. Many of them saw Ho Chi Minh as a master tacti-
cian and expressed grudging admiration. Enlisted and drafted men below
the officer cadre had a less articulated and thought-out position but expressed little enthusiasm for the war. Few naval personnel, of the hundreds
interviewed, had been traumatized by the war. They were on shipboard or in
planes, removed from the trauma and largely unaffected as far as my evaluations could detect.

This was in great contrast to the marines, both officers and enlisted
men. Where the naval personnel were troubled by the futility of the war,
marines were confused and furious at the lack of support for the war on the
part of their fellow citizens. Many had seen combat, some for two years and
most for one, and at least a third suffered nightmares, flashbacks, and
emotional instability. Many went AWOL (absent without leave) after returning to the United States, as if the military was the situation they were
avoiding. Many of these servicemen were abusing drugs, most commonly
marijuana and alcohol. Some were abusing or addicted to heroine. Almost
all of the drug abusers claimed to have begun their use and abuse before
their overseas experiences but reported that the abuse had become much
more frequent and intense during their time in Vietnam. Recent findings
indicate that WTC survivors who abuse alcohol or drugs to deal with the
sequelae suffer greater, prolonged symptoms. About 30 percent of those
seen who were suffering from some form of PTSD or related condition
were sufficiently dysfunctional so as to merit discharge and eventual dis-
ability pension. My patients appeared to be much more vulnerable to dysfunction and discharge if one or both of two conditions prevailed—first, if
they had a history of psychiatric illness or substance abuse before their service, and, second, if they lacked a real support system, specifically family
or friends who admired their service and conveyed a sense of being proud
of them. Although the first has been reported in the literature (personal
and family histories of illness and substance abuse bearing on response to
trauma), I remain unaware of any scientific literature bearing on the significance of support systems.

As my two years of active service wore on, I became increasingly troubled by my "military" status and supported the desire for discharge of any
person with a convincing degree of suffering. My sympathy and identification with their wish to avoid further service was partly an outgrowth of
professional assessment. It also expressed a kind of countertransference,
an identification with those exposed to trauma as I was increasingly exposed to their horrible stories of danger and loss. On reflection, during my
own training analysis I recognized that this identification was based on

some personal childhood trauma but also on the professionally denied, but unconsciously experienced, sense of dread that I would go through in empathy with the patients as they recounted their dreadful war experiences.

Viewing the events of the war on television became increasingly painful and caused transient nightmares for me, provoking an avoidance of news broadcasts in favor of other television programming. I found a support group among other naval officers, including my commanding officer, Captain Walsh. He shared views on the war and would support me in battles with marine Colonel Savage (yes, that was his name) who objected to the stream of honorable discharges and felt the "Corps could make men" of these marines, most of whom were seen while imprisoned or awaiting trial for going AWOL.

An interesting and revealing set of experiences occurred because the marine captain who was directly responsible for the brig became concerned about the brutality that his marine guards would sometimes visit on the prisoners. He supported my decision to run ongoing groups with the guards. Once they believed the promise of confidentiality, the guards began to talk of their fury with the many marine prisoners who were trying to avoid service by going AWOL, who had gone AWOL, or who ran into other disciplinary difficulty following service in Vietnam. "These guys are un-American" and "Let them go live in a communist country" were the kinds of remarks made during the early weeks and months of the group.

As time went on, however, a different set of feelings emerged among the guards. They were jealous of the prisoners who were refusing to go to Vietnam or were rebelling against military authority on return to the states. "We have to," "I had to go to Vietnam," "I have to do this shit guard duty," and "These guys can sit on their cans and get out of the service" were frequently heard remarks. A sense of unfairness and a jealousy of the prisoners' antiauthoritarian actions appeared to be revealed as the main reasons for the abuse of the prisoners. As this emerged, a considerable diminution of the abuse took place. The obedient marine guards appeared to remain obedient but somewhat sadder and less angry when they dealt with the prisoners.

Less clear and perhaps distorted by my own views of the war, was the feeling of disillusionment with their earlier, patriotic support of the war. In addition to identifying with the prisoners who sought to avoid the war, I found myself identifying and admiring the guards and others who had honorably served, many in heroic individual efforts. Ambivalence reigned and still does with regard to my views of those who participated and those who shunned involvement for moral and personal reasons.

The World Trade Center

My direct exposure to the events at the Twin Towers was simultaneously viewing the TV coverage and seeing the first fire, the second crash, and the collapse from my apartment window. My bedroom houses a computer setup that is immediately to the left of a large TV, which in turn is immediately to the left of a large window that faces downtown and the upper two thirds of the WTC. I was working at this computer and listening to the news on TV when the first crash was described by the announcer. I stood and went to the TV and then the window where I viewed the subsequent crash and eventual collapse, turning from the window to the TV and back again. The entire experience, not unlike the feelings provoked by the stories of the Vietnam veterans I'd interviewed, was fraught with a sense of distance, disbelief, awe, incredulousness, and emotional denial. Within a few minutes, as it became clear that this was an act of terrorism, a sense of being violated and of retaliatory rage was experienced. This was very much like the feelings I'd had toward Presidents Kennedy, Johnson, and Nixon, who I felt were responsible for the war in Vietnam and its tragic toll of Vietnamese and American lives. Now this rage was directed toward a faceless enemy called al-Qaeda. Over the next few days, as this became President Bush's and the country's shared emotional response to a considerable degree, my feelings reverted to long-standing pacifism and skepticism about war-solving problems. This was modified by feeling that self-defense was involved, and perhaps necessary because of the intentions of the fundamentalists to destroy the United States and make war on innocent civilians. A strong desire to help the victims and their rescuers and families surged up without any of the ambivalence I had experienced over service during the Vietnam disaster.

Disaster Psychiatry Outreach contacted me, along with many other New York and U.S. psychiatrists, asking for volunteers to provide psychiatric assistance to people affected by the attacks. Both my wife and I signed up and went through a training session, and shortly thereafter I became a clinical director at the Family Assistance Center on Pier 94, working on Tuesdays and Thursdays for the weeks and months after the center's inception and until it closed. Much as the Vietnam War had stimulated a desire to serve, first as an antiwar activist and later as a professional evaluating and treating the military personnel involved, a desire to serve the victims was and remains my strongest reaction to the WTC disaster. One felt a need to be helpful to others but this was not a purely altruistic impulse because it involved a sense that helping others was the one thing one could do to assuage one's sense of helplessness, victimization, and personal violation.

The first surge of interviewees were survivors who had managed to get out of the buildings before they collapsed, family members of those lost but quickly presumed dead by the professional community and sometimes by the families, and police and firefighters who would informally approach me during lunch or while I would make rounds of the pier's various areas. Among the family members of the missing, many refused to acknowledge overtly their loved one's death while at the same moment grieving. Some did manage to simply deny the loss, both verbally and emotionally, and were engaged in a uniformly fruitless search, going from Ground Zero to the medical examiner's offices, to hospitals, and to Pier 94. As time wore on and the mayor announced the futility of hoping for more survivors, they nearly all came to accept the deaths while some retained an interesting balance of belief and disbelief. This mirrored the experience of cops and firefighters, survivors, families and helpers like myself, an experience made of a sustained derealization. We all believed in the fullness of the horror and yet nagging at our consciousness lay a sense of doubt. It couldn't have really happened, could it? Not a single person I spoke with during formal interviews and informal conversation failed to express some form of this derealization. For me it lasted months, and I still occasionally look out that window to rediscover the reality.

A striking example of this derealization was experienced by an architect in his 50s. His office building was not directly affected by the WTC disaster, though it was only a block away. After he heard the noise and felt the shock, he went to the roof of his building to see what had happened. After gazing in wonder at the site, he noticed that the roof around him was covered with recognizable body parts, an arm here, a leg there. It all seemed unreal two weeks later when I interviewed him. He had all the symptoms of PTSD, and, although authorities had promised that his business could reenter the building in a few weeks, he refused to return even to get his belongings. In addition, he refused to return to his apartment in Liberty City and moved his wife and children to Long Island.

Because his response was so intense, I explored earlier life trauma and he revealed that at age 10 he and his parents were in a car crash in Bulgaria (his native country), and he had been seated in the front passenger position. He immediately saw that his father was dead, impaled on the steering wheel. He had minor injuries as did his older sister. His mother was hospitalized for depression, and he lived with an uncle for several months until she returned, separated from the sister as well. The WTC catastrophe and his own exposure to body parts, clearly mobilized the traumatic memories of his father's death, and this explained his severe symptoms and avoidance. It was striking to me that his symptoms of avoidance caused him to duplicate the displacement he'd experienced following the car crash.

After the first few weeks of work on the pier, I'd sent several colleagues to the site of the disaster. Boats were taking family members down to the site, and the police asked for mental health personnel to accompany them. Our DPO psychiatrists, police personnel, Red Cross mental health volunteers, and New York State and City Offices of Mental Health personnel were mobilized. After about two weeks, I decided to go myself, and this experience was one of melancholy, fear, love, and trauma. I served two groups on this trip. The first was the wife, two young-adult sons, the brother, and the sister-in-law of a broker who'd been on the upper floors of the WTC. The second was a young man who was in the World Financial Center and who'd watched many victims leaping from the towers before it dawned on his consciousness that his closest friend, a cousin who lived directly next door to his family, was on the top floors of one of the towers. While this young man talked and mourned in an appropriate fashion, as did the large family group, there was an exception. The younger son of the family remained separate from the remainder of his family and refused to join in their expressions of grief and loss. I tried but failed to help him to verbalize his grief and facially expressed rage, but a Catholic priest from the coast guard was on the boat with us. I asked him to try. He seemed to make some headway, and as we approached the viewing platform, the boy rejoined his brother and showed his grief. None of this seemed unique to the WTC disaster. I'd worked with families of suddenly and violently deceased persons before when I'd run the Mount Sinai Hospital Emergency Psychiatry Service in New York City over a five-year period.

Once the boat reached the site, the viewing of the area brought home to me the horror of this event and mobilized a sense of personal trauma. Seeing the enormous swathe of twisted steel, rubble, smoke-spewing clefts, and hazily perceived rescue workers and equipment was shocking and terrifying. No TV or photographic image had captured the enormity of the sight and its surreal quality. One imagines feeling something akin to the utter sense of helplessness, the overwhelming violence of those last moments of the victims' lives, although clearly this exercise of imagination pales besides the reality. That night I was awakened repeatedly and finally gave up trying to sleep. I spent the hours between 2:00 and 8:00 in the morning composing a poem in an attempt to reach some sense of perspective and understanding of what I'd seen and experienced. As I worked on the pier during the following months, I experienced no recurrence of the nightmares but did avoid taking the trip back to Ground Zero until months later at the time of the first memorial services. Rather than intensifying the sense of de-realization, this second visit to Ground Zero actually helped me to accept the horror and to listen more fully to the stories of survivors and family members as they imagined the horrors of their loved ones' experiences during the disaster.

Much as I came to admire the Vietnam veterans, the survivors of the WTC disaster took on a heroic coloration, as did the families. They struggled first to sustain their denial and yet eventually had to deal with their grief while seeking help amid the enormous waits and bureaucratic maze on the pier. The police and firefighters became for me, as they appear to have done for so many, newly anointed knights of New York's round table. A recurrent theme of many survivors was the sadness at their memory of descending the stairs; helping others, being helped, or both; and encountering panting, exhausted firefighters and police on their way up the monstrous heights bearing the weight of rescue equipment. Many had this image as the center of recurrent nightmares and flashbacks. This is as poignant an example of survivor guilt as any I encountered during the Vietnam era.

Finally, up to two years after the disaster, I've had the opportunity to interview several firefighters, both professionally and informally. The firefighter and police unions had informed volunteer groups that many of their personnel will not use departmental in-house counseling services but will speak with volunteers. I've joined the New York Disaster Counseling Coalition, which offers free therapy and psychopharmacology to firefighters involved in the WTC disaster. While some have thus far been identified as PTSD victims, many have retired early leaving massive gaps in the ranks beyond those who lost their lives. An explanation is offered, and is undoubtedly a contributory cause, that so much overtime was accrued in the rescue efforts that retirement now is beneficial because benefits are determined by the last few years' earnings. One wonders whether an element of avoidance isn't a natural consequence of the horrors of the disaster, the rescue, and the cleanup which is comparable to that experienced by marines in the Vietnam era. Like the marines going AWOL, perhaps this avoidance underlies the retirements beyond the financial factors.

As time has gone on, I find myself avoiding TV coverage of the disaster and the memorials like that held on the anniversary of the WTC disaster, much as I did coverage of Vietnam during and following my service. From the perspective of one psychiatrist who participated in both types of traumatic events, wartime trauma and peacetime disasters leave their victims with similar adaptive and maladaptive responses. Those who try to assist them, at least in my own case, may also have similar responses to working with victims of war and civil disasters. Although there must be differences that I have failed to recognize, I am left wondering what justification exists for distinguishing between the emotional and mental responses to civilian and military catastrophe.

Contributors

Eraka Bath, M.D. is a part-time clinical instructor at the New York University School of Medicine, where she is completing her Child and Adolescent Psychiatry Fellowship. She has recently been awarded a SAMSHA grant as an APA Minority Fellow.

Raquel E. Cohen, M.D. is Professor Emeritus of the University of Miami Psychiatry Department and consultant to the PanAmerican Health Organization, which recently published her disaster training book in English and Spanish.

Lynn E. DeLisi, M.D. is Professor of Psychiatry, New York University, and Associate Director for Clinical Studies, Center for Advanced Brain Imaging, The Nathan S. Kline Institute, Orangeburg, New York. She is a Fellow for the American College of Neuropsychopharmacology, co-Founder of the International Society of Psychiatric Genetics, and co–Editor-in-Chief of the journal *Schizophrenia Research*.

Mark L. Dembert, M.D., M.P.H., CGP, FACPM recently retired from the U.S. Navy after a 27-year medical career, much of it spent in the fields of public health, environmental medicine, psychiatry, and disaster medicine. He is board certified in psychiatry and in public health/general preventive medicine. He currently is the Virginia Department of Health's Eastern Regional Medical Consultant for All-Hazards Emergency Preparedness and Response, based in Norfolk, Virginia.

Pamela J. Edwards, M.D. is Assistant Professor of Psychiatry, Director of Disaster Planning for the Department of Psychiatry, and Staff Psychiatrist for the Intercultural Psychiatry Program at Oregon Health and Sciences University.

Jennifer M. Finkel, M.D. is a fourth-year psychiatry resident at New York University Medical Center. She volunteered with Disaster Psychiatry Outreach in the relief efforts after September 11 and is currently serving as Senior Resident at Bellevue Hospital's Psychiatric Emergency Room. She plans on pursuing a fellowship in Consult-Liason Psychiatry after graduation.

Diana R. Graham, M.D. completed the adult psychiatry residency at New York University Medical Center in 2003 and is now an attending physician in the Comprehensive Psychiatric Emergency Program at Bellevue Hospital Center. She is a graduate of Harvard Medical School.

Desmond Heath, M.D. is a child and adolescent psychiatrist in private practice in New York City and attending at Mount Sinai Hospital, New York City. He attended medical school at Trinity College, Cambridge, and St. Mary's Hospital, London, United Kingdom, and did his residency training at Bellevue Hospital and Columbia University Presbyterian Hospital and New York State Psychiatric Institute.

Kristina Jones, M.D. is Assistant Professor of Psychiatry at Cornell Medical College and an Assistant Attending Psychiatrist at New York Presbyterian Hospital in Manhattan. She has been working with the Fire Department of New York and with Project Liberty since October 2001.

Craig L. Katz, M.D. (Editor) is Director of Acute Care Psychiatry Services at the Mount Sinai Medical Center in New York City. He is also a founding member and president of Disaster Psychiatry Outreach, the only organization in the world devoted to disaster mental health services.

Carol Luise Kessler, M.D., M.Div. is a Child and Adolescent Psychiatrist who works with families affected by HIV at New York Presbyterian Hospital. She also serves as an interim minister at Transfiguration Lutheran Church in the South Bronx. She lives in Ossining, New York, with her son, Rafael.

David C. Lindy, M.D. is Clinical Director/Chief Psychiatrist with the Visiting Nurse Service of New York's Community Mental Health Services. He is Associate Clinical Professor of Psychiatry, College of Physicians and Surgeons, Columbia University, and is on the faculty of the Center for Psychoanalytic Training and Research of Columbia University.

Joseph P. Merlino, M.D., MPA is Director of Psychiatry at New York City's Queens Hospital Center and Clinical Professor of Psychiatry at New York University School of Medicine. He is President of the American Academy of Psychoanalysis and Dynamic Psychiatry.

Arthur T. Meyerson, M.D. is Clinical Professor at New York University School of Medicine. He is a Distinguished Life Fellow of the American Psychiatric Association, a Fellow of the American College of Psychiatrists, and author of five books and many articles and chapters.

Joseph C. Napoli, M.D. is Assistant Clinical Professor of Psychiatry, College of Physicians and Surgeons of Columbia University; Chairperson, Disaster Preparedness Committee, New Jersey Psychiatric Association; and Chief, Crisis Response Team, Office of Emergency Management, Fort Lee, New Jersey. He was recently given the American Psychiatric Association's Bruno Limo Award for outstanding contributions to the care and understanding of victims of disaster.

Anand A. Pandya, M.D. (Editor) runs the ADEPT Program at Bellevue Hospital and serves on the faculty of the Department of Psychiatry at New York University School of Medicine. A cofounder of Disaster Psychiatry Outreach, he is active in the American Psychiatric Association and serves on the board of directors of NAMI, the National Alliance for the Mentally Ill.

John W. Raasoch, M.D. is Clinical Director for the University of Texas Medical Branch correctional managed care psychiatric hospital in East Texas. He has lived in the Gaza Strip and worked with the Palestinian Mental Health Center.

Beverley Raphael, M.D. is the Director of the Centre for Mental Health for the New South Wales Department of Health in Australia and Emeritus Professor of Psychiatry for the University of Queensland. She is Past President of the Royal Australian and New Zealand College of Psychiatrists and has been awarded an Honorary Fellowship of the American College of Psychiatrists.

Donald E. Rosen, M.D. is Residency Training Director at Oregon Health and Sciences University, where he has worked since 1999. A graduate of the University of Kansas School of Medicine, he worked for 15 years at the Menninger Clinic, where he served as founding Director of the Professionals in Crisis program, Associate Director of the C. F. Menninger Memorial Hospital, and Director of Psychiatry.

Manoj R. Shah, M.D., FRC Psych. (London, UK), DFAPA is Assistant Professor of Psychiatry, Albert Einstein College of Medicine, Yeshiva University, New York, and Medical Director, Recognition and Prevention Program (RAP), Schneider Children's and Hillside Hospitals, North Shore–Long Island Jewish Health System, New Hyde Park, New York.

Claudia T. Sickinger, M.D. serves as Medical Director for Westchester ARC in White Plains, New York. She is an alumna of Columbia University's Public Psychiatry Fellowship Program, Mount Sinai School of Medicine's Psychiatry Residency Training Program, and Mount Sinai Medical School, all in New York City.

Margaret E. Tompsett, M.B., B. Chir., F.A.A.C.A.P. is an Assistant Professor of Psychiatry at the University of Medicine and Dentistry of New Jersey at Newark and cochair of the Disaster Preparedness Committee of the New Jersey Psychiatric Association. She is in private practice as a child and adolescent psychiatrist in New Jersey.